"Bob Williams has written an insightful, clear, and up to date book that brings economics and ecology together in a fruitful way. Highly recommended!"

– *Professor Herman E. Daly, University of Maryland, USA*

"*Greening the Economy* breaks new ground in articulating the critical relationships between ecosystem services upon which our lives depend and the difficult policy choices that must be made to restore and preserve those services. The book offers concrete local examples and a fresh roadmap to policymakers, academics, and citizens interested in market-based solutions to environmental challenges".

– *Trip Van Noppen, President, Earthjustice*

Greening the Economy

Drawing on both economics and ecology, this book offers telling insights into the confusing "jobs versus environment" debates as well as charts a recommended path towards a more co-habitable relationship. Avoiding the extreme views that economic growth will either destroy or save our natural environment, *Greening the Economy* takes a more discriminating stance and illuminates why our nation's natural environment is both better and worse than it was forty years ago. From the perspective of ecology, the book identifies twenty-four key ecological services essential in supporting our economic well-being. An explanation of these services and their underlying ecology distinguishes those services that are especially vulnerable to our expanding economy from those that are not. From the perspective of economics, the book examines those conditions under which markets function effectively, then distinguishes them from conditions under which they do not.

Professor Bob Williams examines the essential elements that give ecosystems their durability. These key characteristics are: self-regulating cycles of key materials, a plentiful and durable energy source, an ability to adjust to changing circumstances, and the capacity for resiliency in the face of unpredictable disruptions. In separate chapters, each of these natural attributes is applied to our economy and twenty policies are recommended to shift our economy toward these objectives. The policies include marketable waste-emission permits, a carbon tax, split-rate property taxation, environmental assurance bonds, a revamped home mortgage deduction, and an inheritance tax. Such policies would function to implement the principle of full-cost pricing in order to ensure market incentives that encourage environmentally temperate behavior and decisions.

This book will be of interest to students of Ecology and Economics, at undergraduate and postgraduate level alike, as well as anyone seeking an understanding of key ecological concepts that are critical to fully appreciating the role of natural capital in our economic affairs.

Bob Williams is Professor of Economics at Guilford College, North Carolina, USA.

Routledge Studies in Ecological Economics

1 **Sustainability Networks**
Cognitive tools for expert collaboration in social-ecological systems
Janne Hukkinen

2 **Drivers of Environmental Change in Uplands**
Aletta Bonn, Tim Allot, Klaus Hubaceck and Jon Stewart

3 **Resilience, Reciprocity and Ecological Economics**
Northwest Coast sustainability
Ronald L. Trosper

4 **Environment and Employment**
A reconciliation
Philip Lawn

5 **Philosophical Basics of Ecology and Economy**
Malte Faber and Reiner Manstetten

6 **Carbon Responsibility and Embodied Emissions**
Theory and measurement
João F.D. Rodrigues, Alexandra P.S. Marques and Tiago M.D. Domingos

7 **Environmental Social Accounting Matrices**
Theory and applications
Pablo Martínez de Anguita and John E. Wagner

8 **Greening the Economy**
Integrating economics and ecology to make effective change
Bob Williams

Greening the Economy

Integrating economics and ecology to make effective change

Bob Williams

Routledge
Taylor & Francis Group
LONDON AND NEW YORK

First published 2010 by Routledge
2 Park Square, Milton Park, Abingdon, Oxon, OX14 4RN

Simultaneously published in the USA and Canada
by Routledge
270 Madison Avenue, New York, NY 10016

Routledge is an imprint of the Taylor & Francis Group

Typeset in Times New Roman by
Pindar NZ, Auckland, New Zealand
Printed and bound in Great Britain by
The MPG Books Group in the UK

British Library Cataloguing in Publication Data
A catalogue record for this book is available from the British Library

Library of Congress Cataloging in Publication Data
Williams, Bob (Robert B.)
Greening the economy: integrating economies and ecology to make effective change / by Bob Williams.
p. cm.
Includes bibliographical references and index.
ISBN 978-0-415-57056-5 (hb) — ISBN 978-0-203-85044-2 (eb) 1. Environmental economics. 2. Economic policy—Environmental aspects. 3. Environmental policy—Economic aspects. I. Title.
HC79.E5W5288 2010
333.7—dc22 2009049405

ISBN 978-0-415-57056-5 (hbk)
ISBN 978-0-203-85044-2 (ebk)

Contents

Illustrations

Figures

Tables

Acknowledgments

Writing is acutely private and surprisingly collaborative. Of course, writing entails countless hours of individual toil as I struggle to capture my elusive thoughts onto the page. I find it a daunting challenge and one that I never enjoyed in the past. My thoughts, which often seem so brilliant and convincing in my mind, rarely look that way on paper. It is so much easier simply to leave them where they remain untarnished. Thinking through ideas ever more carefully and then finding the words to express them are activities that do not come easily to me. What exactly am I trying to say? How do I express it clearly and succinctly? Even now, as I work on this culminating piece, I find myself, once again, stymied by these two questions.

Thankfully, this book has given me the opportunity to appreciate, and even enjoy, the craft of writing. Two particular joys stand out. The endless hours of writing, editing, and rewriting require a commitment to some regular routine. The discipline and structure provided by scheduled writing give an order and purpose to my life that serves like "comfort" food, familiar and often replenishing. Yet, within this discipline of writing lies an even greater source of joy. I speak of those moments when I find myself lost in the world of ideas no longer confined by the passage of time. Working on some thought, I would realize that several hours had elapsed since I last considered such matters. Sometimes these ruminations led to a refined idea or an elegant expression; most times, they did not. No matter; the real payoff was getting lost in the moment and becoming fully engaged in whatever I was working on. That these moments led to some novel understanding or creative expression was an added bonus. Learning these joys is but the first debt I have incurred in writing this book.

Despite its solitary nature, I find writing to be a collaborative exercise. Of course, a writer is always in the room with the reader. What do I need to share with you so that you can follow my argument easily? How can I best share it with you? What is too much? At what point have I communicated something effectively and can I move on to the next thing? At what point am I losing you? Even alone in my study, I am in continual conversation with you, the reader, as I work to answer such questions.

Beyond the reader, I bring many more collaborators into my study; in fact, I have a roomful who are working with me as I write. There are far too many to acknowledge singly, which is why there exists a bibliography to do so, though less personally. This whole book reflects the ideas of those who have written before me; I have simply refashioned their ideas. I am deeply in their debt.

A number of colleagues and friends offered valuable advice throughout my time at work on this book. I owe a particular debt to two colleagues in the Biology Department, Chuck Smith and Lynn Moseley, who patiently answered my questions and directed me to valuable sources as I grappled with concepts in both ecology and biology. Conversations with two other colleagues, Jeff Jeske and Jeff Thigpen, helped to crystallize my thinking regarding the use of vignettes and concrete public policy remedies in the book. Other colleagues, including Elwood Parker, Edwins Gwako, Peter Wycoff, and Lisa Young, suggested valuable sources. David Landrigan gave me permission to use his rendering of the young beauty–aging matron image. In addition, I want to thank my good friend Andy Rowland, whose curiosity about the project and openness about the challenges of writing served me as a continual source of support. Each of these contributors has given the book substantial added value.

Teaching at a liberal arts college, I subjected countless classes of students to reading the early versions of different chapters. To my students, your comments and suggestions gave me a constant reality check and shaped the eventual form of the book. Thank you for your willingness to believe that you could make a difference; in this case, your faith has been realized.

Many friends and colleagues gave considerable time to reviewing the manuscript and offering invaluable criticisms. Early on, Rich Thompson, Steve Williams, and Larry Morse plowed through a very rough manuscript and gave me thoughtful and much-needed advice. While I fully anticipated getting cogent feedback from these three, I was very surprised by the gift I received from Rand Cork. Not expecting more than an honest appraisal, I was overwhelmed by your perceptive and exhaustive copyediting. I am still moved by your generosity. Bobby Wayne Clark, thank you for your offer of considerable time and amazing talents in pruning and refining my wordiness and clumsiness. Though your efforts did not reduce the length by 20 percent as you suggested, they did lead to a more streamlined book. Any excessive verbiage that remains cannot be laid on your back.

For a first-time author, navigating the book publishing process can be daunting, frustrating, and frequently opaque. I owe much to my colleagues, friends, and court rivals, Richie Zweigenhaft and Bob Wineburg, who willingly shared their experiences and offered their counsel. Thank you, David Perry, for giving me invaluable advice on how to approach publishers and frame a book proposal. Both Todd Baldwin and Don Riesman gave me thoughtful and useful feedback after reading the manuscript. Late in the process, two anonymous readers offered valuable advice on how to strengthen the book. Thank you, Virginia Ferguson, for your technical help throughout.

Like all authors, I owe much to my editors at Routledge. As Senior Editor, Rob Langham saw the potential in this manuscript; in addition to wholehearted support, he has offered perceptive advice due to his considerable familiarity with the literature. Thanks to Emily Senior and Louisa Earls who helped to shepherd the book through the publishing process.

I want to thank my Wednesday afternoon group. You have supported me throughout with your unstintingly honest feedback, even though it was not always appreciated. You have offered me more than I can express. Perhaps above all, I appreciate your encouragement to find my voice and to trust my instinct that I could and should write this book. I do not see how I could have written it without your help.

Lastly, I want thank those who gave me the "time" to complete this project. Thanks so much to Guilford College and its study leave program for its support of this project. Teaching at a private, liberal arts college is frequently more than a full-time affair, leaving little time for research and writing. Thankfully, I received two study leaves that gave me the time and space to conceptualize the book and eventually complete it. And thanks to my colleague, Robert Williams, for picking up the slack during my leaves.

Between these leaves, I spent the bulk of my summers as well as evenings and weekends slowly completing it. Throughout this long process, I received the forbearance and loving support from both my son, Samuel, and my partner, Mary Beth. I know that I was unavailable for innumerable hours, sometimes even when I was physically present as I sat mulling over some idea or vexing problem. Thank you for your continual curiosity about the book, your patient listening to my frequent diatribes, and your love.

1 Dueling paradigms

Browsing through the "Environment" section of my local bookstore can be a confusing if not depressing experience. Lined up across the bookshelves are titles that convey their focus on the current environmental "hot" topic, global climate change. Most, like the well-known *An Inconvenient Truth*, offer a disturbing future that includes warmer temperatures, rising sea levels, more violent storms, receding glaciers and polar ice, and stranded polar bears. Some titles, such as *Boiling Point*, *Climate Crash*, and *The Suicidal Planet*, convey this view more provocatively. These books explain how our modern dependence on fossil fuels has raised carbon dioxide levels in the atmosphere, thereby fueling the conditions causing global climate change. However, other book titles like *Unstoppable Global Warming: Every 1500 Years* and *Meltdown: The Predictable Distortion of Global Warming by Scientists, Politicians, and the Media* suggest a very different point of view. These books insist that the dire predictions of climate change are based on an incomplete reading of historical records, poor understanding of the natural forces that influence climate shifts, unreliable computer models, and the political agendas of their authors.

Further inspection of the bookshelves reveals other contrasting viewpoints. Many books focus more broadly on the state of the world and our natural environment. Some have illuminating titles like *Plan B 4.0: Mobilizing to Save Civilization* or *When the Rivers Run Dry*, while others such as the annual *State of the World* series are more neutral; however, each argues that our current decisions threaten the natural environment. Our ocean fisheries are collapsing around the world as we continue to "mine" this important source of protein and use the oceans as our global sewer. Similarly, our agricultural methods, though highly productive, are depleting the fertility of our soils and undermining the habitats of numerous species as we transform the landscape. Our affluent lifestyles cause us to place ever-increasing demands on our local environments as we spew fumes into the air, flush sewage down our pipes, and cram our landfills with endless garbage. These books and others offer a variety of statistics that convey an earth in decline as we deplete resources and dump mounting effluents into our environment. In many cases, they assert that these declines are the result of modern technologies and unquenched appetites that drive the pursuit of increased economic growth. They argue that we must revamp present policies and behaviors if we are to avoid a further decline, even collapse, of critical natural systems.

Adding to the confusion, other books like *The Skeptical Environmentalist* and *The Improving State of the World: Why We're Living Longer, Healthier, More Comfortable Lives on a Cleaner Planet* offer a wealth of statistical information, though in support of the contrary view. They argue persuasively that our economic decisions have created unprecedented prosperity in recent centuries. Using a variety of measures, they argue that humans today are better fed and educated, live longer and healthier lives, and earn higher incomes than at any time in human history. They insist that this unparalleled increase in human prosperity is due to the harnessing of modern technology and economic growth. Though they concede that some environmental problems have arisen, they contend that both technology and economic growth offer us the means and capacity to solve current and future environmental problems. Rather than viewing them as major contributors to our environmental problems, they tout them as the key contributors to their solution.

Though no one disputes the critical role that energy plays in fueling our modern economy, there are plenty of books that quarrel over our energy futures. Some, like *The End of Oil: On the Edge of a Perilous New World* or *The Empty Tank: Oil, Gas, Hot Air, and the Coming Global Financial Catastrophe*, herald the rapidly approaching moment of "peak oil," in which world oil production begins its inevitable decline. According to many, this end of "cheap oil" will likely bring an era fraught with financial crises, economic dislocations, wars over energy supplies, and massive human migrations.[1] Without adequate fuel, the industrial engines that have spawned modern technology and our contemporary affluence will sputter haltingly. Other titles like *A Brighter Tomorrow, The Bottomless Well: The Twilight of Fuel, the Virtue of Waste, and Why We Will Never Run Out of Energy* and *The Hydrogen Economy* all suggest a much different, and certainly brighter energy future. Though they focus on different energy solutions, each contends that we can transition to an energy future in which supplies are secure and ample and harmful emissions are negligible. Each of these books suggests we stand on the threshold of an energy transition that will appear as significant to our descendents as the transition from wood to fossil fuels appears to us now.

My confusion goes beyond the provocative and suggestively conflicting book titles. Most provide careful and thoughtful arguments as they plausibly make their case. They support their key assertions with ample statistical information. Moreover, the pedigree of the various authors, with their degrees and experience, along with the testimonies provided on the book jackets, make it difficult to dismiss easily one view or the other.

As I consider how the changes discussed in the books have affected my local community, Greensboro, my confusion deepens. Relying solely on my errant memory, recent winters have seemed unduly warm, as I have missed those brief cold spells that seemed to come each winter and evoke a surprising longing for the hot days of August. In my yard, the fall vegetable garden seemingly survives longer through the winter and my spring replanting date arrives earlier each year.

Each spring, the songs of the migratory songbirds seem slightly less loud and the summer sightings of Monarch butterflies slightly less frequent, even as I make my yard more hospitable to both.

Driving around town, the evidence of economic growth is apparent. At the edges of my city, shopping centers and housing developments dominate the landscape. These developments bring jobs and incomes that contribute to the increased prosperity of my community. New arrivals bring new tastes and novel skills. For example, the variety of cuisines and the quality of restaurants currently at my disposal far outstrip the offerings of even a decade ago. New businesses and service providers offer me a range of new choices in countless other areas as well. A decade ago, my city's downtown was a dreary and sleepy place after 5 p.m.; today it is alive with a multitude of cultural choices. Local investment and increased incomes have fueled a variety of cultural offerings ranging from a new baseball stadium to a thriving regional theater company. Economic growth has spawned many new opportunities.

At the same time, these changes aggravate many of my city's problems. I find it increasingly difficult to reach the peacefulness of the countryside from my downtown home as the ring of development expands outward. Traffic congestion is worsening and travel times are lengthening as more cars clog the limited roadways. Summer comes with its visible haze of smog on the horizon as local officials post warnings discouraging outside activity. Further development and more concrete increase the urban heat sink, making the already sweltering summers seem ever hotter. As I consider these changes to my community, both the benefits and the problems, my confusion intensifies. I turn to some key statistical measures of change in my community to see what clarity they reveal.

Measuring change in my community

Though unique in some ways, the changes that have shaped my community are similar to those that have influenced communities all across this country in recent decades. The key figures in Table 1.1 indicate that my local community has prospered over the years. Like much of the Sunbelt, Guilford County, North Carolina, has attracted many new residents and has doubled in adult population (25 years and older) since 1970. Over the same period, its non-agricultural employment growth has more than kept pace with this surge in population, although manufacturing jobs clearly have not.[2] Further, this employment growth has encouraged rising average pay.[3] In inflation-adjusted figures, the average annual wage in the county has increased by 16 percent over the twenty-year period from 1980 to 2000. One measure of economic strength, gross retail sales, has doubled during the thirty-year period, indicating a robust, local economy. The surge in population and the increasing incomes have contributed to the dramatic increase in local property values, a key measure of local wealth. Using inflation-adjusted figures, local property wealth has nearly doubled in just the past twenty years. Taken collectively, these measures indicate a stronger, more prosperous economy than a generation or two ago.

Table 1.1 Key demographic and economic trends of Guilford County, NC

	1970	*1980*	*1990*	*2000*
Adult population	152,736	186,981	225,647	274,942
Non-agricultural jobs	142,930	177,180	231,281	285,880
Manufacturing jobs	58,580	57,250	58,790	55,550
Average annual real wage ($)	NA	27,700	29,129	32,225
Real retail sales ($ millions)	4,394	5,561	6,874	9,244
Real property values ($ millions)	NA	17,807	23,365	30,010

Source: LINC (Log into North Carolina) Database.

This economic prosperity has brought widespread benefits to my community. Since 1970, the county's median family income has grown nearly 23 percent, even after adjustments for changes in the cost of living. The typical family now earns about $10,000 more than they earned a generation ago. Since our homes represent the major source of household wealth, changes in median home values measure the relative wealth status of the typical family. Since 1970, median home values in the county have increased by two-thirds, exhibiting dramatic improvements in typical family wealth. These income and wealth gains have allowed more residents to complete a college education and the percentage of college graduates has more than doubled.[4] The declining infant mortality rates suggest that the recent prosperity has improved health outcomes and eased access to health care for many residents.

Regrettably, not all of the figures in Table 1.2 indicate that this prosperity has led to widespread and substantial improvements in well-being. Economic prosperity has not dented local poverty. Though the local poverty rate did decline modestly from 1970 to 1990, its stubborn reluctance to fall further during the 1990s is a source of concern. Even with the declining poverty *rate*, the number of persons

Table 1.2 Key trends of economic well-being in Guilford County, NC

	1970	*1980*	*1990*	*2000*
Median real family income	$42,837	$40,858	$48,424	$52,638
Median real home value	$69,679	$91,116	$103,557	$116,900
Percentage college graduates	12.8%	19.7%	24.8%	30.3%
Infant mortality rate	23.8%	11.1%	10.4%	7.2%
Poverty rate	12.2%	11.1%	10.1%	10.6%
Poverty disparity	NA	3.49	3.16	3.00
Mean family disparity	60.5%	62.3%	56.1%	NA
High rent burden	19.3%	24.0%	26.6%	27.4%

Source: LINC Database.

and households in poverty has *increased* over the period.[5] Further, the disparity in poverty rates is disturbing. Poverty disparity measures the ratio of poverty rates among black families and white families in the county. As this measure suggests, poverty rates among black families have remained three times the poverty rates among white families, despite the economic gains experienced. Even more troubling, the mean income for black families has not kept pace with the growth in average income among white families. During the period the data are available, the average black family's earnings fell from above 60 per cent to just 56 per cent of the average white family's earnings.[6] The racial income gap appears to be growing, not diminishing within the county. Lastly, the percentage of rental households that spend more than 35 per cent of their income on rent, defined as high rent burden, has risen from 19 per cent to over 27 per cent of households. The rise in property values that has benefited most property owners has increased the rent burden on lower-income households. Taken collectively, these figures suggest that the benefits of recent economic growth are many, but they are not shared throughout my community. In particular, the economic prosperity has not adequately buoyed the prospects of many county residents, whether from lower-income or black households.

Increased growth in population and employment opportunities has led to a loss of neighboring green space and rural landscapes. We have used our neighboring farms and woodland to make room for new housing developments and office buildings to lodge and employ our newer residents. At the same time, local officials have worked to offset these losses with increased park acreage to provide local residents with a variety of recreational opportunities. Table 1.3 crudely measures the impact of both developments on our local quality of life. On the one hand, farm acreage in the county has declined by over a fourth in just twenty-five years. Although not all of this "lost" farmland has become new housing and shopping malls, other undeveloped tracts not counted as farmland have been developed. Park acreage has nearly doubled, though it has not kept pace with the diminishing farmland.

Increased population and economic activity place further stresses on our environment. More people and more businesses normally generate more garbage and pollution in addition to the increased products and services they provide. Over the twenty-year period covered in Table 1.4, both solid waste disposal and hazardous wastes generation increased through 2000 and then declined subsequently.[7] At the same time, vehicle registrations have grown dramatically, without any hint of peaking in recent years. As a result, our roads are more congested and one would imagine our local air is more polluted. However, the latter is not necessarily the case.

Table 1.3 Green space trends in Guilford County, NC

	1982	*1992*	*1997*	*2002*	*2007*
Farm acreage	135,965	113,654	111,882	111,382	96,519
Park acreage	3,956	5,943	6,954	7,555	7,822

Sources: LINC Database, compilation of local sources.

Table 1.4 Key environmental trends in Guilford County, NC

	1985	*1990*	*1995*	*2000*	*2005*
Solid waste disposal (tons)	NA	a 471,541	449,957	730,012	703,606
Hazardous wastes (tons)	6,317	5,477	b 8,613	c 9,238	5,566
Vehicle registrations	236,995	268,068	287,763	319,756	333,992
Toxic air emissions	NA	2,702,254	2,041,034	1,010,032	513,410
Air quality index 90th	NA	NA	d 51	78	73
Water use (millions gpd)	41.76	44.24	42.74	56.65	45.94

Note: a = 1991–92 figure; b = 1994 figure; c = 1999 figure; d = 1996 figure.
Sources: LINC, NC DEHNR Solid Waste Annual Reports, EPA TRI Explorer Report, EPA Air Quality Index Report.

Different measures of air quality suggest different trends. The reductions in both toxic air emissions suggest that our "airshed" is less polluted and healthier than in the past. Other data suggest that we have witnessed dramatic declines in lead and carbon monoxide levels since the 1970s.[8] Yet, one key measure of air quality is suggesting a different trend in recent years. The Air Quality Index 90th percentile measures the level of air quality that the dirtiest (10 per cent) days exceed.[9] Over the past decade for which data are available, this measure has risen, thereby indicating substantial reductions in air quality. Recently, the biggest air quality "offender" is ozone, a key byproduct of cars and other gasoline combustion engines. Lastly, water use generally has increased, though perhaps peaking in 2000. Given Greensboro's position at the peak of its watershed, this has created some periods of distress, particularly during times of extended drought. Very recently, the city along with other regional partners has supplemented the local water supply by building another reservoir that will likely lead to future increases in water consumption.

My city's location at the upper end of our watershed raises another issue as well. We have little worry of what upstream neighbors may be doing to our drinking water supplies. Our reservoirs largely capture runoff from local rains. However, the same conditions that limit our water supply (quantity) also hamper our waste treatment efforts. Being located at the high end of the watershed means our local creeks and streams rarely have strong water flows, except during periods of extended rain. Thus, there is limited water flow to help dilute the treated wastewater that is returned to our local streams or the untreated stormwater that carries with it the runoff from our yards and streets. Both rising population and expanding development place greater pressures on the local streams that receive the wastewater. Despite our substantial effort in making improvements, the water quality assessments at four sites below the city have remained partially or significantly impaired by our water use, as Table 1.5 suggests. Redoubled efforts in recent years have led to some marked improvements. Nonetheless, our thirst for water exerts significant pressures on the local water systems' capacity to treat and receive the wastewater generated.

Table 1.5 Water quality trends in Guilford County, NC

Monitoring locations	*1988*	*1993*	*1998*	*2003*	*2008*
Horsepen Creek	NA	Fair	Fair	Poor	Fair
N. Buffalo Creek	NA	Poor	Poor	Poor	Fair
Reedy Fork	NA	Good–fair	Good–fair	Fair	Good–fair
S. Buffalo Creek	Poor	Poor	Poor	Poor	Fair

Source: Basin wide Assessment Report – Cape Fear River Basin, August 2009, Division of Water Quality, NCDENR.

Taken collectively, these varied measures of "development" give us a mixed and complicated picture. They fail to clarify my confusion, as they support varied conclusions. Local pessimists and environmentalists can point toward specific environmental quality measures and conclude that the quality of life has declined substantially over the period. In particular, they can cite the solid waste figures, the water quality data, and certain air quality measures to support their conclusions. Quite compellingly, they can argue that much of the prosperity is not fully shared throughout the community. At the same time, local optimists and civic boosters can point to the economic and water quality data as evidence that conditions have improved. Both of these views are prevalent in our local discourse, just as they are regionally, nationally, and even internationally. Though each side tends to focus on certain data and ignore other, contrary statistics, we should explore both perspectives before dismissing them as incomplete.

The Neo-Malthusian view

About two centuries ago, a rather obscure English parson published a startling book entitled *An Essay on the Principles of Population*. He offered a grim outlook to a nation on the doorstep of its Industrial Revolution. This country parson, Robert Malthus, argued that humanity faced a bleak future due to two relentless realities. On the one hand, human populations, just like other forms of life, reproduce in an exponential fashion. Assuming a modest two children per generation, each two-parent household would produce two offspring who would subsequently produce four grandchildren, eight great-grandchildren, sixteen great-great-grandchildren, and so on. Prosperous times that accompanied expanding harvests, higher incomes, and improved standards of living would only encourage this growth in human population. At the same time, Malthus argued that the stinginess of nature would permit increases in food production that would only grow arithmetically. Improvements in farming techniques and more lands in production could increase food harvests, but only at an incremental pace. Thus, Malthus offered the very gloomy prediction that the contemporary prosperity experienced in the England of his day was *inevitably* a temporary phenomenon, at best.

Malthus articulated a rather simple and commonsense proposition: on a finite planet, growth cannot continue without limit. Biologists encounter evidence of this reality in the natural world in countless ways. Indeed, it is the fertility of life that drives natural selection and evolution. Too many offspring competing for scarce resources is what permits some particularly well-adapted organisms to outlast and reproduce in greater numbers than their rivals, thereby influencing the genetic make-up of future generations. Recognizing the limitations placed by specific natural conditions, biologists use the concept of *carrying capacity* to describe the upper limits on the growth of a given species. In this way, biologists view growth as a local and temporary phenomenon that is constrained by some physical limit, often food supply.

This biological concept of *carrying capacity* is controversial only when applied to humans. Even Malthus noted our unique position. He argued that two other forces – which he called positive and preventative checks – could curb our tendency toward explosive population growth. Positive checks – like famine, pestilence, and war – increase mortality rates, thereby restraining population growth. These effects are largely found in the natural world as well. Preventative checks like prostitution, abortion, and infanticide reduce birth rates. In later years, Malthus raised the issue of moral restraint and the possibility of celibacy and late marriage as further ways that birth rates may decline over time.[10] Awareness, foresight, and self-restraint, all elements of our human potential, could prevent his gloomy predictions from becoming reality. Presumably, his disposition and experiences as a parson caused him to consider this outcome as unlikely.

Malthus's central point that there exist ultimate limits on human economic growth seems clear and sound. I suspect that most would agree. Yet, substantial disagreement hinges on how binding and how close these limits actually are. For example, local limits are not always binding. Rainfall in a specific locality does place limits on the local flora, fauna, and human populations that can exist over time. Yet, human ingenuity can and does overcome local limits. Pumping water from underground aquifers, piping it over long distances, or supplementing it with desalination plants are all ways that humans have overcome this local limit. While many regions of the world suffer from inadequate supplies of fresh water, the potential supply of water on earth far outstrips what our thirsty behaviors currently consume.[11] More broadly, regional and international trade can supplement shortages imposed by local limits. High water-consuming produce can be grown where water is abundant and shipped for sale in drier locales. Trade and technology have eroded the seasonal limits on local food supply. The fresh produce section in the supermarket during winter provides one obvious example. For thousands of years, humans have engaged in trade; a primary aim of interregional trade has been to overcome the geographical vagaries of nature.

Further, we have overcome past resource limits using our ingenuity in a different way. Eighteenth-century Great Britain experienced dwindling forests as a swelling human population sought more firewood to heat their homes and cook their food. A subsequent switch to coal as the primary fuel source reduced this pressure and permitted some reforesting to occur. In the nineteenth century, declining coal supplies brought new worries that energy limits were being reached.[12] These fears proved unfounded as Great Britain and the rest of the industrial world switched to plentiful oil and natural gas. These historical examples should serve as reminders that not every physical limit is indeed binding on our activities. At the same time, history (along with new archeological) research should teach us the perils of ignoring critical environmental limits.[13] Evidence of past societies litters our soils, their collapse often the result of not respecting their local resources and ecological constraints.

The Environmental Kuznets view

Many who argue that the Malthusian view of human growth is too simplistic base their ideas around those of Simon Kuznets, a twentieth-century economist and Nobel laureate. Among his many accomplishments, Kuznets identified specific patterns that resulted from rising household income and its varied impact on consumer purchases. Specifically, rising household incomes caused households to increase their expenditures of some goods, called superior goods, and to decrease their expenditures on other goods, called inferior goods. According to Kuznets, economic development would favor superior goods, because their appeal would grow disproportionately as household income increased. Steak and champagne are two obvious examples of superior goods. Kuznets himself never applied his framework to environmental goods and services; later individuals made the connection. As one contemporary has characterized it, "only when we become sufficiently rich can we afford the relative luxury of caring about the environment."[14]

Formally called the *Environmental Kuznets effect*, the argument goes like this. People in poverty have little luxury to take measures to protect their environment. Gaining access to adequate amounts of food, water, shelter, and clothing are necessary for short-run survival. Particularly in periods of stress, these short-run survival needs will outweigh longer-term concerns. For example, periods of hunger or extreme cold may force excessive harvesting of local food sources or local forests for fuel, regardless of their longer-term impact. As societies embark along the path of economic development, they often must exploit their local environment as they compete against rivals to increase production and lower costs. In this way, economic development may bring material prosperity at the expense of the local environment. Such prosperity provides personal wealth that prevents the stark dilemma that the very poor often face. Further, increased well-being encourages a re-evaluation of the value of the local environment as suggested by Kuznets. Enhanced concern for the quality of the environment encourages policy changes that counteract prior behaviors that led to a degraded environment. These changes can occur by two primary avenues.

First, market prices can frequently serve to protect our environmental resources. As economic growth proceeds, rising consumption of specific natural resources will lead eventually to emerging shortages. These shortages can trigger higher prices, thereby discouraging their consumption while encouraging additional supply and the search for cheaper substitutes. Rising timber prices encouraged the switch to coal as a source of heat and power for homes and factories in nineteenth-century Great Britain. Later, rising coal prices encouraged the exploitation of oil as a new energy source. More recently, we have responded to rising lumber and fish prices by developing new practices to supplement nature's fertility, for example with agro-forestry (plantation forests) and aquaculture (fish farming). As implied by the phrase "Necessity is the mother of invention", higher prices encourage new inventions and technologies that resolve critical shortages. Higher prices for natural resources cause a multitude of behavioral changes that limit further depletion of these critical resources or reduce their importance as we switch to substitute products or alternative technologies.

Second, as economic growth encourages rising household incomes at the expense of a deteriorating natural environment, increased awareness will foster changing attitudes and decisions. Increasingly aware of the hazards of pollution, citizens will pressure government officials to legislate and enforce laws that restrict further pollution. Water and air quality standards, zoning restrictions, landfill requirements, and bans on highly toxic materials offer some examples of how citizen pressures can lead to improving environments. Though sometimes costly to implement, these measures become affordable by the rising prosperity. Regulations can encourage businesses to explore new technologies that limit the offending pollutants. As economic growth further satiates our material needs, we increasingly look toward improving our local environment to enhance the quality of our lives. Responsive government should reflect this increased desire to protect our natural environment in its public policies. As the argument goes, economic development initially encourages a decline in the natural environment. However, at some point the relationship switches and further economic development fosters an improvement in the natural environment. Rising incomes give societies both the means and the motive for protecting and improving the quality of the environment.

Critics take issue with this view on several points. Sure, market prices can encourage prudent and even capable stewardship of many of our natural assets. Yet, markets do not adequately represent many environmental resources and services. Market prices of many environmental assets, if they exist at all, do not reflect their underlying scarcity or value. Under these circumstances, specific resources or services can dwindle without triggering the "alarm" of rising prices. For example, many species of migratory songbirds are under significant threat as development reduces their natural habitats and human-made chemicals affect their health and reproductive capacity.[15] As bird counts continue to decline, no market price will serve as a siren to change our practices; only their dwindling numbers and fading songs will herald their further decline. Going further, we already have the technology to "substitute" for their declining absence. To offset their silence, we can play tapes of their songs. Yet, would anyone really argue that having a high-quality recording is an adequate replacement for their songs *in vivo*?

In addition, critics argue that government is not always responsive in protecting the public interest. In some parts of the world, government institutions do not represent public sentiment. Even where democratic traditions and representative government are established, they function imperfectly. While the majority of citizens may prefer more restrictive pollution regulations, a few well-funded interests may oppose these changes. They may make their opposition effective either by reframing the public debate or by lobbying key lawmakers and public officials. In either case, their focused and well-financed opposition may overcome a more widespread, but less intense desire for increased restrictions. Substantial flaws in both markets and government mean that many environmental problems can worsen even if the public wishes otherwise.

Assessing the two paradigms

Both paradigms just discussed are true and both are wrong. Like most widely held worldviews, they each offer penetrating insights even as they each limit our understanding. It is true that our current phase of exponential human population growth cannot continue for long or certainly not without limit. Undoubtedly, there is some finite limit or carrying capacity for human population, no matter how clever we are.[16] Moreover, we cannot expect a limitless future where we consume more and more. It is extremely doubtful that our natural environment could cope effectively if all humans alive today lived the American lifestyle. As an example, consider momentarily if the rest of the world drove cars to the extent that Americans do – a scenario that would easily quadruple (or more) their numbers on the road. Their impact would create staggering consequences on local air pollution, greenhouse gas emissions, and oil markets. Clearly, there exist limits to certain forms of economic growth and it is likely that as we approach these different limits, we will find some more binding and harder to evade. In the eighteenth century, economic growth led to an alarming thinning of the English forests. In the twenty-first century, our economic policies in support of continuing growth are contributing to global climate change. Not only has our modern limit become global rather than local in scale, but it also offers us a breadth of challenges that did not confront our ancestors.

Though our current challenges are daunting, we do have significant tools at our disposal as the Kuznets view posits. In some areas of the world, past policies have created a material prosperity that is unprecedented in human history. Our level of affluence gives us the means, if not the motivation, to halt further damage and restore critical elements of our degraded environment. We can afford to pay for restoration efforts and select policies that will mitigate future harm. Further, our ingenuity, knowledge, and technology will inform many of the solutions available to us and provide us with choices that are more palatable.

However, we cannot simply assume that our current policies will create more solutions than problems. Economic growth, as we currently practice it in this country, is fundamentally antagonistic to our natural systems, despite the gains in technology. For example, thanks to new technologies the typical car sold today gets nearly twice the mileage and emits one-tenth of the pollutants than cars sold in 1970.[17] Yet, our unabated appetite for personal mobility caused a near doubling of cars on the road and miles driven since that date. As a result, ozone levels are lower in many locations, but gasoline sales and CO_2 emissions are higher.[18] We have spent much of the impressive gains from technology on our desire for more and bigger cars. Although our appetites appear to expand without limit, there are physical limits to what new technologies can accomplish for us.

Even though each of these significant paradigms is incomplete and limiting in their perspective, we should not necessarily reject them. Rather, we should view them as partial insights to a much more complex reality, one that will always challenge us and cause us to come up short. Holding both perspectives and understanding their competing, yet complementary, insights can offer us a better guide than merely adopting one or the other. There exists a well-used image to illustrate this point. In Figure 1.1, most people quickly see either a young, beautiful woman or aging matron. Only with some effort and time can most of us see both images. While we may be predisposed to see one figure initially, we can see both with some help. Possessing both views, being able to switch back and forth, is certainly richer and more interesting than experiencing just one image. More importantly, our initial perspective may limit our viewing of either the younger or older woman, despite the presence of both images. Unless we are willing to look beyond our initially comforting perspective, we may never see the other facet of reality contained in this image.

In the same vein, we must integrate the two competing paradigms as we examine our prevailing economic policies. We cannot continue our current path in assuming that "more is better." We will encounter binding, natural limits, some of which can be quite devastating. Yet, this should not suggest that we cannot develop society in ways that can improve the well-being of humanity. We can realistically aspire

Figure 1.1 A young beauty or an aging matron?
Source: David Landrigan.

to a brighter, more fulfilling future. However, we must learn to adapt our ingenuity, our technologies, and our policies in ways that improve the human condition without further undermining our natural environment. We can move toward a path of "green development." An understanding of both ecology and of economics can ease our way to this new path.

Focus of this book

This book takes the ecological economics perspective as it integrates two – often conflicting – disciplines, economics and ecology, to reveal new insights. Not only does this dual framework illuminate the limiting aspects of each individual discipline, but also it distinguishes those environmental challenges that are likely to persist from those that are more susceptible to human solution. The twin perspective facilitates the development of solutions and policies that are effective in both the natural and economic worlds. Moreover, this synthesis encourages an awareness of the limitations even of this combined perspective. Let me explain each of these points in turn.

Economists have long ignored the full value of nature in our economic debates. Though they consider nature as one of three key *factors of production* critical to any economy, most debates have relegated *land* to an inconspicuous corner as the focus has turned to *labor* and *capital*. Economists have generally viewed nature's bounty as being largely limitless or endlessly substitutable, thereby justifying its dismissal. In Chapter Two, I redress this neglect by identifying the critical services that nature provides our human economy. Many of these services are essential to life and have no easy substitutes. This fuller recognition of the economic value of *land* or nature gives rise to the concept of *natural capital*, one that is both comparable and distinguishable from the related concepts of *human*, *social*, and *physical capital*. In Chapter Three, I discuss these natural services to distinguish those that are most vulnerable to over-exploitation and neglect from those that are more susceptible to policies that encourage effective stewardship. In Chapter Four, using the "1970s energy crisis" as a case example, I show how markets largely "solved" that crisis, though in a manner that has led to the much greater energy crises we face today. In Chapter Five, I explore the circumstances in which markets suffer failure. Taken collectively, these four chapters distinguish those environmental problems that can be resolved relatively effectively from those that will require much more creative and concerted effort.

At this point, the book shifts its focus toward policy solutions. As a conceptual guide for the remainder of the book, Chapter Six examines how natural systems function and persist over long periods. In particular, the chapter identifies four key attributes of sustainable natural systems: self-regulating recycling of key resources, a plentiful and durable energy source, an adaptive capacity, and system resiliency. The chapter examines the importance of each in sustaining the essential character of ecosystems and preserving their functional effectiveness over time. In turn, I discuss over the next four chapters each of those attributes as well as specific policies that could encourage their development in our economy.

Chapter Seven identifies the importance of materials recycling to our economy. I propose a variety of policies to encourage increased recycling and reduced depletion of key resources, particularly non-renewables. Chapter Eight examines the significance of moving toward a plentiful and more durable energy source. This chapter identifies a variety of policy options that will reduce our current dependence on fossil fuels and encourage a shift to a variety of alternative, less harmful energy sources. By eliminating current subsidies to the non-renewable sources and implementing emissions fees, these policies will encourage an energy transition that must come sooner rather than later.

Chapters Nine and Ten continue this analysis as they consider attributes of nature that go beyond those characterized as *natural resources*. Similar to nature, market economies respond and adapt to changing external circumstances. In this way, promoting market outcomes should ensure that our economy continues to evolve and adapt as circumstances dictate. Yet, markets do not capture the full environmental costs of development and therefore encourage growth that is more environmentally damaging. Chapter Nine examines several policies that would encourage greater market accountability of environmental costs and environmentally benign development. In Chapter Ten, I apply the concept of resiliency to our economic circumstances. Rather than expressing complete shock when natural and human-created disruptions occur, we should anticipate their likelihood even as they are unpredictable in time and location. As such, we should ensure that our citizens, communities, and economies have the capacity and resiliency to absorb and recover relatively quickly from such disruptions. In this chapter, I discuss a number of public policies that could increase our capabilities.

In Chapter Eleven, I remind the reader of the importance of integrating both economics and ecology and the insights raised throughout the book. I note how each discipline reveals limitations of the other and provides a richer, more complete understanding of the world and our pressing challenges. Throughout the book, an understanding of natural systems enables us to see which components of our natural heritage are most susceptible to our neglect and squandering as well as to understand what structural changes we must make in our economy. Similarly, an understanding of economics offers a guide toward effective policies. One of the secrets of organic farmers is that they are relearning how to harness rather than fight the natural functions that nature provides for free. Environmental policymakers need a similar grounding in economics to develop policies that harness rather than fight market incentives. Taken together, this dual perspective of ecology and economics offers key insights toward understanding and effectively resolving many of our current environment problems. Nonetheless, even this rich perspective has its limitations and I discuss these before concluding the book.

Re-examining the local conditions

Recall that my community has undergone changing circumstances that are not unlike those found in many other communities across this country. Our manufacturing base has lost its prominent role in the local economy as many of our traditional industries have closed their doors. Despite this development, Greensboro has witnessed a surging population that has brought new jobs, businesses, and an expanding economy. Average pay, median family income, and median home prices have all increased, bearing witness to the increased prosperity experienced by the typical family. Despite the increased population, air quality is generally better today than in the 1970s and water quality is improving. Yet, not all of the changes have been positive nor have they brought uniform benefits. Black households continue to experience disproportionately lower pay and suffer from higher unemployment and poverty rates. Not all air quality measures, particularly ozone, suggest improved air quality. Local green space appears to be in decline.

This picture suggests a mixed and confusing set of trends. The remaining chapters of this book will clarify much of this confusion. In particular, the sections that explain the selective strengths of markets in resolving different environmental problems will illustrate why some improvements in this area have been witnessed. Therefore, a fuller interpretation of these local trends must await the upcoming analysis. I will return to these issues in the last chapter.

Further reading

Ronald Bailey, *Earth Report 2000: Revisiting the True State of the Planet*, offers in its first chapter an engaging argument for how humanity can avoid the Malthusian trap.

Lester Brown, *Plan B 4.0: Mobilizing to Save Civilization*, offers an updated assessment of the perils we face if we continue to exceed nature's limits, as well as an alternative path of development.

Robert Costanza *et al.*, *An Introduction to Ecological Economics*, provide an excellent overview of the field of ecological economics.

Herman Daly, *Ecological Economics and Sustainable Development: Selected Essays of Herman Daly*, includes two dozen recent articles, speeches, and expert testimonies by Herman Daly, the pre-eminent scholar in ecological economics.

Matthew Kahn, *Green Cities: Urban Growth and the Environment*, provides an excellent discussion of the Environmental Kuznets curve that is the basis of the view discussed in the chapter.

Bjorn Lomborg, *The Skeptical Environmentalist: Measuring the Real State of the World*, offers a massive, though controversial, use of evidence to argue that economic growth has improved the natural environment.

Donella Meadows *et al.*, *Limits to Growth: The 30-Year Update*, offer an update to prior works that sparked the neo-Malthusian critique of modern economic growth.

2 Our precious endowment

The Catskills Watershed

Somewhat surprisingly, New York City has a reputation for high-quality tap water, enough so that it has been bottled and commercially sold in the past.[1] The city draws its water largely from the famed Catskills Mountains, an area that lies 100 miles north of Manhattan. Largely forested and sparsely populated with farms and small communities, this area comprises 1,600 square miles and embodies two watersheds, the Delaware and the Catskills. The area operates as a large basin capturing the falling precipitation as it slowly flows into the public reservoirs and eventually to the city's nine million customers. Due to the absence of development in the region, the water requires only minimal treatment, the primary reason for its untainted taste and reputation for quality.

In the 1990s, New York City officials gained further appreciation for their unusual water supply. New federal water-quality standards gave New York and other cities an expensive choice: filter your drinking water or provide proof that you are safeguarding water quality through watershed protection. City water officials estimated the cost of installing filtration plants to be $6 billion or higher, with an annual operating cost of $300 million, each a sizable figure even for New York City. To avoid this substantial investment, the city petitioned for a filtration waiver promising to protect the watershed. City officials pledged to fund improvements in the local septic systems and sewage treatment plants, to restrict the use of de-icing compounds on roads, and to limit the construction of impervious surfaces like roads and parking lots.[2] In addition, the city agreed to purchase land buffers along streams and around reservoirs to limit further any chemical runoff. Such watershed protections would cost the city up to $1 billion. Given the substantial disparity in costs between the two alternatives, it is apparent why the city chose to protect its current watershed rather than build new water filtration facilities.

For a variety of reasons including terrain, economics, political muscle, and luck, New Yorkers had a choice unavailable to most other cities. Like many municipalities, New York long ago secured water rights to much of the watershed. However, in other cities development pressures and poor watershed protection led to municipal water supplies needing filtration and treatment to meet federal guidelines. New York and the Catskills have largely avoided this fate. Although once a region filled with farms, the forests have reclaimed much of the land as farmers moved elsewhere in search of land that is more productive.[3] Nearly half the land is now state owned. Though the city itself owns relatively little land in the watershed, a 1913 state law allows it certain rights to protect the watershed. For all of these reasons, New York retains a water catchment system capable of providing water of both adequate quantity and quality to meet its current needs. This option can save billions of scarce tax dollars as long as water officials prevent further development that would damage the watershed and degrade their drinking water. It is now their clear responsibility to either preserve or squander this natural asset.

New York's decision represents a significant transformation for the Catskills, which moves from water source to protected watershed. As long as New York cared simply for water quantity, officials could view this area solely as a large reservoir valuable for its capacity to provide ample water flow. Adding the concern for water quality requires care for the network of complex natural systems that produces this highly prized and relatively pure water. If these natural systems become impaired, then New Yorkers face Environmental Protection Authority (EPA) sanctions and the cost of building water filtration facilities. New Yorkers now have a substantial financial interest in protecting these natural systems.

However, this region serves New Yorkers and others in neighboring communities as more than a source of untainted fresh water. The Catskills Watershed offers a variety of goods and services that both make our earthly existence possible as well as desirable. Not only does it provide a source of livelihood and community to those who live there, but it also bestows many recreational and cultural opportunities. It offers a haven to wildlife and flora, cleans the skies of noxious pollutants, and moderates our climate. These different services and the human claims on them offer a recipe for acrimony and conflict. New York City water customers may agree in keeping the Catskills as pristine as possible, but the area's local residents may have different aspirations for the region. Resolving these competing interests will require discussion, negotiation, and compromise. However, we must first recognize the different benefits and services we receive from these natural systems.

Just like the Catskills, any area provides a vast array of freely provided services resulting from a myriad of complex and interrelated ecological processes. Their variety provides testimony to the complexity of the natural environment and to its generous contributions to our individual well-being, our communities, and our economies. Rather than viewing the environment merely as source of valued resources, we must consider it as a provider of a web of interconnected services, some of which are critical while others are merely delightful. Yet, simply appreciating these varied services is not enough; we must also understand the underlying ecological systems that provide these services. Otherwise, we are liable to squander opportunities such as the one New York City seized. To realize fully the bounty that nature provides us, I now turn to a discussion of the full breadth of these ecological services. Only as we understand these services and their value to us can we appreciate our natural endowment. In this way, we learn the lesson of New York City and its acclaimed tap water.

Table 2.1 Ecological services

Life-support services	*Provisioning services*
Atmospheric gas regulation	Food production
Climate regulation	Raw materials
Disturbance regulation	Genetic resources
Water regulation	Cultural services
Water supply	Aesthetic and spiritual
Soil formation	Educational and informational
Erosion control and sediment retention	Carrier services
Nutrient cycling	Human habitation
Waste treatment	Cultivation and pastoralism
Solar energy fixation and biomass production	Commerce and transportation
Biological control	Energy conversion
Pollination	Recreation
Maintenance of biological diversity	Refugia

Natural benefits

Over the past decade, several different researchers have catalogued the range of benefits or ecological services we obtain from our natural environment. Gretchen Daily[4] identified thirteen different ecosystem services, Robert Costanza (with others[5]) listed seventeen different services, and Rudolf de Groot[6] did not stop counting until he named thirty-seven different benefits. Actually, these lists are more alike than the numbers suggest. There is little argument over the ways we benefit from nature; the differences revolve over how we categorize and articulate these multifaceted gifts. My own list falls conveniently in the middle, as it cites twenty-four different services rendered. Like de Groot, I place these different services into four categories that reflect their relationship with humans. I shall discuss the importance of each in turn, starting with the life-support services, followed by provisioning services, cultural services, and carrier services. I have enumerated the full list of services in Table 2.1.

Life-support services

Through our myths, religious faiths, art, and oral traditions, humans have long acknowledged the varied roles that the natural world plays in our lives. Our ancestors did not understand how nature provided these essential services; yet, their stories, paintings, fertility festivals, and cultural expressions all give testimony to the importance they attached to these gifts. In contrast, we understand better the incredibly complex processes that continually provide us with protective climate, food, water and other essentials we need to exist. Despite our scientific understanding, we, ironically, pay scant attention to these vital gifts from nature. Increasingly, we rely on our modern technologies to insulate ourselves from the vagaries of nature. As we do so, we slowly lose our appreciation for nature's gifts.

Atmospheric gas regulation

Comparing the earth's atmosphere to those of its planetary neighbors illustrates the importance of this crucial service. Venus and Mars have similar atmospheres, comprised of carbon dioxide (about 95 percent), nitrogen (about 3.5 percent), trace gases and water. Initially similar to Venus and Mars, our atmosphere is now comprised of 78 percent nitrogen, 21 percent oxygen, traces of carbon dioxide (surprisingly, only 0.04 percent), noble gases, and water. Over the eons, our planetary atmosphere and life have co-evolved to create the current mixture of gases we now find, a balance that is critical to life in so many ways. Too little atmospheric oxygen, about 15 percent or less, and most life that needs oxygen for respiration would suffocate. Too much oxygen, about 25 percent or more, and the planetary surface would ignite in a massive flame of spontaneous combustion, leaving little chance for terrestrial life to survive. Fortunately, complex natural systems work effectively to keep the gas balances in check. For example, a continual balance between animals and plants works to maintain the balance of both oxygen and carbon dioxide in our atmosphere. Evidence suggests that our current composition of gases has been relatively stable for the past seventy million years.

Our current atmospheric composition is essential to terrestrial life in another way, as it protects us from life-threatening, ultraviolet solar energy. It was not the presence of atmospheric oxygen (O_2) that allowed life to leave the safety of the oceans, but rather the presence of ozone (O_3) in the upper atmosphere. At this level, ozone shields the harmful ultraviolet light which, if permitted to pass through to the earth's surface, would threaten all land-based life. (The less harmful ultraviolet rays that do reach the surface cause the sunburn we get at the beach.) Yet, these ultraviolet rays exact a toll as they convert the protective ozone (O_3) into regular oxygen (O_2). Fortunately, natural atmospheric systems function to create more ozone in the upper atmosphere to replace the depleted ozone. Without these replenishing processes, virtually all terrestrial life would perish or return to the safety of our oceans.

Climate regulation

Many of the same natural processes that regulate our protective atmosphere also provide hospitable and stable climates. For example, the regulation of gases between plant and animal respiration has maintained a level of carbon dioxide that has sustained life on earth. Without this carbon dioxide (and other gases), the earth's surface temperatures would crash to a chilly 1° Fahrenheit, creating a frozen planet hostile to nearly all forms of life. Carbon dioxide permits some, though not all, of the solar radiation to warm our planet to the comfortable temperatures we normally experience, thus creating the "greenhouse effect." Our atmosphere moderates our climate in another key way. Primarily due to the angle of the incoming solar radiation, surface areas near the earth's equator receive more solar heat than do latitudes further away. This heat differential drives the trade winds and other atmospheric forces that dominate our weather and climate. These winds disperse heat and moisture around the world, thereby moderating conditions in both the tropic and temperate regions. This climate moderation tends to limit the temperature extremes that can place undue stress on most forms of life.

Each of us can easily appreciate the obvious benefits of moderate temperatures and the absence of extreme weather conditions. Yet, we receive a variety of less visible rewards from these climate-moderating processes. Milder climates enable plants and animals to thrive more broadly across the planet. Their extended reach has meant that humans can prosper in more areas as well. Climate moderation also allows plants and animals to devote fewer energy resources to merely surviving their environment. Plants can devote more energy toward plant production and less toward overcoming the stress caused by extreme conditions. More efficient use of solar energy leads to more bountiful plant growth and greater food sources for grazing animals. In stable, temperate climates, humans and other animals require less energy to protect themselves from their environment, freeing energy to serve other purposes. In these ways, stable, temperate climates lead to a more prolific world filled with flora and fauna.

Disturbance regulation

However, neither our climate nor its shorter-term counterpart, weather, is fixed and unchanging. Severe and extreme conditions do occur, sometimes with ruinous effect. Yet, natural systems mitigate the most harmful effects of these storms as well as encourage recovery from their damage. In cases of major hurricanes and rainstorms, vegetation absorbs the worst effects of the storm. Trees restrain the power of surging winds while their canopy of leaves protects the ground from the full power of pelting rain. The capacity of vegetation and soils to absorb massive amounts of water alleviates some of the worst effects of flooding. Certain soils act like sponges, absorbing huge amounts of water during periods of torrential rain and only slowly releasing it into watersheds initially overwhelmed by the deluge. Alternatively, in conditions of drought, most plants and animals have behavioral responses that limit water loss to endure the dry conditions. In addition, many trees and shrubs have fire-resistant barks that allow them to survive all but the hottest of fires.

Natural systems are capable of restoring areas traumatized by natural or human-caused calamity. Lands denuded by fire, flood, or severe drought attract enterprising plants, animals, and micro-organisms once the source of trauma has subsided. These pioneering species migrate into the newly created void to begin a process of rehabilitation. This capacity for self-healing is a crucial service that sustains the long-term health of ecosystems. This process of recovery, known as *secondary succession*, grants natural areas the capacity for restoration, though not necessarily to the original state. Given our capacity to affect and even scar our environment, this service of recuperation offers us some valuable insurance against past, present, and future mistakes.

To be sure, we do not always welcome this critical recovery service. In modern agriculture (and in the typical suburban landscape), we have taken the challenge of overcoming the forces of succession. In creating fertile conditions to grow selected plants and crops, we simultaneously encourage the growth of pioneering "weeds," which are simply undesired plants. Understandably, farmers concerned with increasing their yields would rather avoid these competitors for water, nutrients, and solar energy that displace their cash crops. They spend hundreds of millions of dollars annually to restrain this key response of nature. Similarly, homeowners spend considerable amounts in battling weeds that mar the look of their verdant and weed-free lawns.

Water regulation

Water is the stuff of life. Humans are fully two-thirds made up of water. Fortunately, our planet is blessed with lots of water, though virtually all of it is largely unavailable.[7] Some is locked up in glacial ice while most resides in the oceans. If not for the global systems of evaporation, winds, and precipitation, we would quickly run through our supplies of fresh water on land. As water runs downhill with gravity, rain that falls on the land eventually returns to the oceans, either through the surface water systems of streams and rivers, through the groundwater aquifers, or through evaporation and another cycle of rainfall. Whatever the route taken, fresh water eventually ends up in the salty oceans where it is of little use to most terrestrial life. Fortunately, solar energy heats and returns the ocean waters back to the atmosphere as water vapor, leaving the unwanted salts behind. Atmospheric winds carry the moisture to the distant corners of the planet. When sufficient amounts of water vapor collect and accumulate, rain is the result. Without this complex set of planetary mechanisms, life on land could not continue. While the amount of water available on the earth is assuredly finite, the relentless nature of this cycle makes it elastic, almost infinite over time. Though the regularity and amount of rainfall varies with a given location and is often a source of extreme frustration, its broader dependability is crucial to land-based life.

Water supply

Knowing that it is raining somewhere on earth at any moment of time gives little solace when you need water now, at a given spot. Even when the rains do come, the falling water acts like an itchy traveler ready to resume its travels back to the oceans. Most rain that falls on the land returns to the atmosphere via the dual mechanisms of evaporation and transpiration. The remaining water either becomes runoff or infiltrates through the soil into the groundwater system. Given the penchant of water to seek the lowest level, the surface water found in our rivers and lakes quickly runs toward the oceans. It takes less than three weeks for this surface runoff to return to its ocean home. This easy source of water quite literally runs through our fingers.

Fortunately, nature offers various means of water storage to extend its availability between rainfalls. Low-lying areas serve as ponds and lakes to catch the surface water flows, acting as natural reservoirs. Below ground, the soil absorbs water during heavy rainfalls and slowly releases the water into aquifers that carry it toward surface streams. This sponging process slows the pace at which fresh water returns to the salty oceans and explains why creeks and rivers continue to run even after days of no local rain. In addition, the soils and groundwater provide vast, natural reservoirs that allow water withdrawals as need dictates rather than when the weather permits. This captured water provides us with dependable sources of water to quench our thirst and irrigate our fields. Level terrain, extensive forestation of the land, and specific soils all encourage this water retention process. Deforestation decreases the soil's ability to absorb rainfall, causing more to flow as runoff. Eroded soils and those packed by the pressure of direct rainfall absorb less water. Even worse, paving over soils to erect roads and parking lots encourages flooding, as it prevents any water infiltration. Less water refills the underground reservoirs and more flows as runoff that quickly dissipates. We can offset any losses in water regulation by building reservoirs. However, we pay dearly for the loss of this freely provided service.

Soil formation

Soil represents perhaps the clearest example of nature serving as a source of natural endowment or capital. For thousands of years, humans have fought over fertile lands in recognition of their substantial value. Soil is important to plant life for several reasons. It provides a medium for plants to cling to in periods of strong winds and lashing rain. Richer, deeper soils provide a better means of anchor. Further, soil permits the retention of key plant nutrients as well as the massive numbers of micro-organisms that help plants to use these nutrients. Fertile soils are those rich with these elements. Lastly, soil serves to store water as previously mentioned. Fertile soil creates a hospitable home for plant life to thrive and offer an essential sanctuary for our farming economy.

Somewhat surprising to some, soil represents a renewable resource, though one with an extremely slow reproduction rate. Soil formation is part of a larger, global system of erosion that relentlessly transports sediments from one spot to another. The weathering of rock – be it by wind, water, or chemical reactions – slowly yet persistently fragments bedrock into ever-smaller pieces. Wind and water insistently drive these particles from place to place, as they land temporarily in the local soil. Eventually, they settle as sediments in the ocean depths. Over the eons, they may reappear as magma during times of volcanic activity. Then the cooled lava becomes the bedrock that erosion will eventually transform to make new soil. Moreover, soils are more than tiny pieces of rock; they also require organic matter to provide space for air and water to reside. Complex biological processes must supply these sources of organic matter, usually decayed plant life tunneled into the soil by earthworms. Together, these sources slowly work to build the depth of soil.

Erosion control and sediment retention

Yet, what comes around goes around. The vast and relentless processes that create new soils also work to separate the particles from their current home and to transport them downwind or downstream. Fortunately, vegetation reduces the corrosive power of these forces. Acting as windbreaks, vegetation reduces the amount of soil carried off by powerful winds. A vegetation canopy protects the soil from the force of hard downpours, thereby reducing the erosive effects of rain. Plant roots further restrain the movement of soil as the water washes over it. Often plants provide a barricade behind which sediments will accumulate, thereby resisting the tidal force of water carrying sediments further down a slope. In providing these services, the vegetation cover prevents the erosion of an important and visible form of natural capital that has sustained life and human activity for millions of years.

Deep and rich topsoils result from circumstances that minimize local soil erosion to permit their slow accumulation. Unfortunately, modern farming practices leave the soil vulnerable to increased erosion, generating concern that these methods are depleting our soils as erosion rates exceed the soil formation rates. Perhaps new technologies will reduce our current dependence on natural soils to grow sufficient food to meet the needs of humanity.[8] However, until that time, we depend on the continual formation of soils to replace those inevitably lost to erosion to sustain our farm economy and indeed all land-based biotic life.

Nutrient cycling

To flourish, plants require more than just hospitable soils, sunlight, and water. They also need four major nutrients (carbon, nitrogen, phosphorus, and sulfur) and another dozen or so minor nutrients to grow and reproduce. Like all matter, each of these nutrients has limited availability. Yet, plants require ample amounts of each nutrient, on a continuing basis. To satisfy these requirements, elaborate networks have evolved that literally span the earth to ensure their constant recycling. These networks include complex geological, chemical, and biological processes, some of which we barely understand. For example, carbon is recycled in different forms through the earth's atmosphere, waters, soils, living tissues, and molten core. Vast arrays of processes, ranging from cataclysmic events like volcanic eruptions to mundane acts of respiration (as we exhale carbon dioxide from our bodies), participate in this carbon cycle. These cycling processes occur on a global scale, ensuring their dispersal. This dissemination supplies the ongoing fertility to soils that supports plant life. Unfortunately, the pace of replenishment is rarely quick enough for our modern agricultural systems, which have turned to commercial nutrients (fertilizers) to boost yields and offset declines in natural fertility.

Not all nutrient recycling relies on global processes; in fact, much of it is local in nature. We live in a "dog eat dog world," and thank goodness that we do. Plants mostly meet their daily vitamin requirements through nutrients found in the soil. Herbivores then feed on these plants as their source of energy and nutrition, even as they serve as the food source for carnivores. At each stage, the feeders are able to use these nutrients and transform them into new structures. This new form becomes the delicious meal for another feeder. Lastly, certain animals and micro-organisms known as decomposers dine on whatever is left. In doing so, they essentially return each of these key nutrients back into the soil to "finance" new plant growth. These food webs preserve local soil fertility.

The provincial nature of these nutrient loops creates a fundamental problem for our more cosmopolitan agricultural and food systems. The "bread baskets" of our world, say Nebraska, export much of their wheat to feed growing appetites in our cities. In doing so, they are "exporting" the key nutrients that, if left to decompose, would maintain soil fertility to harvest future crops. To offset this withdrawal of nutrients, farmers need to "import" expensive fertilizers to replenish soil fertility. At the same time, we are overloading our urban areas with key nutrients. Some food wastes we truck to landfills where we also deposit toxic materials. We flush our remaining food wastes into local streams and rivers, where they frequently overwhelm these waterways before eventually flowing to the ocean. Neither option allows for the easy recovery and recycling of essential nutrients.

Waste treatment

The bio-geochemical processes that regulate our atmosphere and recycle nutrients provide waste treatment services. Just as every living organism must seek food and nutrients, so it must also expel waste products no longer usable to the organism. Not only are these excretions undesirable, they are usually harmful to the organism. There must be some way to eliminate these wastes to offset their continual creation, otherwise, any abundant life form would quickly suffer from the accumulation of its own litter. Fortunately, nature has created a system in which one creature's harmful waste products are the source of food and nutrition for another.

Many consider oxygen as the first pollutant on earth. As early life forms emerged, they used the available carbon dioxide and expelled oxygen into the atmosphere. As oxygen slowly accumulated, it eventually threatened these same life forms. Simultaneously, the build-up of oxygen likely encouraged the evolution of life forms able to use this increasingly abundant element. Animal life evolved to complement the requirements of plant life, thereby creating a mutual waste treatment system in addition to a stable atmospheric balance. In this way, nature appears to have an entrepreneurial bent, as it offers rewards to species that adapt to consume any build-up in the wastes of others.

Much like beauty, "food" is in the eye of the beholder. The wastes of one organism are the food source of another. A wide variety of animals and micro-organisms called decomposers are attracted to unwanted plant and animal wastes and transform these wastes into more useful forms. They provide an essential link in the nutrient recycling chain. Further, these organisms offer a variety of specialized services. Scientists have found a number of different bacteria whose appetite for petroleum is nearly insatiable. We now use these bacteria to combat the ravages of coastal oil spills. In consuming the petroleum, they transform it into a much less damaging form. Long before humans drilled for oil, these bacteria likely evolved in areas of naturally occurring oil spills. Consequently, not only do these waste treatment services function to clean our environment, but we can also use them to mitigate some of the injury caused by our modern way of living.

Fixation of solar energy and biomass production

As discussed previously, vast and complex natural systems encourage the cycling of vital elements of life, including water and key nutrients. To function effectively, these global systems require energy supplied by the sun. Solar heat drives the evaporation process and powers the winds that scatter moisture across the planet, eventually falling as rain or snow. Each organism participating in the nutrient cycles requires energy to transform food and water into usable materials. Unlike water and key nutrients that can be endlessly recycled, the energy that we use can be used once and once only. This is the depressing consequence of the Law of Entropy, or the Second Law of Thermodynamics. According to this law, the work potential of any energy source inevitably declines as it is used. Yet, each of the natural services already discussed requires a dependable energy source. Fortunately, the sun should serve as a reliable source for the next hundred million years or so.

Though all living organisms require energy to survive, only a few can directly use sunlight as a source of power. Animals may bask in its warmth and they may value (or alternatively fear) the visibility it provides; however, they cannot use sunlight directly to fuel their biological functions. Only plants can. Through the process of photosynthesis, plants use solar energy to transform nutrients and water into stored chemical energy, known as carbohydrates. Whether directly or indirectly, virtually all other living organisms feed on these created carbohydrates and thus satisfy their energy needs. Solar energy supports virtually all life on earth. Not only does photosynthesis create a different and more usable (to animals and some plants) form of energy, it also creates a more concentrated form of energy. Though plentiful, sunlight is a highly diffuse form of energy. Photosynthesis concentrates the energy from sunlight as well as transforming it. In this way, it eases the burden of life for all plant-eating creatures, providing a relatively rich fuel source as compensation for any foraging costs.

Biological control

The web of life includes a number of highly complex systems and mechanisms that keep the populations of different species roughly in balance, thereby preserving the diversity of life. A variety of behavioral relationships – predation, competition, mutualism, and parasitism – serve as methods of biological control. Each functions to prevent one species from capturing the full range of energy opportunities, dominating the others, and blocking other species from finding new niches in which to survive. A world dominated by a few key species would not only be less interesting, but would also be less adaptable and more vulnerable to disruptive changes.

Many cat owners cringe and complain about the brutality of nature when we observe our pets killing some unsuspecting bird in our yard. Yet, this process of predation is an important mechanism in the service of biological control. Any change in circumstances, whether natural or human-induced, may favor certain species. An unusually mild winter may permit more deer to survive than normal. If unchecked, their increased numbers strip the local area of undergrowth that serves as fodder. Overgrazing leads to erosion and depletion of the soil. Not only can these losses lead to starvation among the deer, but also to reduced populations in the future. In places where wolves and other predators of deer remain, a different scenario unfolds. The expanding deer population leads to greater opportunities for these predators and swells their numbers. The predators curb the explosive growth in deer, saving the local woods from overgrazing. Further, predation culls the deer population of its weaker members, thereby strengthening the overall health of the herd. A falling deer population causes the wolf population to suffer decline as the kills become less frequent. In the end, both prey and predator return to some balance, albeit an uneasy one. Although predation can lead to extinction of the prey species, that rarely results. The more likely outcome is that the biological controls work to maintain, and in some cases encourage, the further diversity found in our natural systems. This increased diversity strengthens the integrity of our natural systems and encourages their continued viability.[9]

Pollination

Beyond survival, all living organisms live to reproduce themselves. Reproduction among plants offers interesting contrasts from animal reproduction. Unlike animals, plants generally produce both male and female gametes, therefore giving them the potential to engage in self-pollination or asexual reproduction. Curiously, most plants shun this option for a much riskier gamble offered by cross-pollination and sexual reproduction. In contrast to animals who are mobile and can seek out potential mates, plants are sessile and unable to "search" for likely mates. Instead they rely on blind luck, hoping that either the wind or water will carry their seed to nearby cousins or that some insect or bird will visit carrying suitable pollen. Most plants have evolved to rely on animal pollinators to provide this critical service.[10]

Why would most plants ignore the relative safety of self-reliance and throw their lot toward such a risky gamble? Although relatively safe, asexual reproduction carries a risk in that it creates offspring with an identical genetic code. In cases where the plant is perfectly adapted to its environment, this is actually an advantage. In the absence of random mutation, each offspring receives the parent plant's positive characteristics. However, self-fertilization generates less genetic variety within the species and provides less opportunity for genetic adaptation as the plant's environment changes. Plants that use cross-fertilization have higher genetic diversity within their population and greater adaptability to changes in their environment.

However, they are subject to the risk that pollination will not occur and they will leave no offspring. Who thought that gambling was solely a human vice?

The availability of abundant pollinators is crucial not only to plant productivity, but also to biodiversity, both within and across species populations. While most of us think only of the "birds and bees" as plant pollinators, other insects such as flies, wasps, beetles, butterflies, and moths, as well as bats, all supply pollinating services. However, bees are the most important pollinators, pollinating over 70 percent of the 1,500 major crops and medicinal plants.[11] Unfortunately, there is evidence of their decline over the past half-century. Honeybees face a number of diseases that are reducing their numbers. In addition, there are new threats, including the encroachment of African bees that are reducing honeybee populations. Already, there is evidence that this reduction in numbers is having an impact on American agriculture.[12] While we can supplement natural pollination by private means, it does cause a significant increase in the cost of farming. The decline in natural pollination services means that farmers likely will see increased costs, either in the form of reduced yields or the increased cost of contracting pollinating services.

Maintenance of biological diversity

Just as death is the only certainty in each of our lives, so is extinction the only certainty for any given species. Even without the heavy footprint of modern humans, climatic changes and other natural events cause species to become extinct as a normal consequence. Scientists estimate this "background" extinction rate as being one species or so per year.[13] In addition, scientists have found evidence in the fossil records of five mass extinctions, with the last one occurring sixty-five million years ago along with the demise of the dinosaurs.[14] Experts believe that virtually every species that has ever lived on the earth is already extinct (99 percent).[15] Extinction is the rule, not the exception.

With all of this death and destruction, it is fortunate that nature has created mechanisms that spawn new species to offset the impacts of extinction. Through three biological processes – genetic mutation, sexual reproduction, and speciation – nature continues to replenish and expand the world's genetic resources. This biological diversity is significant both *within* species (known as genetic diversity) as well as *across* species (known as species richness). Random mutation and sexual reproduction both serve to expand the genetic diversity within a species. Random errors in the genetic reproduction lead to new genetic possibilities. While most of these chance occurrences are "mistakes," an infrequent number lead to advantages that improve survival. Natural selection then encourages this trait to become more common within the species' genetic pool. Sexual reproduction encourages mates with different genetic types to create new combinations of genetic prototypes. Both mechanisms work to expand the genetic material available to a specific species, thereby providing increased adaptability in the face of changing circumstances.

At the same time, the several methods of speciation encourage the creation of new species. Biologists believe that speciation occurs when a sub-group of a given population is somehow isolated from the rest of the group. This isolation may be geographic, ecological or behavioral. In the case of geographic isolation, the different environmental conditions facing each sub-group encourage a different evolutionary path. Their isolation prevents any changes occurring in one sub-group from evolving in the others as well. Eventually, the different paths lead to sufficient differences that the sub-groups become distinct species. Darwin's finches that inhabit the Galapagos Islands offer a clear example. Thought to have a common ancestor, these birds were able to evolve into distinct species due to the relative isolation of the islands. Each evolved over time to become better suited to the particular conditions and food sources found on their specific island habitat until they became separate species.

Among other benefits, biological diversity (biodiversity) serves as a comprehensive ecological insurance policy.[16] Both genetic diversity and species richness offer insurance against future changes and uncertainties. Species with broader gene pools have greater adaptability in the face of changing environmental conditions. Genetic combinations that offer few advantages under existing conditions may emerge as essential attributes under future conditions. In a similar vein, the future viability of ecosystems is dependent upon their species richness. As different species often provide redundant services and roles within a given ecosystem, each provides a "back-up system" in case extinction strikes the other species. Just as investors are warned against placing all of their assets in one stock, so should we avoid reducing the variety of our biotic endowment. Doing so would increase the risk that key ecological services we presently count on will diminish or even vanish.

The thirteen life-support services (see Table 2.1) share a common trait: they provide and maintain the essential conditions for life, including our own. The elimination of any one of these services would eradicate virtually all forms of life. On the positive side, these thirteen services do more than just permit our existence. They provide a habitat that is welcoming, generous, and forgiving. These services not only protect us from the hazards of a universe that makes life so rare, but they also provide all of the critical functions needed to make our existence possible and appealing.

Provisioning services

Unlike the life-support services, provisioning services are those that capture our interest. All of the material goods that quench our thirst, satiate our hunger, clothe our bodies, shelter us from the elements, power our tools and machinery, and satisfy our every material desire are provided as a bounty of nature, often freely. Humans have long recognized the value of these services; past and present, they have been the source of conflict and war. The goods that result from these services constitute what economists call *natural resources* and they make a significant contribution to our material well-being as measured by such indices as GDP (Gross Domestic Product). Every commodity produced by humans requires the fruits that result from nature's provisioning services. Indeed, given the reaches of modern biotechnology, we are recognizing the role of diverse gene stocks as the building blocks of this nascent industry. A more diverse gene pool provides a wider selection of basic ingredients available for creating biotechnology recipes.

Food production

Natural systems that provide us with life-support services also create the food (and drink) services that meet our dietary needs. All of the foods that we consume – the fruits, vegetables, grains, legumes, nuts, meat and fish, and herbs – are created from largely self-regulating systems of nature. The liquids we drink, including those from animals, also result from the same set of natural systems. For thousands of millennia prior to the emergence of agriculture, humans survived and even thrived on these naturally provided goods. They foraged for fresh water, wild grains, vegetables and fruits, and hunted for wild game. Nature freely gives these gifts, only requiring human labor to collect or capture them.

In the last 10,000 years, we have supplemented these naturally provided food sources with significant investments of our creative culture. First, we domesticated certain wild animals and later wild plants and trees. Both innovations enabled our ancestors to increase the yield from these food sources. To boost their harvests, our ancestors created irrigation systems to supplement irregular rainfall and to replenish the soils with nutrients. They imported other natural fertilizers to raise yields further. While these innovations often generated impressive harvests, in some cases they led to long-term decline in the local soils. Once known as the Fertile Crescent, the deserts of contemporary Iraq are partially the result of past irrigation practices.[17] The continual irrigation of these soils slowly brought to the surface the salts located in the subsoil, thereby making the surface soils inhospitable to most vegetation.

In recent decades, we have become more proficient in substituting human-made capital for natural capital. Complex machinery, chemical fertilizers and pesticides, genetic engineering, greenhouses, and hydroponics farming have all expanded the natural limits and increased crop yields to feed our growing human population. Despite these innovations, our food production system still relies on a number of natural systems that are extremely complicated and poorly understood. The continued effectiveness of our food production systems requires that we understand and maintain the integrity and effectiveness of these underlying systems. Unfortunately, there is evidence that some of our innovations are undermining their effectiveness. Chemical pesticides kill not only the pests that feed on our crops, but also the natural predators that limit those pests. In solving one problem, our commercial pesticides create another problem as an unintended consequence.

Raw materials

Our lives are not simply about bread and water alone; they are warmed by the shelters we build, brightened by the clothing and ornaments we wear, and enlivened by the instruments and products created from our vast imaginations. Nature generously provides all materials needed to produce the huge array of human-created products. Some, like the fibers and flowers from plants and trees as well as the fur and feathers from animals, are renewable resources that are created by the same natural systems discussed above, subject to seasonal and annual variations. Their natural replenishment permits continual use over time. Other resources like minerals and precious stones are not renewable. However, virtually all of these limited resources are reusable. Depending on our purposes, we can reuse these resources repeatedly to meet our needs over a substantial period. Moreover, we are constantly finding new uses for certain materials. As an interesting example, the blood of the horseshoe crab contains a unique substance that supports ongoing medical science. Only found in the crab, this compound serves as an effective "test for contaminants in every drug and vaccine, every artificial limb and every intravenous drip in every hospital in America."[18] Scientists have been unable to create this compound synthetically, so far.

As previously mentioned, there exists one significant exception to our reuse of non-living resources: energy. According to the laws of thermodynamics, energy can neither be created nor destroyed. However, its usefulness does decline as we use it. When we burn coal to generate electricity, we transform the energy into different forms, but we destroy none of it. Most of the energy in the coal becomes heat energy. As the heated steam drives a turbine, we transform some of the heat energy into physical energy. The remaining heat energy quickly declines in usefulness as it dissipates into its cooler surroundings. Once used, energy becomes more diffuse and therefore less useful for future work. To be sure, this degradation of energy from highly concentrated to less concentrated forms occurs even without our intervention, though at a much slower pace. Because of this, some view our world as a huge battery that is inevitably depleting its energy charge. Fortunately, all signs suggest that our primary battery, the sun, is well charged. Yet, not all of the batteries (energy sources) we currently use are so reliable.

Genetic resources

As explained earlier, biological diversity makes natural ecosystems more productive and more durable in the face of changing environmental conditions. As critical as these life-support services are, we also benefit more directly from nature's provisioning of genetic resources. Not only does this genetic generosity provide us with a vast assortment of fruits and vegetables to select from, but also a variety within a given species, say apples. The benefits extend beyond the pleasures of choice. Essentially half of our current array of medicines and pharmaceuticals owe their origins either to plants, animals, or micro-organisms.[19] Who can tell which chemical compound residing in some unlikely plant or animal may serve as a future cure for cancer, HIV, or some other disease? Not only do these drugs save countless lives and reduce human suffering, but they serve key sectors of our economy like the pharmaceutical and chemical industries.

Humans have long made use of this vast genetic collection. Starting thousands of years ago, our ancestors learned to "improve" the wild animals and plants they valued through selective breeding. By favoring individual animals and plants with desired traits, they developed hybrids that exhibited desirable characteristics and repressed undesirable traits. Over time, selective breeding led to less aggressive and more productive animals as well as plants that produced larger fruit, even as they could no longer reproduce without human help. These improvements boosted yields as they cut production costs. In favoring these selected breeds at the expense of their wild cousins, we have let many of the disfavored varieties disappear through extinction.

As in financial management, a broad and diverse investment portfolio lessens risk. Though our current plant and animal hybrids have been carefully adapted to modern conditions, circumstances necessarily change. Alterations in climate and precipitation patterns, soil fertility, and pest mutations can all alter the suitability of any variety. Without a broader genetic base to rely on, future changes in these selected hybrids are limited. Further, successive inbreeding of plants and animals eventually creates genetic vulnerabilities. Modern hybrids have little of the natural durability and pest resistance of their "wild" cousins. Their widespread use creates a natural "siren song" to any pests able to overcome any remaining natural as well as human-made defenses. While modern agricultural methods have largely masked this vulnerability, occasionally it becomes a significant problem. In 1970, 70 percent of the commercial seed corn used by American farmers came from six inbred strains. That year, a leaf fungus blighted the Corn Belt and destroyed 15 percent of the crop, sharply reducing farm income and raising food prices.[20] Fortunately, researchers found a wild, and nearly extinct, strain of corn that was naturally resistant to the leaf fungus. Plant breeders were able to integrate this characteristic into the ensuing commercial strains, thereby protecting the vast corn industry from the ravages of the fungus. Without a broad library of genetic resources, breeders have limited options in how they can respond to future pests and blights. As bioengineering techniques progress, the variety of genetic resources available will determine solely our capacity to respond to future problems.

Cultural services

Unlike the services just discussed, cultural services provide us with direct benefits that are non-consumptive. Rather than consuming these services in the way we consume food or raw materials, we benefit from them without needing to use them up. These services range from the awe-inspiring grandeur of sites like the Grand Canyon and Niagara Falls to the commonplace quietude we gain from walking through nearby woods. Nature offers us nearly limitless inspiration as our spiritual and artistic selves attempt to interpret our world and express that understanding in a variety of forms. In virtually all cases, we can choose to benefit from these services of nature without having to consume or threaten their offerings to future generations. Yet, as we will shortly see, our actions are threatening these services nonetheless.

Aesthetic and spiritual

Nature has long held our fascination, eliciting both trepidation and awe. The ancient cave paintings found in southwestern France give testimony to this enduring fascination as the painters took great pains to draw the animals that contributed to their livelihood. Through time and across cultures, our ancestors have adorned their pottery and ornaments with scenes from nature. In our modern era, the landscape canvas serves to meet our contemporary need to relate and connect with the hidden magic contained in nature. The dizzying arrays of shapes, forms, and materials found in nature have inspired other art forms, including sculpture and architecture. The oblique complexities shrouded in nature have fueled the imaginations of countless storytellers, writers, and musicians, giving us a myriad of entertaining and educational stories.

The aesthetic power of nature reaches far beyond our artistic expressions and affects even the way we live. Early in the twentieth century, the appeal of the bucolic countryside increasingly lured prosperous city dwellers to relocate. Modern transportation extended to the masses the opportunity to live in the country and work in the city. Suburbs sprung up to meet this desire to leave the noise and congestion of urban apartments and to gain the peace and privacy of our countryside "estates." The mass migration to the suburbs has brought many of the same problems and new ones as well, encouraging some to move even further out. Flourishing developments and soaring prices for homes located on the seashore or nestled in the mountains give further evidence to the value we attach to natural settings. The Biophilia Hypothesis argues that humans are innately attracted to nature and its vitality. Recent research suggests that even images of nature can improve recuperation from both mental and surgical trauma.[21] This idea is spawning new directions in architecture as designers seek ways to integrate nature into our built environments to improve employee morale.

Often, we seek sanctuary in natural areas for spiritual enrichment. Most major religions and forms of spiritual practice encourage quiet meditation as a means of achieving spiritual renewal. The relative quiet offered by natural landscapes offers us the perfect setting for this respite from our busy lives. For some, a walk in the woods can provide this opportunity while for others there exist spiritual retreat centers. Unsurprisingly, the overwhelming numbers of these centers are located in secluded, natural areas. Regardless of our affiliations, visits to natural areas offer each of us an opportunity to shed the distractions of our modern lives and reconnect with our inner selves and natural roots.

Educational and informational

Nature's vast biological diversity offers us a huge library of informational sources – one that we have just recently begun to catalogue and understand. As mentioned earlier, many of our current drugs and pharmaceuticals result from natural compounds. Few doubt that future cures will result from an increased understanding of the potential benefits of chemicals from this plant or that insect. Many key oils and gums used in various industrial processes are derivatives of plant oils taken from leaves or seeds. Certain species of trees – including oak, beech, sycamore, and willow – are particularly effective at cleansing our air of such noxious pollutants as sulfur dioxide.[22] This knowledge can inform our urban foresters as they prepare landscape guides for our cities. Over the eons, different species have evolved in countless ways as they have adapted better to defend themselves from hungry predators or from their changing habitat. Understanding this full variety can help us to develop biological solutions to current and future problems.

A better understanding of natural systems can foster more effective agricultural practices. Simply spraying chemical pesticides to rid our crops of their natural pests rarely works in the long term, even when these chemicals produce no collateral damage beyond their intended victims. Continual spraying encourages the emergence of pesticide-resistant strains that usually require ever-increasing doses to keep them at bay. In understanding nature's processes, integrated pest management encourages the use of varied chemical and biological controls to vary the attacks on the offending pest and to keep it off-balanced by this variety. As in so many other areas, this knowledge of natural systems allows us to design chemicals and processes that are both more effective and less costly.

As a well-spring of useful information, nature can teach us much about our own heritage. Information gleaned from long buried fossils and core samples from ice fields can inform us about our past. Discovered fossils give evidence of the process of evolution and have caused us to re-examine our origins and our relationship with the divine. Archaeological digs allow us to understand how our ancestors lived and whether their practices undermined the durability of their societies. Ice core samples offer evidence of past climate and temperature fluctuations, helping us to understand our history as well as our likely future. Each of these lessons and more can guide our efforts as we attempt to live in a manner that will offer substantial opportunities to our own descendants.

Carrier services

In addition to life-support and provisioning needs, all living organisms have space requirements as well. These requirements include not only the physical space needed for habitation but also adequate space for meeting their material and refuge needs. Each organism needs ample space to meet its provisioning needs and to permit sufficient assimilation of its natural wastes. In a similar way, we value the use of space for a variety of functions and uses. Not only do we need physical space to build our homes and raise our food, we also need land (and water) to transport desired products, to derive recreation, and even to convert necessary energy. Lastly, we have recognized that some land must remain as a refuge for nature. Unfortunately, the carrying function of any piece of land is subject to largely zero-sum constraints. Two different organisms cannot occupy the same physical space at the same time nor can a given piece of land generally serve two carrying functions simultaneously.[23] To those of us who tend home gardens for their fresh fruits and vegetables, this rule may appear fluid and flexible. Yet, any expansion to the footprint of our house requires the loss of garden space. Perhaps more than other natural limits, physical space places the most severe restraint on how we may use our natural world.

Human habitation

Each of us requires a place to reside and lay our head. As we continue to multiply as a species, the physical space we need to devote to human habitation must inevitably increase. Yet, more than just our numbers are driving this increase. Our affluence, technology, and cultural decisions are contributing to the housing boom that is transforming fertile farmland or undeveloped areas into residential developments. In countless communities across our country, individuals are recognizing and lamenting the loss of local farms and green belts. Urban sprawl is affecting most communities as we attempt to meet the needs of a growing population with an expanding cultural definition of what constitutes a "home." Obviously, huge sectors of our economy, including the residential real estate, homebuilding, and home furnishing industries, are dependent on this expansion's continuing.

Cultivation and pastoralism

Growing human population and our cultural appetites for an expanded diet are fueling the need to devote more land to raising crops and animals. Already, we have transformed much of our available fertile land into homesteads due to its desirable location. To compensate, we have shifted previously undeveloped areas, forests, and steep hillsides, into farms and ranches. Fortunately, modern technology has reduced the amount of land needed to raise our food. New crop varieties that produce larger yields, along with "factory farming" of animals, have mitigated the need for more acreage. While effective at reducing our land-use needs, these practices do place other and more insidious pressures on our natural systems. In both cases, these intensive food-raising practices require substantial importation of nutrients or feed and generate significant "runoff" problems, as the unused wastes must go somewhere. Further, rising income throughout the world is shifting food consumption towards more land-intensive foods, particularly meat. All of these factors combine to place ever greater pressures on providing adequate lands to grow ample food.

Commerce and transportation

Only as societies learn to boost their food production and move away from agrarian economies does this category take on much significance. Yet, in our contemporary economy, commerce is a major consumer of land, particularly since it includes retailing, government, and industry. Thus, population growth and material prosperity are the twin drivers of this land-use form. Fortunately, one can expect some restraint to occur here. In their drive to prune expenses, businesses seek to reduce unnecessary property costs and thereby limit their land-use needs. As one example, modern building technologies and materials have permitted businesses to limit their space needs and "stretch" the available land by building skyscrapers and other multiple-story buildings.

We need land for another function as well. Modern industry requires access to markets in order to sell the merchandise and services it produces. In addition, these businesses require reliable access to key resources, including raw materials, energy, and a labor force. In both instances, businesses need reliable and convenient transportation networks to facilitate this flow of resources, people, and goods. Consequently, our modern economy devotes an increasing percentage of land to roads, railroads, port facilities, and airports. Increased commerce will require additional infrastructure of this form. Not just land, but also surface water in the form of navigable rivers, lakes, and oceans serve as important conveyances of goods and people to and from their workplaces. Though it may seem that this use of the waterways does not hamper other uses of the same water, it actually does. Damming rivers to store water and provide timely electricity hampers this carrier use of the same waterway. Even if one builds a system of locks to permit water transport, the water used to permit the carrier use cannot be used for its other purposes.

Energy conversion

Given the importance of energy to any human settlement, some land must be devoted to this use as well. Traditionally, human societies have relied on forested lands to provide firewood to fuel their needs. Today, the land requirements for this function reflect our current emphasis on "mined" energy sources. Some energy sources, like petroleum, natural gas, and deep-mining coal, require relatively little surface area. Other key sources, like surface coal and uranium, require larger tracts of surface land and frequently yield devastating results. Overall, the amount of land devoted to energy conversion is relatively small compared to our other needs. Yet, as we deplete our current sources of oil and natural gas, we will need to develop alternative energy sources, many that require more land. Wind power and solar power both are relatively benign sources of renewable power; yet both require substantial amounts of space if either is to play a significant role in our energy futures.

Recreation

Human societies have long used the land for recreation and sport. As dense urban settlement makes nearby undeveloped land scarce, the need emerges to set aside land for recreational purposes. Urban parks and village greens offer two examples of this impulse. Nationally, concerns about the disappearing wilderness instigated our national park system. Today, much of our land, particularly in the West, is devoted to wilderness areas, private hunting preserves, natural parks, and camping areas. Their use testifies to the tremendous interest our public has in pursuing these rather traditional forms of recreation, including hunting, fishing, riding, and hiking. We dedicate other land to our fascination with sports, as golf courses, soccer fields, baseball diamonds and tennis courts dot our suburban landscapes. Indoor pursuits including music, theater, film, and the arts require other venues and space. Lastly, affluence and technology have combined to create new recreational venues, including sports coliseums and amusement parks.

Refugia

This last carrier function of land refers to the needs of non-human species. Just as humans have the need for physical habitat to provide comfort and protection as well as food sources and assimilation services, so does every other species as well. Insects, birds, and small animals require plants and trees to provide natural cover as well as sources for nesting materials. They require the same for their natural predators to help keep their own population in balance as well as for those species that decompose their wastes and return nutrients back into the ecosystem. Thus, refuge areas must provide healthy and durable ecosystems, not just adequate habitat for specific species. For some mobile species like migratory birds, these refuges must exist in multiple places, including birthing areas, "rest stops" along key migratory routes, and summer havens. Without these areas, we will lose varied species and squander ecosystem services already discussed throughout this chapter.

Not all of the other carrier functions are anathema to this function. For example, areas left undeveloped for "wilderness" use can frequently serve as effective wildlife refuges. Good fishing and hunting areas require healthy ecosystems. Hikers usually seek areas that will offer a variety of (non-threatening) animals and exotic plants. Yet, even these activities tend to place some selective pressure on species, particularly those that are sensitive to human disturbance or the target of human activity. The other forms of carrier functions are even less hospitable to most species. Our modern homes and businesses are off limits to all but the most persistent animals and a few favored species. Our surface transportation systems are deadly to most species that attempt to share them intemperately. While forested land used as a source of firewood can be quite hospitable to many species, lands used to mine surface coal and uranium are largely unappealing to most species and harmful to many.[24] Lastly, fields used to raise crops and animals are quite inhospitable to most species. The success of our modern farming in raising yields has been at the expense of these natural competitors. We spray chemicals to eliminate rival pests that dare to eat our crops. Other chemicals eliminate weeds that might compete with the favored plants. To make modern farming practices cost effective, we clear broad swaths of land of any competing plants and level the ground to permit more efficient use of machinery. Virtually all of the focus on our modern farming technologies is to eliminate any refugia opportunities provided by our farmlands. Indeed, one can say the same about most of our land development and landscape practices.

Returning to the Catskills Watershed

Though New Yorkers no doubt appreciate the clean taste of their tap water, I doubt that they fully grasp the precious endowment they have in the Catskills Watershed. While most Americans can realistically expect access to inexpensive, yet safe drinking water, few urban dwellers have tap water untainted by chlorine and other purifying chemicals. Yes, our water-treatment technology has largely eliminated past scourges like typhoid, thereby justifying our public investments in these facilities. Yet, the Catskills Watershed offers us a clear illustration of nature as capital, or *natural capital*. New York officials have the choice to invest in new water treatment and storage facilities or to invest in watershed protection to preserve the naturally provided water-treatment services. Both investments offer water users valuable services. In recognizing our endowment from nature as a form of capital, an important shift occurs. Instead of viewing nature as something to exploit and consume, we are encouraged by the concept of natural capital to conserve nature and act as stewards. Just as it is folly for the young heir to consume their inheritance, so it is calamitous for a society to exhaust its natural endowment.

In several respects, viewing nature and its underlying processes as a form of natural capital is an apt analogy. In the case of productive capital – items like buildings, machinery, and tools – what we really appreciate is not so much the objects themselves, but the services they provide us with. Physical assets generate benefits or income for their owner, thereby giving them value. In a similar vein, we may marvel at the complexity of design in the water cycle; yet, what we most value is the replenishing supply of fresh water that this cycle brings us. The stream of services we receive from these natural systems is like "income," either for our benefit or to share with others. In addition, we can enjoy the income or benefits provided by these natural systems without threatening the assets or principal that provides them. We can enjoy the harvest of nature – the wild berries, wood from our forests, food from our fields – without undermining the future capacity of nature to provide these goods. Generously provided by nature, these life-support services are self-generating so that reasonable use of these services does not harm their functioning. We can depend on these natural systems to function effectively, reliably, and continuously, without need for human attention. However, unreasonable use or destruction of these natural assets will lead to a loss of ecological functioning. Just as our human-made machinery may suffer harm or injury when used in ways "not intended by the manufacturer," so it is with our natural endowments. Human actions that eliminate or impair these systems will inevitably lead to a loss of the benefits they generate. Too often, we have treated nature like a limitless source of "resources" only to realize that we have squandered the natural capital that provides these services.

On the other hand, analogies can mask important differences. Strictly viewing our natural systems like any other form of financial capital can be misleading. An example is instructive here. Concerned about the decline of our nation's forests, forestry experts have promoted the concept of "sustainable yield." The concept targets the maximum harvest that one can take from a forest on a sustained basis. To calculate this yield, one could turn to financial guidelines regarding prudent use. In the case of a simple savings account, one can draw upon its balance as long as one does not consume more than the annual interest. By not depleting the principal, one can count on receiving comparable levels of income into the future. Applying this rule to sustainable yield of our forests gives us the following guideline: as long as we do not harvest more lumber than the annual growth of our forest stock, we should expect that stock to remain unthreatened by our use. If the forest has annual growth of 2 percent, we ought to be able to harvest 2 percent of it without reducing the principal, according to this guide. Unfortunately, things are not so simple.

Living capital responds to rules beyond those that apply to financial or physical (machinery) capital. Making even what appears to be "sustainable" withdrawals from our forest resources can lead to problems. Cutting timber for sale as lumber can threaten the integrity of the forest system. Taking out trees also removes key nutrients that would normally rot to replenish forest soils and fuel future growth. Exporting these nutrients without some compensatory action will slowly rob the forest of its fertility and vitality, likely generating reduced yields in the future. Just as modern agriculture quickly depletes soils of their nutrients, so can the application of agro-forestry methods. Additionally, the manner of forest "withdrawals" is important. Clear-cutting the forests to capture this "income" will likely damage the natural systems as the action leaves the area unprotected and vulnerable to the cascade of harms already discussed. Selective harvesting of only certain species or the best specimens will leave the forest with a less diverse and lower-quality wood stock that will serve as the source of future replenishment. Even cutting older, diseased trees creates problems. Many species reside solely in these older, even rotten trees; removing their habitat threatens the biodiversity of the forest system. Harvesting followed by monoculture tree plantations may increase future yields and generate an increased "principal" for future generations. However, such forests experience much lower levels of biodiversity and provide reduced levels of ecological services.

Given this discussion of natural services, it is unsurprising that preserving the Catskills Watershed is the cheaper of the two options. The underlying processes that contribute to water regulation, water supply, and waste treatment services, require no human compensation. Natural precipitation provides the initial source of water. In leaving the harmful salts and chemicals behind, the processes of evaporation and transpiration largely purify this water source. Dense vegetation protects the soils that then absorb the rainfall and slowly ease it into the area streams, thereby offering cost-free water storage. Healthy streams filled with aquatic plants and wildlife can further eliminate any impurities and enhance the "taste" of the water. Even when storms and other natural calamities damage the area, the natural system has the capacity to recuperate and replenish its services over time. Nature provides each of these services for no charge. In strategically using these services, the city Water Department can offer its customers quality water at a very reasonable cost. As is frequently the case, it is cheaper to protect our environmental endowment than to restore it in the aftermath of disregard and damage.

Even Water Department officials who understand the water regulation and waste treatment services provided by the region are likely to underestimate its value. The watershed protections are doing more than ensuring an ample and safe drinking supply for New Yorkers. Dotted with farms and small communities, the area does provide limited carrying function for the local population, including human habitation, cultivation, industry and transportation. Most of the area remains largely undeveloped as forests. As such, the area provides substantial refuge services for resident plants and animals. Certain lands provide recreational outlets for hunting, fishing, and hiking. The woods offer local citizens numerous opportunities to find spiritual renewal as well as to uncover evidence of past human settlements in the area. In addition, these lands offer substantial contributions to each of the life-support services discussed earlier, not just those that relate to provisioning fresh water. The dense forest growth functions to regulate atmospheric gases and the local climate, to capture solar energy, to protect the soils, and to offer habitats and resources to other wildlife. While difficult to evaluate, these varied services no doubt add significantly to the total value of the region.

Despite the exceptional value offered by the Catskills Watershed, the choice given to the New York City Water Department officials is an exceptional one. Few major cities have the option that this area offers to New York. While most major cities had at one time the choice to preserve natural catchments that could serve as their source of clean water, nearly all have subsequently lost or squandered this opportunity. The lure or pressures of development led to the degradation of local watersheds and the need for water treatment. Only recently have we appreciated the value of these naturally provided services and the natural systems that provide them. However, simply appreciating our bounty is not sufficient to prevent its decline. Even today, our decisions and policies do not give adequate due to these natural services. I leave the challenge of explaining why we continue to squander so much of our valuable natural endowment to the next chapter.

Let me make one last point. In this particular case, our ingenuity and technology provide us with an alternative or substitute for the natural provision of fresh water. We have the expertise and physical plant to treat impure waters and make them safe, if not always appealing, for drinking. As one surveys the full list of Table 2.1, this alternative does not always seem apparent. Do we have an economical substitute for depletion of the upper atmosphere ozone layer that protects all terrestrial life forms from deadly solar radiation?[25] Which human technology will enable us to generate fresh water if shifting circumstances cause a reduction in regional rainfall patterns? What would it cost to transport this water? Are our agricultural systems ready with an economical replacement for the steep declines in our natural pollinators? Are our insurance companies ready to reimburse for any increased risks and damage that may occur because of declining disturbance regulation services? While we can supplement and even replace some of these freely provided ecological services with technology, many other services are irreplaceable. As the next chapter suggests, our policies and behaviors do not always safeguard those services that have no substitutes.

Further reading

Robert Costanza *et al.*, 'The Value of the World's Ecosystem Services and Natural Capital', tackle the daunting task of measuring the value the world's ecosystem services and compute an estimate, though one that has been widely criticized.

Gretchen Daily (ed.), *Nature's Services: Societal Dependence on Natural Systems*, offers more in-depth discussion of various ecosystem services as well-known scientists review the current research on the significance of these services.

R.S. de Groot, *Functions of Nature: Evaluation of Nature in Environmental Planning, Management, and Decision Making*, provides a thorough explanation of the varied benefits we derive from the many ecological services offered by nature as well as a rationale for the four functional areas largely followed in this chapter.

Peter Kahn, Jr., *The Human Relationship with Nature: Development and Culture*, offers a thorough assessment of the Biophilia Hypothesis and reviews current research of its significance.

Mark Sagoff, 'On the Value of Natural Ecosystems: The Catskills Parable', gives more background on New York City's experience with the Catskills Watershed.

E.O. Wilson, *The Diversity of Life*, provides an extremely readable exposition of the complexities of natural systems and their significance to us.

3 Understanding our natural endowment

Near where I work lies a large parcel of land, over 400 acres, that is currently undergoing dramatic change. Owned by the local insurance company Jefferson Pilot, this property served for decades as a recreational refuge for its employees and their families.[1] Largely untouched, the tract combined rolling hills forested with towering hardwoods alongside open fields and meandering streams. Nestled on an overlook sat a stone-faced clubhouse that hosted countless company gatherings. For years, families would dine regularly on Sundays to enjoy the comfortable atmosphere, delicious food, and company-subsidized prices. Nearby, a small lake served those who liked swimming or boating on warm, summer days. Another lake offered the opportunity to fish. Hiking trails through acres of woods provided both solace and exercise to those who sought them. During the summer, the company ran a day camp for children of employees, giving them the opportunity to swim, play tennis, and enjoy the outdoors. At a time in which Greensboro had few public parks, this refuge offered valued recreational benefits. Neighbors who grew up locally light up at the mention of the property as they share warm memories of times past.

In its largely undeveloped state, the property offered the local community a variety of services beyond those given to the corporate family. The dense groves of trees served to cleanse the local air of pollutants, to provide cool relief from the hot summers, and to buffer the strong gusts of wind that often accompanied summer thunderstorms. The open fields and meandering streams protected downstream property owners from the ravages of flooding and cleansed the water of impurities before emptying into the municipal water supply. Local residents benefited in other ways as well. The woods and fields provided a welcoming habitat to a variety of plants and trees that stood in stark contrast to uniform lawns and shrubbery that dominate the encroaching neighborhoods. The diverse, natural foliage offered refuge to an assortment of animals, birds, and insects. These natural residents offered valuable services to neighboring lands as they fed on local pests or pollinated the plants of nearby farms or suburban gardens. Though discouraged by "No Trespassing" signs, some neighbors walked the trails while many others who only drove by could enjoy the property's beauty and serenity. Even if never invited as a guest, many of us in the community benefited from this land and its multiple offerings.

Yet, change is endemic. Nothing stands still, not in nature or in society. When purchased eighty years ago, this parcel of land was largely indistinguishable from the surrounding farmland. Since that time, the area has undergone tremendous change as the pressures of population and economic development have increasingly enveloped the park. Networks of roads, suburban neighborhoods, and shopping centers have sprung up on adjacent properties. Increasingly, this tract of land stood in open relief, a green parcel of calm, to the more cramped and bustling areas surrounding it. At the same time, use of the corporate facilities slowly declined. For years, corporate gatherings on July 4 were important events that drew most employees and their families. In recent years, such gatherings lost their appeal and turnout suffered as a result. In its heyday, the summer camp accommodated nearly 300 children; in its last decade, enrollment dwindled to around 100 per summer.[2] Over time, the once bustling dining room lost its cachet and increasingly stood unused.

Certainly, many factors led to the declining use of this corporate retreat. The emergence of other recreational alternatives, including city parks, summer camps, and area restaurants, competed for both the leisure time and wallets of company employees. Changing corporate culture also played a role. As this company morphed from a small-town business to a nationally known corporation, organizational changes inevitably occurred. Top management placed less emphasis on cultivating the "corporate family atmosphere" that the park provided. At the same time, younger employees were less attracted to the paternalistic strings that came with the park's benefits. Increased incomes enabled the employees to choose other available alternatives. The aging of the workforce reduced interest in the summer camp as many now had grown children and grandchildren who lived in distant cities. Within the industry, increased focus on profit margins and rates of return on corporate assets took greater priority. An enclave amid a prosperous area of the city, the property increased in value as local developers considered its potential uses. At last, the lure became too much and the property's development became inevitable.

A decade ago, the corporate owner presented a development plan designed to fit within the confines of Greensboro's long-run growth plan as well as promote shareholder returns. Specifically, the proposal targeted more than half of the acreage for residential development, three-quarters of which would be single-family homes and one-quarter, multifamily apartments. Retail and office space would occupy another quarter of the total parcel. The rest, about a fifth of the total land, would remain as open spaces to accommodate the tract's creeks, lakes, and wetlands. Implementing this development plan offered the corporate shareholders many tens of millions of dollars. At the same, its realization would transform the property and the local area. To accommodate the new homes, businesses, and roads, the developers would remove many trees and pave much of the land, thereby reducing its offering of life-support services. Office buildings, restaurants, and retail stores would attract more traffic, creating more congestion, noise, and pollution. Many local residents joined in an outcry against the proposed development, fearing the loss of services and changes to their neighborhoods. Many called on local government officials to purchase the land to preserve its value as a green enclave. These calls never stimulated a credible public response, largely due to the ballooning value of the land and our local government's limited purse.[3]

Across this country, communities face such decisions every day. Newly arriving residents require additional housing, stores, and offices to live, shop, and work. New developments must materialize to accommodate the needs of a growing population and an expanding community. Thus, our day-to-day decisions of where to live, work and shop clearly affect our local environment and the quality of our lives. These new developments bring more traffic, congestion, and pollution as they eradicate fertile farmland and local green spaces. Area residents are naturally concerned about the impact of these changes on their lives (and property values). Recognizing the mixed results of any new development, some argue that markets effectively adjudicate these costs and benefits. They argue that markets are well suited to identify the highest value use of a given parcel of land. Further, as community needs change, so will the prevailing market prices as they reflect the changing valuations of competing uses. Our economic decisions to develop different properties inevitably affect the endowment of natural capital. Though some view this influence given to markets with alarm, others do not. Those predisposed to markets view them as effective stewards of capital, of whatever form. By allowing markets to dictate how we use the natural capital, we can ensure that the same institutions that sustain and promote private forms of capital will do the same with naturally provided capital. This argument is worth considering in depth.

Functioning markets

Markets are simply "places" where prospective buyers and sellers can trade goods and services for payment. No matter their form, whether local or global, online or a physical location, markets serve a variety of uses. First, markets convey a price for most valued commodities and services, thereby giving each a comparative value. The price of a particular parcel of land reflects the value attached to comparable land nearby. Merely because of its location, any block of land found on Manhattan, New York, will command a much higher value than a similar-sized lot found in Manhattan, Kansas. Yet, any specific parcel of land has its own particular attributes that add or subtract value from the locally prevailing price. The value attached to these attributes may change as the expected use of the land changes. For example, a developer interested in building low-density housing may view a parcel of land with rolling hills as particularly attractive. The hilly terrain may permit the developer to offer "unique" lots to prospective homebuyers. The presence of mature trees may give the residential development a "natural look" that may further inflate subdivision prices. To the developer envisioning a new shopping mall on this site, these same features would appear as added costs, not unique benefits. To facilitate the construction of the mall, the developer may need to level the land and raze the trees, adding to the cost of the project. A nearby parcel of land that is flatter in terrain and devoid of trees will hold greater appeal for this developer.

In assigning different values to different commodities and services, markets further influence our decisions. Most of us want to improve our material well-being. Hence, we seek to make decisions that increase the flow of benefits and services and decrease any costs or outlays. Somewhat surprisingly, pursuit of our individual interests often leads not only to personal advantage, but to decisions that favor our broader communities as well. In the example discussed above, economic interest will likely cause the mall developer to bid on the flatter, less forested parcel of land. Rather than expend additional costs in modifying the hilly site, the mall developer will choose the alternative site, leaving the trees and hilly terrain as an amenity for future residents. In this way, markets encourage decisions that retain these desired features. What makes sense for the individual developer can also make sense for the broader community – an insight that Adam Smith articulated with his "Invisible Hand" concept over two centuries ago.

The reach of markets extends far beyond land-use decisions. As consumers, we consider the price of any item in comparison with its expected benefit. Higher prices encourage some sacrifice and conservation as we temper the adverse impact on our family budgets. We frequently respond to lower prices by purchasing more of the commodity to take advantage of the savings. While we make these decisions to protect our household budgets, they generate broader benefits to the community as well. Resources, goods, and services that become increasingly scarce relative to their demand will rise in price. These price increases encourage each of us to prune our purchases of these items, thereby easing the budding shortages. Other resources, commodities, and services that become more plentiful relative to their demand will drop in price. Falling prices encourage each of us to buy relatively abundant items, easing the emerging glut and discouraging wasteful production. Markets function to balance the demands for key goods and services with their available supply. More importantly, markets provide self-correcting feedback when imbalances occur. In this way, markets mimic the self-correcting processes found in many of the natural processes discussed in the prior chapter. Market imbalances encourage a multitude of responses that function to restore market balance.

Market pricing also encourages stewardship of our property and assets, whether real, financial, or natural. Our ability to buy and sell property gives us an ongoing stake in their value. It is in our material interest to preserve the value of these assets and limit any changes that may undermine their value. The power of these incentives is undeniable as one contrasts how homeowners and renters maintain and improve their homes or how we care for our own versus rental cars. These incentives do extend to natural assets as well. Private owners of forested areas have substantial incentives to ensure the healthy growth of their trees, particularly as lumber prices rise to reflect the increasing scarcity of wood products. Similarly, owners of natural gas fields face financial incentives to undertake costly recovery methods to remove as much from the subterranean field as is feasible. Both actions, taken for individual material gain, serve the broader social need for more wood-based products and for cleaner energy.

Market incentives function most effectively when the key participants, the buyer and seller, are collectively responsible for the full range of benefits and the costs of any given transaction. Under these circumstances, markets generally guide the actors toward decisions that are socially beneficial as well. Problems emerge when the decision-makers ignore or undervalue some of these consequences. Faulty or incomplete information hampers all economic decisions. Each of us has experienced this phenomenon as we recall purchases in which our actual experience did not match our expectation of product benefits or costs. With this knowledge, we can anticipate future mistakes and thereby avoid repeating them. Additional problems emerge when our decisions generate consequences that are not our personal responsibility. Though most of us complain about the reduced visibility and sting of urban smog, we continue to drive our cars. Most of us recognize the connection between our individual driving and the increased smog, but it rarely has much impact on our driving decisions. Compare this to the impact that soaring gas prices can have on our driving habits! Largely because we lack direct accountability for the full consequences of our actions as we drive, we make decisions that not only harm others, but ultimately ourselves as well. To consider how effectively markets capture the various benefits offered by our natural capital, we need to return to the categories of ecological services discussed in the prior chapter. We can then distinguish those circumstances in which markets offer reasonably effective incentives from those where they perform poorly.

Market pricing and ecological services

Without question, nature poses substantial challenges to markets and their ability to assign accurate prices. Some of these difficulties are common to all of the twenty-four services discussed in the prior chapter. In some cases, particular attributes of the four functional areas either mitigate or exacerbate these challenges. In other cases, the specific attributes create other causes of concern for specific functional areas. As I will argue, certain areas of our environment pose particular challenges for markets and their capacity to price our ecological services accurately. It is important to discern these impacts so that we can understand the uneven impact our economic development paths will likely have on our natural environment.

Common to all of the ecological services is our tendency to take nature's bounty for granted, despite the fact that most of these services are essential for life. This paradox is not simply due to hubris; some blame is attributable to the way nature provides these services. The ecological systems that generate these services are complex, vast, and frequently operate on a global scale. Their seemingly limitless nature encourages the perception that these systems are impervious to human harm, thereby leading to a sense of complacency. Two centuries ago, the passenger pigeon was the most prolific bird on earth.[4] Early nineteenth-century accounts spoke of flocks of passenger pigeons flying overhead and darkening the sky for hours. Less than one hundred years later, the last bird of its kind would die in captivity in the Cincinnati Zoo, the victim of endemic slaughter. Today, considering the vast size of our atmosphere, we have difficulty comprehending that we are altering the balance of key gases and thereby changing our planetary climate. Yet, the evidence confirms that levels of carbon dioxide have increased by over one-third during the past 150 years. Too often, we ignore or question the impact that our individual actions could possibly produce.

Nature encourages our ingratitude for its services in another way. Nature provides these services freely from natural systems that operate in self-regulatory systems. Their continued existence requires no human intervention, management, or conscious thought. Good environmental management requires only that we leave these systems relatively undisturbed to maintain their level of functioning. For example, the natural water cycle provides us with an endless replenishment of fresh water supplies. Though the timing, duration, and spatial distribution of the rainfall may frustrate us, we are the fortunate benefactors of this continual renewal of fresh water. We can expect its continual operation without any effort. As nature places no requirements on us, it is understandable that we may become complacent and neglectful. However, our negligence can wreak harm on this system, at least locally. Stripping the landscape of its natural cover will reduce the natural evapotranspiration that fuels local rainfall. Though nature requires nothing from us in providing these services, it does require that we do no harm.

Strictly speaking, the above point is true for provisioning services and carrier services too, though we have learned ways to "improve" what nature provides us with. Nature offers the essential goods and services we need for sustenance from the same natural systems just discussed. For thousands of millennia prior to the emergence of agriculture, humans survived and even thrived on these naturally provided goods. Our ancestors foraged for fresh water, wild grains, vegetables and fruits, and hunted for wild game. Over time, our ancestors learned to fashion naturally provided plant fibers, leather, and minerals into clothing, tools, weapons, and ornaments. Seasonal and annual variations aside, they could count on their natural replenishment as long as the underlying ecological processes remained unharmed. Some examples like ocean fishing persist today. Similarly, nature provides us with the land required to meet our space needs, giving us the room to live, work, and play. In these two cases, we have learned ways to enhance nature's bounty. In agriculture, we have applied our knowledge to enhance the yields supplied by nature at the same time as our building technologies have permitted us to use the land in more satisfying and complete ways. In both cases, our efforts to develop these services still rely on the natural processes offered by nature as part of their foundation.

These attributes of nature and its ecological services not only encourage our ingratitude, but they lead to other challenges. Frequently, the natural systems that generate these services function in interdependent ways across space and time. Local actions do have regional and even global impacts. The use of the atmosphere to disperse unwanted pollutants can affect areas hundreds of miles downwind and threaten the health and productivity of these distant ecosystems. Deforestation in one region can reduce rainfall in adjacent regions, thereby reducing what these affected areas can support. Using a property to build a factory, landfill, or an airport will undoubtedly affect neighboring residents. Under these conditions, our decisions as market participants generate consequences – sometimes beneficial, frequently harmful – for those excluded from the market decision. Further, the passage of time can cloud the link between the offending behavior and its ecological impact. Current activities that spew greenhouse gases into the atmosphere will manifest climate changes whose full impact will only be clear decades in the future. Long lag times between a given cause and its uncertain effects make it very difficult to assess accurately the impact of our current decisions and practices. Because of such spatial and temporal interdependencies, individuals far removed or distant in the future bear the consequences of specific activities, producing what economists call "market externalities."[5] More importantly, such complex interconnections insulate the market participants from key consequences of their decisions, thereby reducing market accountability.

Nature's generosity leads to another serious challenge to markets and their capacity to value accurately natural services. Nature offers these services to all of us without conditions and frequently on demand *in the absence of human-created limitations*. By virtue of our existence, we are each able to use these services. We all benefit from the earth's hospitable climate, its fecund offering of flora and fauna, its innumerable secrets and mysteries, and its vast offering of land on which to roam and roost. In most cases, we have the opportunity to make use of these services as much or as little as we choose. Under these "open access" conditions, markets for these services cannot emerge. Markets for any product or service can only arise if the service provider can supply those individuals willing to pay some market price while excluding those unwilling to pay the fee. No shopkeeper will survive for long if they must provide their wares to all who want them, whether they are willing to pay for them or not. Given the choice between paying for some item or not paying for it and getting it nonetheless, most of us will behave as "free riders". Each time we listen and ignore the on-air solicitation of either public radio or television, we make this choice. Even those of "us" who do respond to these appeals usually make contributions that understate the actual value of the service. Since we can freely avail ourselves of these services, few of us offer to pay for them.[6] Would you not scoff at the local crank who proposes that each of us pay for using the warmth of the sun or the rainfall that benefits our yards and gardens? We tend to view these services and our use of them as something we are entitled to, not something we should pay for.

Given that nature freely provides these services, why should we pay for them? The sun will continue to shine and the rain will continue to fall whether we make payments for them or not. Or will they? Market prices convey underlying value to us and encourage us to behave in corresponding ways. Most of us will drink a $100 bottle of wine differently than a $10 table wine, even if our palates are unable to distinguish the difference. The absence of any market price, more specifically a zero price, for these services conveys to each of us their apparent lack of value. Consequently, we are encouraged to consume them as if they were limitless. In a world of overwhelming natural bounty and small human populations, this illusion is insignificant. In a world of stressed natural systems, stretched and challenged by unprecedented human populations with unceasing material appetites, this disconnect has untold ramifications. Free access to these services encourages their overuse, often leading to their depletion. More insidiously, a zero price for these services discourages actions that could preserve or restore the natural systems that provide these services, as there is no financial reward for doing so.

Not always does our tendency to "overuse" these environmental services lead to environmental harm or even to their depletion. Sometimes, use of these services can occur without limit. Each of us can enjoy simultaneously (and without limit) the protective qualities offered by the upper atmosphere ozone layer and the natural systems that maintain our hospitable climate. We can each benefit from the myriad of natural systems that encourage biological diversity and sustain highly functioning ecosystems in the face of dynamic change. The discovery of a life-saving drug taken from some obscure plant or animal can save or improve untold lives in the future. Countless art lovers can savor a specific Monet landscape when it is hung in a public gallery; even more can enjoy it almost without limit as a high-quality reprint. We can use these services largely without limit and without cause for worry for others. These services are what economists call *non-rival*, in that my use of such services does not diminish your enjoyment of them.

However, our use of other ecological services does lead to rival outcomes. Most of the provisioning services are actually physical commodities that are subject to rival consumption. Fresh water that slakes one person's thirst cannot also quench another's simultaneously. Another cannot utilize food already consumed by one individual. People can share an article of clothing, but not at the same time. This attribute of rival consumption necessarily creates a condition of scarcity, since a limited number of these goods can only meet a limited number of human needs. Similarly, the availability of land limits carrier services. No two people can occupy the precise spot simultaneously nor can we generally use a particular spot to satisfy two different carrier functions. Even some life-support services are subject to this conflict. Prodigious production of waste products is taxing the assimilative capacity of natural systems and creating problems for our neighbors. The chemical runoffs from farms and urban areas pollute local streams, damaging their capacity to cleanse the water. We are rapidly filling up our landfills with an ever-increasing volume of solid waste, with new disposal sites becoming harder to find and more distant. Natural limits place thresholds on the use of these services. Yet, since we largely view these services as "free," there exist few restraints on our use of them. Unrestricted use can damage these ecosystems, undermine their ecological functioning, and diminish their offered level of services.

Our "open access" to these ecological services leads to another difficulty.[7] Consider for the moment a large house that is open to any who might want to use its accommodations, for whatever period they choose. Under these circumstances, what incentive is there for any individual to maintain, much less even improve the accommodations? Since the resulting benefits are open to all, what reward exists for any individual willing to expend their own time, effort, and resources? Indeed, improving the accommodations may only attract others who value the changes. Since we each can use many of the ecological services at will, there is little incentive for any of us as individuals to protect or even to improve the underlying processes that generate them. Who among us takes active measures to strengthen the upper ozone layer that protects all of life? Locally, many of us walk along trails through our local woods to escape from the pressures of modern society. Yet, few hikers take the responsibility for maintaining these trails in order to mitigate the impact on them. Sometimes we are moved to action for emotional reasons; rarely do we gain financial reward for acting as stewards of these natural assets that offer benefits without restraint.

Although all twenty-four ecological services and each of the four functional areas are subject to the challenges just discussed, they are not uniformly affected. Specific differences among the four functional areas clearly exist, thereby explaining their uneven treatment by markets. In some cases, these differences are due to dissimilar features among the four. In other instances, we have developed institutions that resolve these difficulties. Together, these differences explain the uneven impact of economic development on the natural endowment, threatening some elements while allowing others to thrive. Let us turn to these differences now to understand better the uneven outcomes.

Life-support services

As discussed in Chapter Two, the environment provides thirteen life-support services that produce the essential conditions for life on earth. The elimination of any one of these services would end life. Despite their undeniable importance, we take these services largely for granted. Certainly, nature freely offers these services on vast scales that dwarf our individual existence. Each is sufficient to explain our neglect. However, there exists a third complementary reason as well; these services rarely satisfy our human needs *directly*. Instead, they contribute to the underlying infrastructure essential to life. When confronted with a buzzing bee, we are more likely to consider the threat of its stinger rather than the fresh fruits and vegetables that it pollinates. Yet, the demise of all bees would devastate our harvests.

Not only do these life-support services meet our needs indirectly, but most do so in ways that are not easily observable. Only with the powerful tools of modern science have we recognized the complementary role of plants and animals in maintaining a life-supporting balance of gases in our atmosphere. We are only slowly removing the veil that shrouds the many mysteries of nature. Thus, we rarely value these ecological services in themselves, instead only valuing them as they contribute *indirectly* to the provision of bountiful harvests or hospitable habitats. We overlook their importance until we realize the consequences of their decline.

The natural systems that generate life-support services are not only vast, but they also operate along global scales and over long periods. The complexity of their causal links means that activities in one location and time have perceptible, though not easily traceable effects on distant and future locales. Draining wetlands in one location can reduce water quality and increase erosion downstream. The decision to burn fossil fuels can raise respiratory health risks, threaten downwind habitats with heightened acid levels, and contribute to future climate change. We are unlikely to understand fully the impact of our decisions until decades later. In many economic decisions, the market participants have only a partial understanding of their actions and even these known consequences are often borne by others.

This challenge becomes even more difficult as one considers the complementary nature of these systems and the life-support services they generate. Impairment of one system can degrade the functioning of others. Deforestation or overgrazing of vegetation leaves the soil less protected, leading to increased erosion and nutrient losses. The decline in soil fertility will curtail plant productivity and biomass production. Removing the shade cover will reduce plant transpiration and increase ground temperatures. When rain does occur, it will fall directly on the hardened soil and quickly run off in nearby streams, taking with it fine soil and key nutrients. These losses simply exacerbate the problem.[8] Further, impairment of one system can degrade the functioning of another. Less water vapor in the atmosphere will lead to less rainfall in downwind areas, creating a similar decline in vegetation and cycle. These changes can reduce the effectiveness of natural systems, causing a decline in the life-support services they offer. As these changes can occur imperceptibly, they may remain unnoticed until the damage is substantial. Consequently, neglect or overuse in one area can lead to a decline throughout the whole ecosystem, and across systems, as the damage permeates throughout.

Indeed, these interactions can function in an inverse manner as they complement and reinforce each other in significant ways. Specific conditions can favor increased soil formation and more efficient nutrient cycling, and thereby support a larger plant population. Increased plant cover will minimize water losses and reduce soil erosion, thereby encouraging more plant growth. The increased plant biomass will recycle more water vapor into the atmosphere, increasing rainfall, both locally and downwind. More rain, protected soils, and improved nutrient cycling will encourage even further growth. New plant species able to use these abundant resources will thrive, creating niches for other plants and animals and enhancing local diversity. Increased plant growth will enhance their waste treatment services as they assimilate many airborne and waterborne pollutants. Trees and shrubs can clean the skies of unwanted air pollutants while other plants can cleanse streamwater. Increased plant foliage will provide additional refuges for predators of pests and other species requiring biological controls. These changes combine to increase the area's biological productivity and support a more diverse animal and plant population. The result is a better functioning ecosystem that offers us more and better quality services.

Under normal circumstances, one would expect landowners to follow practices that promote these synergies. However, life-support services suffer the most from the "open access" problem, resulting in a zero market valuation. Consequently, landowners have little financial incentive to make improvements that increase ecosystem functioning and life-support services. In some cases, landowners will invest in these services, not so much for their own sake, but rather for their indirect impact on crop yields. Since we mostly benefit from these services without needing to consume them, a zero price will rarely lead to their depletion through overuse.[9] Rather, their decline is more likely due to neglect, where we simply fail to maintain, much less improve the conditions that produce their provision.

Provisioning services

While we have largely ignored life-support services, we have long valued the benefits of provisioning goods and services. True, nature provides these services from the same vast and complex network of natural systems that generate the life-support services. In contrast, these services, for the most part, directly satisfy our material needs and wants.[10] These are the goods and services that quench our thirst, satiate our hunger, clothe and ornament our bodies, shelter us from the elements, power our tools and machinery, and satisfy countless other wants as well. Humans have long recognized their value and rewarded those who can supply these desired goods and services.

Similar to the life-support services, provisioning services are subject to the "open access" problem, making them susceptible to overuse and depletion. In this case, there exists a complicating factor. Virtually all of these provisioning benefits are actually physical commodities that are subject to rival consumption. As such, a limited supply of these goods can only satisfy so much human want. In circumstances where their obvious value intersects with limited supply, conflict is the likely result. Indeed, these provisioning goods and services have been the greatest source of human conflict and war through the ages, even to the present.

Generously provided by nature, these valued goods are subject to the "rule of capture." Whoever controls or possesses the resource can benefit from its use. In the case of non-living resources like freshwater springs, timber, or mineral deposits, control largely comes down to possession, squatting rights historically and ownership rights today. Whoever effectively controls the local area controls these fixed resources. The assurance of control can lead to careful conservation of these resources. If I expect to have long-term control over the valued resource, say a fruit orchard, I will likely use it in ways that ensure its long-term viability. I might even make costly investments, say an irrigation project, which I hope will swell future harvests.

Mobile resources offer circumstances that are more problematic. Fish and game can freely range across human boundaries. To implement the "rule of capture," one must hunt and kill these resources in order to capture them for private use. Under these conditions, there exists little incentive to conserve biological stocks, particularly since one individual's moderation may benefit less temperate rivals. This dynamic helps to explain behaviors that have contributed to the extermination of so many animal species.[11]

Though some view this problem as being exclusive to animal resources, it has emerged in modern times with inanimate resources, too – like oil, natural gas, and groundwater. In the early days of oil, each landowner whose land sat above the valuable oil reservoir had the incentive to drill quickly to capture as much of the mobile resource as possible. These multiple drillings squandered much of the geological pressures that would naturally and economically lift the oil and natural gas to the surface. Too costly to pump up, vast reserves were left in the ground as a result, wasting a valued resource.[12] Conversely, many aquifers around the world are experiencing rapid declines as landowners pump water to irrigate valuable crops. In neither case does there exist adequate incentives to encourage conservation of these mobile resources.

To limit problems arising from the uncertainties caused by the "rule of capture," we have created a structure of private property rights to encourage stability and better stewardship of these provisioning goods. In the USA, we give title to both the surface and subsurface provisioning services located on or under a parcel of land. Under normal circumstances, this title confers on the property owner the following rights held in perpetuity: to use these resources and services, to exclude others from their use, and to transfer these rights to others as they wish. The granting of these rights provides economic incentives that generally encourage resource owners to act in environmentally sound ways. Long-term ownership rights and the ability to exclude others give resource owners the financial incentives needed to conserve their use. Restraint is rewarded as the owner remains the beneficiary of any moderation in their use. Further, these incentives encourage improvements that increase the provisioning capacity of the land. The landowner benefits either from the increased yields or from the sale of their more valuable property.[13] In these ways, private property rights can encourage effective stewardship of these provisioning goods and services.

Though some argue that private property rights are both a natural and comprehensive solution to our environmental problems, neither is the case. Property rights have evolved through time and in different locations to meet specific circumstances and address critical problems. They reflect human ingenuity, not some innate part of our humanity.[14] Specific institutional arrangements that worked well in the past may need modifications to keep apace with our changing circumstances. Moreover, simply extending private property rights to all environmental assets is insufficient. The Texas oil drilling frenzy is a case in point. Each landowner had clearly specified title to all surface provisioning services and mineral rights to any subsurface resources. Anything that they dug or drilled from their land became their possession. Since both oil and gas are mobile, one landowner can extract oil and gas that may lie beneath another's land. The quicker one drills, the more one will possess and therefore sell for a profit. Showing restraint offers the patient landowner absolutely no advantage. Since the oil and gas do not "respect" the surface property boundaries, the existing arrangements were ineffective in this case. By meeting and agreeing to share the oil royalties on some *pro rata* basis, the landowners could have avoided this problem. However, the decision among a few that it is better to act than to talk would undermine this solution. As nature rarely respects our legal, property boundaries, this example represents a serious challenge to those who argue that we simply need to privatize every ecological asset of value to remedy our environmental problems.[15]

Cultural services

Unlike the services already discussed, one can argue whether these services are necessary for human survival. Perhaps we could survive in a world without natural beauty to inspire and inform us, though it would certainly be a dreary existence. The value we confer on these services is largely the result of our cultural progress. Our capacity to appreciate the complexity and grandeur of nature and to search within for the divine all give witness to our capacity and desire for self-reflection. That we can learn from the wisdom inherent in nature and transmit these lessons from one generation to another is evidence of our intellectual and cultural development.[16] Indeed, our capacity to benefit from these provided services offers the truest measure of our level of cultural advance, including our scientific and artistic achievements. Ironically, we have probably done more than any other species to harm these natural areas.

Despite our current level of appreciation for these services, we still take many of them for granted. Similar to life-support services, cultural services are of most benefit to us when we simply leave nature largely undisturbed. For most of us, a walk in the woods is most valued when the human footprint is absent. In addition, the vast scale in which nature provides these services encourages us to take them for granted, except perhaps for the truly unique sites. There is some truth to the famous presidential exclamation: "If you have seen one redwood … you've seen them all."[17] We are easily consoled to cutting this grove of trees, knowing that another still stands nearby. Lastly, we should expect that as our cultural development continues to progress, so will our appreciation for these services continue to expand. Who knows what obscure insect could offer us a cure for cancer? Which undisturbed areas can enhance our understanding of the perils of climate change as we learn how natural processes have adapted in the past to changes in planetary climate? As much as we appreciate the variety of cultural services offered by nature, we must recognize that we remain ignorant of much that our descendants will come to appreciate in the future.

Like many life-support services, most of these cultural services are enjoyed, but not necessarily consumed, permitting them to offer non-rival benefits. Information gleaned from unlocking many of nature's secrets can simultaneously benefit many of us. New discoveries of natural substances that can mitigate disease or bring added comfort to our lives can offer future generations virtually limitless benefits. As we rarely consume these cultural services, their use will rarely lead to their depletion. One exception to this is the impact of visiting outstandingly attractive sites, like Yellowstone and Yosemite, which leads to problems of congestion and degradation. In these cases, higher admission fees and increased restrictions on more damaging uses can limit overuse and its harm.

With the exception of unique sites of remarkable natural beauty, conventional markets are as unlikely to reflect the benefits of these services as they are to reflect those of life-support services. As urban sprawl continues to eradicate the natural areas closest to our growing urban populations, real estate markets will not reflect adequately the decreasing availability of these services. The open access problem makes it very difficult for landowners to devise ways to effectively capture the cultural benefits of undeveloped land. Most of us know local trails through the woods that we can use without payment to escape our current stresses, making it difficult for some to charge for the experience. While some developers do include some greenway areas, these are usually too small to support significant cultural services. Thus, it falls to public officials and the vagaries of government revenues to ensure that these services are preserved through land purchases and development restrictions.

More significantly, there is legitimate concern that we are rapidly eliminating much of the genetic storehouse that has developed over the past few billion years. Much of this unexamined treasure resides in a dozen or so key countries. Under current institutional arrangements, the costs associated with preserving this biodiversity fall largely on the host countries. Frequently, this requires precluding economic development that could improve the livelihoods of local residents. At the same time, any visiting prospector can easily appropriate the benefits locked away in this genetic treasure chest without having to pay the host government for any of the foregone opportunities that economic development might bring. Scientists who discover the benefits of some obscure plant can simply share this discovery with whoever is willing to pay for it, leaving the host country uncompensated.

Carrier services

Finally, we return to the last of the four groups of ecological services: carrier services. Historically, carrier services suffered the same problem as the provisioning services, the "rule of capture." Possession of land is required to make use of its carrier services, whether one wants to use the land for residence, for industry, or for some other wealth-creating activity. As long as one's possession is fluid and uncertain, there is little incentive to make the costly investment needed to "improve" the land. Hence, the creation of social institutions that convey clear rights of possession. In modern times, we have largely turned to private property rights. These rights permit the landowner to exclude use by others and to decide how to use the land in order to capture the accruing benefits. In many cases, these rights encourage landowners to make choices that are beneficial to the natural environment as well. Developers of low-density housing projects have a financial incentive to retain as many trees and as much natural vegetation as possible to keep the natural "feel" of the subdivision. In suburban industrial parks, corporations frequently maintain a natural landscape to attract employees and to provide them with fitness and recreational opportunities that can lower employment costs. Given the added right to sell the land, the owner is encouraged to make these improvements even if the expected tenure of ownership is likely to be temporary. Economic benefit often coincides with retaining the ecological integrity of the land.

Yet, not all is well. Land is easily divisible in economic terms, but not so ecologically. Land-use decisions made for one tract of land will inevitably spill over to adjacent tracts as well. Clearing the land of trees to increase acreage for farming reduces the habitat of many birds and insects that prey on crop-ravaging pests. In this case, the landowner captures the full benefits of his clearing while sharing with neighboring landowners (farmers) the loss of natural pest management. New development for industrial, commercial, and retail purposes requires huge chunks of land not only for the building sites, but also for roads and parking lots. The loss of natural areas reduces the land's capacity to absorb water and regulate its runoff. Downstream areas are now subject to increased flooding and water impurities as the cascading waters accumulate chemical residues left from cars. Though these costs can be substantial, they are ignored since their impact affects individuals and communities unrelated to the offending developer. Zoning restrictions and land-use planning have emerged to remedy the more obvious harm caused by certain development decisions, but these tools rarely consider the losses of diminished ecological services. Even today, development that further fragments remaining natural areas and thereby diminishes their capacity to provide the full range of ecological services will occur with little regard for these losses.

Answering the paradox

In Chapter Two, I explained how a comprehensive understanding of the full range of ecological services provided by nature gives us a much fuller picture of the concept of "natural capital." Such an understanding is essential if we are to appreciate these critically important services. We must not simply be aware of these ecological services; we must understand their underlying complexities to avoid a simplifying and inaccurate understanding of how nature can serve as capital. To appreciate more fully and to avoid squandering our natural endowment, we need to understand some basic ecological concepts and processes. In this chapter, I explain how economics and its financial incentives influence our day-to-day decisions as they affect our different forms of natural capital. Each of the four functional areas offers special circumstances that shape our decisions. In some areas, like the provisioning services, our current market-based institutions function reasonably effectively in acting as good stewards of these forms of natural capital. In other areas, particularly life-support services, our current market-based institutions function ineffectively. Simply put, the analysis suggests that markets will not provide equal protection or sensible stewardship of all our natural endowments.

We can return to some of the controversies raised at the book's outset. Too often, we characterize "the environment" as some homogenous system that is either improving or collapsing, depending on our viewpoint. Actually, it is a complex web of separate systems interrelated and interdependent on each other. This variety and complexity belies any simple perception of the environment as some uniform concept. Instead, this analysis suggests that various elements of our environment are faring disparately under our impact. Some natural systems that provide us with critical ecological services are undoubtedly under grave threat; there exists ample evidence to support this claim.[18] Their vulnerability results in part due to their limited range and adaptability to new conditions. Other natural systems are so vast that they are impervious to all but the most destructive human behaviors. Short of some "nuclear" mistake, these natural systems can accommodate the worst of our behaviors without much effect.[19] Some highly damaged systems can recuperate and recover relatively quickly from past abuses as new policies, economic incentives, and human behaviors take root.[20] Other forms of damage, like the extinction of species, are irreversible. Rather than view our environment singularly, we should always expect different natural systems to suffer our presence in varied ways.

The differences in these natural systems and in the services they provide evoke varied human responses and create different challenges for us as well. In some cases, market institutions have evolved that function effectively in encouraging good stewardship of our natural capital. Most provisioning services are subject to clear private-property rights.[21] Particularly as their value rises, market prices will respond and encourage conservation on both sides of the market. Higher resource prices encourage reduced demand as manufacturers modify their production methods to reduce waste or switch to more plentiful substitutes. In the case of renewable resources, higher prices encourage resource owners to make investments that expand the future supply of services. Even for non-renewable resources, higher resource prices can encourage conservation – particularly as the prospect of even higher prices in the future encourages patience. Though exceptions exist, notably with the ocean fisheries, most provisioning services are subject to effectively functioning markets.

On the other hand, many important services, including most life-support services, are not subject to effective market institutions. Nature's vast bounty and unrestricted provision has made it difficult for market institutions to function effectively. As such, the price of these services remains at zero, suggesting the absence of value. A zero price for these services encourages their unrestrained use. As the services become scarce, their prices will fail to rise in response to the changing circumstances, thereby offering no discouragement of their use. A further problem exists. As nature freely provides these services, the value attached to the natural systems that provide these essential services is also zero. This point influences countless decisions. "Undeveloped" land that solely provides life-support services is assessed at zero value. Only as the land is "developed" for some human aim will it gain any market value, providing financial encouragement to such development and an inevitable decline in life-support services. Thus, our market-based institutions neither value the life-support services currently available nor reflect any decline in these essential services. Our decisions therefore assume that these critical services are immaterial and irrelevant. Until we correct this oversight, we will continue to make the same decisions that are currently undermining the many natural systems that generate these critical life-support services.

These market difficulties pose serious challenges to the Environmental Kuznets view discussed in Chapter One. If market prices do not react to environmental shortages, then the expected shortage-resolving responses will not occur. Instead, economic growth will place ever-greater pressures on the shrinking and increasingly vulnerable natural systems. For sure, rising affluence along with the realized losses in ecological services can trigger substantial public outcry and subsequent public policy to limit further damage. Yet, few proponents of this view would argue that the public or governmental response is as effective or as timely as a well-functioning market response. Given the current disposition of market-based institutions to respond to some shortages of services and not others, we can expect a path of economic development that preserves some ecological services at the expense of others. Not only can we expect such, but we can reasonably predict it.

Returning to my local community

In the ensuing years, the development of the land that once served as a corporate park has followed both a predictable path and some surprising curves. Paved roads now crisscross substantial portions of the property. Large houses dot the hilly woods to accommodate the families seeking homes in this part of town.

New shopping centers and office buildings have sprung up along the major thoroughfares that earlier defined the property. To accommodate these changes, the developers cut trees and paved over the fields. Though local residents organized to protest against these changes and appeal for timely government action, none was forthcoming. Events similar to these have occurred in many communities.

However, some critical developments altered the expected outcome. Early in the process, the developers donated a sizeable parcel to the local school system to build a much-needed elementary school. Perhaps, the developers saw this offer as a necessary public relations gesture to a local community already inflamed. In addition, local interests purchased a sizeable tract to create a nationally acclaimed, private high school. The school's founders have demonstrated a strong commitment to respecting the natural attributes of their parcel of land. Lastly, a local benefactor emerged to offer help. Due to their generosity, a local branch of the public library now occupies the site of the old clubhouse and currently sits amid a parcel reserved as a wilderness park. Because of each of these decisions, the property has undergone much less intensive development than the original proposal envisioned and has retained much more of its natural character and value.

This story, like many others across our country, illustrates how our economic decisions reflect certain values offered by our natural assets. As adjacent properties in this desirable area of town became increasingly developed, the value of this last remaining parcel continued to appreciate through the years. As its market value rose, there is little evidence that this appreciation had any connection to the increasingly scarce life-support services that the land brought to this part of town. Instead, the rising values reflected the carrier services that the land could yield, once transformed into upscale residential or commercial properties. Nowhere in any of the financial calculations nor negotiations were there any economic assessments attributed to the lost life-support and other services that development would bring. As such, incomplete information causes these decisions and countless others to be ill informed. To understand where and how these institutional blinders operate, we need to take a wider view of the issues. I leave that to the next two chapters.

Further reading

Garrett Hardin, 'Tragedy of the Commons', is a classic article that explains how markets fail to function effectively in the face of "open access" resources and services.

Geoffrey Heal, *Nature and the Marketplace: Capturing the Value of Ecosystem Services*, provides a more comprehensive and in-depth look at how markets interact with different facets of nature.

Millennium Ecosystem Assessment, *Ecosystems and Human Well-Being*, offers a comprehensive assessment of the role of ecosystem services in meeting human well-being, as well as conditions and trends of the natural systems that provide these services.

4 A tale of two energy crises

The American nightmare

Thirty years ago, we watched in stupefied horror as the American dream that we believed was our future disintegrated into a much grimmer vision. Twice in the 1970s, real or manufactured shortages in the global oil markets sent American fuel prices skyward. Worse, gasoline supplies became unreliable due to the wave of gas station closures, both temporary and permanent. "Sorry, no gas today" signs sprouted like weeds at service stations across the nation. These closures made long-distance traveling by car precarious, at best. Gasless Sundays became the norm as station owners responded to their reduced supplies by cutting hours of operation. Travelers took unwanted hiatuses to avoid being stuck with an empty tank and no open station nearby. The nation's highways, once filled with the drone of vehicles on Sunday afternoons, became virtually empty and quiet. The Sunday drive, once a symbol of American prosperity and leisure, now became a sign of courage or recklessness.

This new reality did more than merely disrupt the Sunday drive. Service stations fortunate to have gasoline attracted long lines of potential customers. Hour-long waits were common. These lines included customers looking to top off their tanks in anticipation of worse shortages to come. Waiting in the long lines, people grew increasingly impatient and frustrated. Occasionally, arguments and fights erupted that led to violence and even death. Service stations capped the amount of gas that a customer could buy in order to stretch their supplies. Nonetheless, their limited supplies would run out, signaling to the remaining customers that their long wait was in vain. The arrival of a fuel truck at another station would immediately attract a new line of customers. To bring some renewed order, states began rationing systems to limit the pursuit of gasoline. These schemes gave drivers a license to hunt for gasoline on selected days, based on their license plate. Our entitlement to cheap and readily available energy had clearly been revoked.

Not only did we Americans suffer long waits for gas, but we also watched its price climb to heights previously unthinkable. First in 1973 and later in 1979, Americans watched as the price of gas doubled in a period of months. Families on tight budgets found these increases more than they could bear. Spiraling oil prices caused other fuel prices to rise as well, and all energy bills climbed beyond the reach of many families. Non-payment of heating bills led some public utilities to shut off the service to homeowners, resulting in some inadvertent deaths. Rising energy prices inflamed the inflationary spiral, causing dramatic price increases in almost every commodity and service. With each purchase, American households faced higher prices that placed increased pressure on already stretched family budgets.

Uncertain gasoline supplies disrupted those occupations and businesses dependent on car travel. Truckers, taxi drivers, and salespeople were frequently unable to work for lack of gas. Businesses could not rely on deliveries, while factories closed temporarily due to the lack of key parts. Rising prices squeezed some activities, making them uneconomical. Farmers could not afford to purchase fuel to harvest crops whose prices had remained unchanged in spite of inflation. Truckers and shippers lost money due to rapidly rising fuel costs. The material shortages and increased fuel prices created dislocations that rippled throughout the economy. The loss of work and business reduced family incomes at the same time as these families were struggling with rising prices. These reverberations rocked the foundation of our American sense of well-being. Taken together, Americans experienced a significant decline in material well-being and faced financial insecurity.

Americans responded as they could. People drove their cars less as they opted to walk more, to carpool, and to use mass transit where available. Residents responded by turning down their thermostats during winter and wearing more sweaters. Neighborhoods once lit up by dazzling Christmas lights now became dark. People exchanged their gas-guzzling cars for foreign imports that were smaller, lighter, and more fuel-efficient. In response to the new sense of national priorities, the Carter Administration created the Energy Department as a cabinet-level post. This reorganization gathered previously dispersed energy programs into one agency to bring coordination and supervision. More telling, the first Energy Secretary, James Schlesinger, was popularly called the "Energy Czar."

These memories embody what we call the "energy crisis" – an uncomfortable accommodation with a new reality, one different from the "good old days" of cheap and abundant energy. Uncertain and expensive energy supplies now threatened American prosperity. Indeed, in his departure from the Carter Administration, Energy Secretary Schlesinger assessed the country's energy prospects as follows: "Today we face a world crisis ... made more ominous by the problems of oil. There is little, if any relief in prospect ... The energy future is bleak and is likely to grow bleaker in the decade ahead."[1] By the end of the 1970s, the world oil situation had upset the American dream and transformed it into a nightmarish era of pessimism and sacrifice.

The aftermath of the first energy crisis

Though respected and knowledgeable about energy issues, Secretary Schlesinger was dead wrong with his prediction of a bleak and ominous energy future. By the end of the decade, the so-called "energy crisis" had been "solved." The oil and gasoline shortages of the 1970s turned into substantial surpluses during the 1980s.

In the decade following Schlesinger's pronouncement, energy prices – most particularly, oil and gasoline – actually fell. As gasoline (and related energy) prices continued to decline in the 1990s, Americans slowly reverted to historical behaviors. Sales of smaller, fuel-efficient models slowed as Americans fell in love with the nascent sport utility vehicles (SUVs) and image took on greater importance than fuel economy. By the late 1990s, light trucks and SUVs had captured fully 50 percent of new car sales in the USA. Americans of all stripes returned to the open road as driving again became a cheap passion. As a crowning reminder that the energy crisis was gone and forgotten, it became socially acceptable once again to exhibit one's holiday spirit through exterior light displays.

Unfortunately, it is both simplistic and incomplete to argue that we solved the energy crisis. True enough, it is a story that illustrates the persuasive and pervasive influence of markets and their financial incentives. It is also a story that exhibits the genius of technology and innovative problem-solving. As such, this story holds powerful lessons for environmental activists and policymakers, who often undervalue the effectiveness of markets and technological solutions. Yet, the same market forces that encouraged effective solutions to the oil shortages contributed generously to our current energy crisis. I am not referring to a return of energy shortages – a real enough concern – but rather to the problem of global climate change. This is indeed the second energy crisis of our generation and one which markets *by themselves* are unable to resolve. Technological optimists and market adherents who argue that we already have the necessary tools to solve our significant environmental problems should pay attention to this part of the story. Though markets and technological ingenuity quickly and effectively responded to the first crisis, they have proved ineffective in response to this second crisis. Complicated and rich in lessons, this tale of the two energy crises illustrates both the genius and limits of market institutions and technological prowess in addressing environmental problems.

Just the facts

As Secretary Schlesinger left the government, world oil prices were close to their historic peak.[2] Crude oil sold at nearly $40 per barrel. Just seven years earlier, the same oil sold for less than $4 per barrel. In that span of time, the price of the modern industrial economy's most vital resource had increased ten-fold. More importantly for the American driver, the price of gasoline climbed to the then unheard of price of $1.40 per gallon. Still fresh in memory was gasoline that sold for less than 40 cents per gallon a mere seven years earlier. As Schlesinger spoke that day about the future, he was unaware of the shifting ground that would lead to a much different energy future than the one he envisioned.

Rather than continuing their price rise, both crude oil prices and refined gasoline prices tumbled from the lofty heights reached in the late 1970s. The price of both commodities fell sharply in the early 1980s and fully collapsed midway through the decade. In the case of refined gasoline, the price fell sufficiently that by late in the decade, the inflation-adjusted price of gasoline was less than in the "good old days" prior to 1973. Oil and gasoline prices sharply increased when Iraq annexed Kuwait in 1990, but both resumed their decline through much of the 1990s. By the late 1990s, gasoline prices in the USA reached historic lows, beating the bargain prices of the 1960s. Only in the last decade have oil and gasoline prices begun to rise again, reaching record highs in 2008. Figure 4.1 illustrates this path of gas pump prices adjusted for inflation.

Not only did prices decline from their stunning heights of the early 1980s, but the oil "shortages" disappeared from view, somewhat perplexingly since oil is both non-renewable and largely not reusable.[3] At the time of the first oil shock in 1973, worldwide production of oil had reached about 55 million barrels per day. After an initial dip, world oil production resumed its steady expansion, topping 60 million barrels by the late 1970s. A second price shock in 1979 caused another

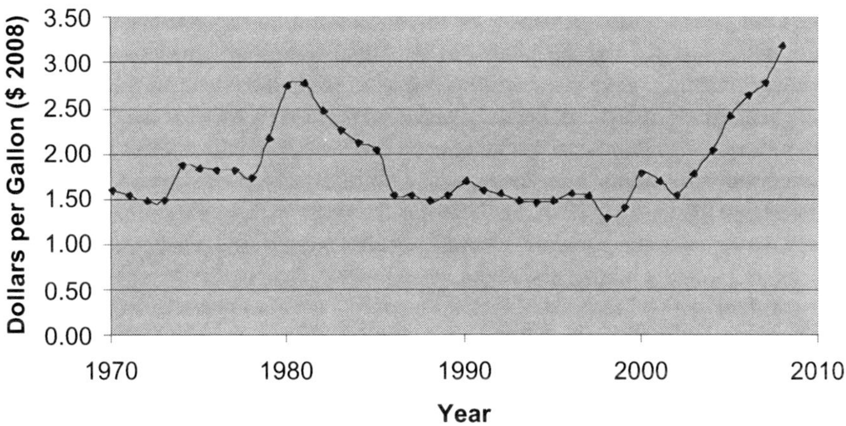

Figure 4.1 Inflation-adjusted gasoline prices.
Source: Energy Information Administration.

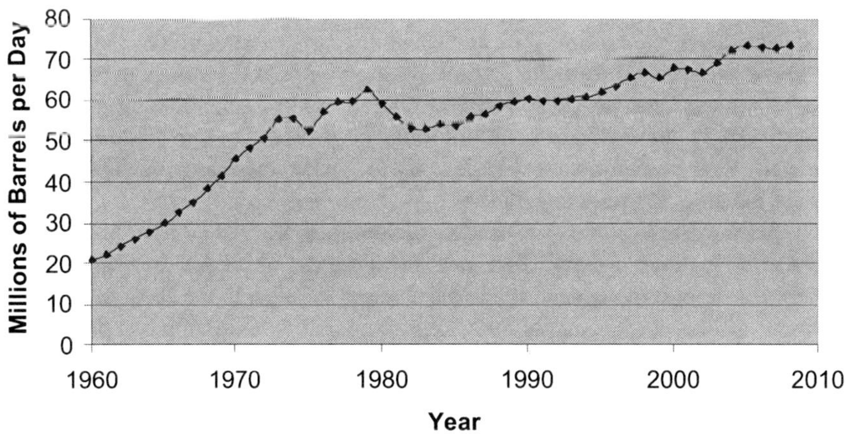

Figure 4.2 World crude oil production.
Source: Energy Information Administration.

decline in oil production, as producers reduced output in response to declining demand. However, by 1985, world oil production resumed its upward trend and continued to rise through the end of the century. World petroleum markets have become awash with oil, causing surpluses to replace shortages. Only recently has our thirst for oil seemingly outpaced production. Lost within this larger trend is a key point. Around 1970, despite many efforts to the contrary, US production of oil peaked and has declined since. Once considered the original Saudi Arabia due to our vast petroleum reserves, the USA's trend illustrates the longer-run future for the world at large as we deplete this non-renewable resource. For this reason, the first energy crisis should be of interest to more than historians.[4]

The underlying conditions

Crude oil prices reflect a variety of factors, including the actions of both the major oil companies and the nations of the Organization of Petroleum Exporting Countries (OPEC). Ever since drilling began in 1856, the world oil markets have rarely been free of the visible hands of major oil producers, whether they are private corporations or governments with major oil reserves. The industry has a legacy of erratic production and wild price swings, with fortunes earned, lost, and regained. Long before the birth of OPEC in 1960, this industry witnessed countless attempts by the major actors to stimulate demand, regulate supply, and raise prices, all with the aim to tame the market and make more money. Despite temporary successes, the world oil market has resisted such tight control and demonstrated independence rarely appreciated. To understand world oil markets, one needs to understand the distinguishing character of oil as a commodity as well as the traditional forces that influence any market for a commodity.

Several factors contribute to the oil market's history of volatility. Though petroleum is relatively abundant in many parts of the world, its location deep in the ground makes its specific position difficult to discern. Further, it is located in reservoirs of varying levels of concentration and ease of extraction. The supply of oil reflects the level of effort, skill, and technological expertise involved in discovering and extracting it from the ground. Rising oil prices encourage producers to invest their time, abilities, and money in finding and bringing more oil to market. Unsurprisingly, these efforts focus on finding large oil fields with vast amounts of crude oil. With their discovery and delivery to market, these huge fields flood the market, causing oil prices to collapse.

On the demand side of the oil market, petroleum is marked by what economists call a *price inelastic demand.* This means that the use of oil and its refined products is largely unresponsive to moderate changes in price. In the early days of the industry, oil was used primarily for heating and lighting. Declining fuel prices had little effect on how much people used. Low fuel prices would encourage people to adopt these new and convenient forms of heating and lighting; however, these changes only gradually boosted oil demand. Even today, as oil and its many refined products have become critical necessities in our modern lifestyle, our use of these products tends to be very resistant to changes in price. While we may grumble endlessly with our co-workers over an increase of twenty cents a gallon in the price of gasoline, such an increase (or price decrease, for that matter) has little impact on our consumption. As a result, fluctuations in oil supplies exert their impact on oil price rather than changes in consumption. Even small fluctuations in oil supplies can wield a noticeable impact on price.

Several other factors can influence this volatility in oil prices. Since oil is a non-perishable product, it need not be rushed to market once discovered. If conditions are not ripe, the owners can simply leave the oil in the ground. Its non-perishable nature gives a patient driller increased advantage in bargaining over price. On the other hand, decisions to develop the oil field and bring it to market offset this restraint. To extract the crude oil from the ground, refine it into products useful to the consumer, and ship it to the point of sale requires a huge infrastructure of oil rigs, pipelines, shipping, storage, and refining capacity. Making these substantial investments generate significant financial pressures to tap the oil reservoir as quickly as possible to pay for them. Only an owner with very deep pockets indeed can resist draining their oil reservoir once they have made these outlays. Moreover, recall the problem discussed in Chapter Three. Where the discovered oil field lies under multiple properties, the "rule of capture" discourages any patience in lifting the oil and creates a free-for-all frenzy of oil extraction, swamping the oil markets with new oil.

For two decades prior to 1973, the world oil market was clearly a "buyer's market." Frequent discoveries of major oil fields brought ever-increasing oil supplies onto the world market. Oil prices declined through the 1950s and 1960s, despite industry efforts to prop them up. Cheap oil encouraged nations throughout the world to follow the economic development path of the industrialized West, whose prosperity rested largely on the foundation of its petroleum-based economy. As a result, world consumption of oil doubled between 1945 and 1960. Between 1960 and 1970, it doubled once again. Despite this worldwide gorging, the new sources of petroleum were sufficient to meet this growing demand and keep prices low. Despite the seeming calm of this golden era of cheap and plentiful oil, there were strong hints of underlying problems that would soon wreak havoc.

While most individuals, business, and nations welcome low oil prices, oil producers, and especially oil prospectors, do not. Low oil prices discourage the costly investment in time and equipment that oil prospecting entails. Although past oil discoveries were ample to meet the rapid growth in worldwide demand experienced during this time, no new discoveries were available to meet future growth. Low oil prices also discouraged significant investment in the costly infrastructure needed to bring ever-greater supplies of crude oil from remote oil fields to the industrial consumer. Without more pipelines, oil tankers, and oil refineries, the world's oil refining system had limited capacity to meet the growing demand. By 1970, world demand for oil was nearing the worldwide production of crude oil. To be sure, there were still plenty of oil reserves, especially in the Middle East. However, both the lack of infrastructure and the calculations of political economy kept these reserves from reaching the world consumer.

Both in 1973 and again in 1979, war triggered the oil price shocks that fractured the industrial bases of the world economies. While OPEC (and its primary clients, the seven major oil companies) were able to profit from these events, their major source of strength came from the recognition that there was little excess supply in the world oil market. Given the central importance of oil in fueling the modern industrial economies, the threat of inadequate supplies created a climate of fear. Oil's role as an essential part of the modern economy meant that any hint of shortages could foster panic as oil consumers considered the alternative of being without. This dire alternative encouraged buyers to offer any price in order to assure adequate supply. Petroleum's central and singular role in the modern industrial economy created the conditions for the tremendous price volatility that would follow.

Solving the initial energy crisis

To understand how market forces worked to resolve the earlier energy crisis, one needs to recognize the twin functions of markets: their allocation function and their less appreciated guidance function. The allocation function refers to the manner in which markets, often rapidly and quite visibly, use prices to ration scarce goods and commodities. The guidance function refers to the ways that markets can marshal resources in response to shortages or surpluses. Both functions are critical to understanding how markets effectively resolve market imbalances.

The allocation function ensures that the price of any market commodity or service responds to changes in underlying market conditions. When permitted to adjust freely, market prices will rise as shortages appear and fall in response to surpluses. Particularly in the case of shortages, price acts to ration the scarce goods among competing buyers. Those customers with the most desire or income to pay for the goods will continue buying them, even at the higher price. The price will rise until enough buyers are discouraged from the market, causing the shortage to dissipate. (Higher prices will also encourage additional supply, as the prospect of making a quick buck will lure some sellers.) In most cases, prices can adjust quite rapidly, thereby ending the shortage. In eliminating shortages, this allocation function reduces the considerable time and effort that is spent waiting in line and searching for available supplies of the scarce, but desired commodity.

While markets are admired for their efficient operation in getting scarce goods to people with the minimum of money and effort, they often pose more problematic equity concerns. Strictly speaking, the rationing function of markets operates as an impersonal mechanism that does not discriminate against specific individuals. Shortages lead to higher prices, a burden that all buyers must bear. However, underlying differences in household income and wealth cause the burden of higher prices to be borne disproportionately. In a world devoid of huge disparities, buyers who have greater zeal or need for the highly priced item will gain a larger share. This would strike most people as both fair and efficient. However, the reality of income and wealth disparities muddies this picture. As these inequalities grow, market rationing causes access to these goods to be determined more by differences in economic power than in varied attraction to the product. Further, markets have a role in creating the vast differences in economic power. Since markets not only price consumer goods, but also the key wealth-creating resources like labor skills, real property, and financial capital, markets do directly influence the underlying wealth disparities that can make their allocating function unfair. There is little evidence that markets tend to moderate the underlying wealth disparities; rather they tend toward the old adage that "the rich get richer and the poor get poorer", at least in a relative sense, if not absolutely.[5]

Unlike the allocation function, the guidance function of markets tends to work more incrementally and less visibly, yet far more pervasively. The shortages that lead to high prices create a host of financial incentives to buyers and sellers as well as to potential rivals. Obviously, high prices encourage buyers to look for cheaper alternatives. In the immediate period of the shortage, buyers frequently have little choice other than to purchase the product at its current price or do without. Over time, they often have additional, less difficult choices. They discover that alternatives do exist or that new ones emerge. They make decisions that reduce their need for the product, thereby easing the pain of doing without. High prices also affect the product suppliers, perhaps even more acutely. Higher prices generally mean higher profits, luring suppliers to expand their production. Potential investors are attracted to the industry to offer additional production. Other inventors, entrepreneurs, and investors are attracted to ideas and potential products that may satisfy the unmet need in alternative ways. New and sometimes better alternatives are developed and marketed that can eventually replace the original product. Manufacturers of related products can modify their products so that their customers have less need of the commodity in short supply. In sum, the guidance function creates a host of incentives that encourage individuals, organizations, and businesses to seek new ways of responding to the unmet need created by the original shortage. Interestingly, as these new efforts satisfy the deferred needs, the price of the original product begins to ease as the underlying shortage abates. The financial incentives continue as long as the original shortage persists. Depending on the importance of the product that is the object of the initial shortage, these financial incentives can extend well beyond the initial industry and engender changes throughout the economy.

How the initial energy crisis was won

Given the indispensable and central role that oil played in the economies of the major industrial nations, its effects spread to all parts of the modern economy. However, in the interests of brevity, I will narrow my focus to what happened in the transportation industry, particularly motor vehicles. In 1973, we burned about 40 percent of the oil consumed in our passenger cars and trucks.[6] What happened in this area of the economy gives us an accurate and detailed depiction of how the whole economy adjusted to the problem of unstable and expensive oil. Clear and accurate records provide evidence of what happened and how significantly these actions helped to resolve the energy crisis.

Though the world oil market in the 1970s was relatively free of any government restrictions (apart from the effective manipulation of OPEC), the domestic oil market in the USA was not. The US market operated under a multitude of arcane laws and regulations that set maximum prices for "old" oil, but not "new" oil. Such regulations aimed to protect vulnerable consumers from the effects of price "gouging" that resulted from past industry efforts to raise prices; however, they effectively limited the rationing role of US oil markets to respond fully to the OPEC-induced oil shocks.[7] While refined gasoline prices did climb in the USA in response to the conditions on the world stage, they did not rise proportionately to the increases in world oil prices. Domestic gasoline prices were not permitted to rise sufficiently to resolve the shortages. Instead, the gasoline shortages persisted, causing long lines, uncertain supplies, and other problems discussed at the outset of this chapter. When we prevent market prices from rationing scarce goods, some other mechanism is required.

By the time of the second oil shock in 1979, political pressures had built sufficiently to suspend the price controls on domestic oil and to allow the market to function without restraint. This time, the supply disruptions caused by the war between two oil producers, Iran and Iraq, had a greater impact on the domestic price of gasoline in the USA than did the events six years earlier. In 1973, a quadrupling of the world price of oil led only to a 50 percent increase in US gasoline prices. In 1979, the doubling of world oil prices led to a comparable doubling of gasoline prices at US gas stations. Domestic markets operated without restraint in responding to this second shortage by rationing scarce gasoline supplies. Fears that uncertain supplies and long gasoline lines would return were largely unfounded.

As expected, higher gasoline prices in both 1973 and 1979 encouraged US drivers to drive less frequently. In the two-year period subsequent to both oil shocks, average miles driven per car declined by 10 percent and 9 percent respectively. Both declines are substantial, though the drop after 1979 was disproportionately low relative to the rise in gasoline prices. However, this anomaly can be explained by examining a related figure. Average fuel consumption per car in a given year measures not only the amount of driving, but also the fuel efficiency of cars. In the two-year period following 1973, fuel consumption per car fell about the same 10 per cent, suggesting that most of this saving was due to less driving. After 1979, fuel consumption fell by a much larger 16 percent, indicating something other than driving habits was the cause. During this period, households increasingly responded to higher gasoline prices by purchasing more fuel-efficient cars. In fact, between 1979 and 1980, the average fuel efficiency of the full passenger vehicle fleet increased over a gallon and a half, the largest single year jump ever recorded. By investing in fuel-efficient cars, consumers could buffer the adverse effects of higher pump prices without having to restrict their driving.

The change in car buying between the first and second oil price shock was not due simply to a difference in customer psychology. In the intervening years, significant changes had occurred in the passenger car market. In 1973, the typical domestically produced (Detroit) automobile was large, heavy, and overpowered to suit the typical American's tastes at that time. Car buyers seeking to gain relief from the escalating gasoline prices of the mid-1970s had few options other than the predominantly Japanese imports. As a result, the sales of imports surged while those of Detroit languished. Sensing the shift in their customers' preferences, Detroit embarked on a massive effort to offer new fuel-efficient models and to downsize many of its traditional bestsellers. By 1980, the "Big Three" domestic car producers had created a number of models that could tempt car buyers seeking fuel economy.

This trend in increased fuel economy has largely continued, though only modestly over the past decade. In the early 1970s, the average car traveled less than 14 miles a gallon while the average car now gets over 22 miles per gallon.[8] Over the years, automotive engineers improved vehicle mileage by reducing the size and weight of cars, increasing aerodynamics, developing improved transmissions, and shifting to fuel injection. To be sure, the federal government's Corporate Average Fuel Economy (CAFE) standards should receive some credit for these improvements in fuel efficiency. These standards mandated that each major car company offer cars that meet a fuel efficiency threshold. For example, a car manufacturer was required to sell enough cars that gained 20 miles per gallon to offset sales of its cars that gained only 10 miles per gallon in order to achieve the mandated average, say 15 miles per gallon. Failure to meet these average fleet standards would bring financial penalties. While the CAFE standards no doubt encouraged manufacturers to offer and sell more fuel-efficient cars in order to sell more of their larger and more profitable cars, most of these gains would have occurred regardless. Without high gasoline prices driving the American car buyer toward more fuel-efficient cars, car manufacturers would have faced severe difficulties in meeting the CAFE standards. This proved true in the 1980s and 1990s when car buyers returned to larger, less fuel-efficient cars as gasoline prices fell.

High oil prices encouraged other changes as well. The astronomical profits permitted by such prices encouraged every oil prospector to seek new sources of oil. And find new sources they did. New oil fields in the North Sea, in Mexico and on the North Slope of Alaska were all developed and integrated into the world oil market. This occurred despite the substantial development costs in drilling and piping the oil from these challenging and remote fields. High oil prices made these investments feasible and economical. As these and other new sources supplemented the existing supply, the pressures that boosted oil prices began to ease. As shortages evolved into oil surpluses, OPEC experienced increasing pressure to cut production in order to prevent the inevitable fall in oil prices. In the USA, OPEC's share of the lucrative market fell by two-thirds from 1979 to 1985 as other, non-OPEC sources filled the vacuum. Despite OPEC's efforts to maintain the high oil prices, these prices continued to slide from their peak in 1981, going from $39 per barrel to $13 per barrel barely five years later. As oil prices tumbled, they brought similar relief to prices at the gasoline pumps. By the mid-1980s, both oil and gasoline prices had returned to levels comparable to the days prior to the energy crisis, adjusting for inflation.

Before their collapse, the high oil and gasoline prices had affected every part of the economy. High oil prices encouraged many large, industrial users to switch to alternative fuels, usually natural gas. Businesses and households alike were encouraged to in invest in energy-efficient equipment, including better-insulated buildings and homes, more efficient engines, and energy-saving home appliances. To make their products more attractive, manufacturers improved their design to increase energy efficiency and lower their operating costs to their customers.

Research and development led to new energy technologies that tapped wind, solar, and geothermal power sources. Nearly all of these extensive and incremental steps added up to a substantial response to the problem of shortages. And nearly all of these responses were directly encouraged by the financial incentives created by high oil prices. Unfortunately, while the collapse in oil and gasoline prices brought welcome relief to energy consumers, they also eliminated most of the financial incentives that encouraged these energy-conscious decisions.

The cloud around the silver lining

The success of the market in solving the early energy crisis has led to the unraveling of its effectiveness. Falling oil prices that reflect more prudent consumption and increased drilling undermine the financial incentives that encourage these behaviors. Low oil prices in the 1990s contributed to the booming popularity of SUVs, as fuel economy faded in importance with the return of cheap gasoline. Low prices discouraged further discovery and development of new oil sources. Taken together, the return of low oil prices encouraged oil consumption over new oil sources and therefore created the conditions for the next oil shortage. Thus, the remarkable market response is a largely temporary one subject to cyclical swings from shortage to glut and back again. Allowing "free" markets to operate in such a cyclical way does not encourage the most effective use of this valuable and non-renewable resource. Public policy remedies do exist that could correct this undesired instability without contravening the effectiveness of markets to ration and encourage socially desirable behaviors. However, this misuse of dwindling fossil fuels looms less important as compared to the larger problem created by their use.

While the earlier energy crisis grappled with the *source* side of the petroleum stream, our current energy crisis is focused on the *emissions* side. The burning of all fossil fuels, including petroleum, releases carbon dioxide into the atmosphere. Since carbon dioxide is naturally present in the atmosphere, these releases were viewed as innocuous, until recently. Fresh scientific evidence indicates rising levels in atmospheric carbon since the Industrial Revolution, which marks the advent of our prodigious use of these fuels. Since 1850, levels of CO2 have increased by over 20 percent and are increasing rapidly, as Figure 4.3 suggests.

Dispersed over a vast atmosphere, increased levels of carbon dioxide pose no direct threat to life, including human life. In such concentrations, they are not toxic; indeed, to all plant life, carbon dioxide is a critical element for photosynthesis. Further, devoid of color or smell, these releases pose no aesthetic problem for humans. Rather, the releases simply enhance the "greenhouse effect" discussed in Chapter Two. Increasing atmospheric carbon levels as we have is like adding additional glass to our planetary greenhouse. Most scientists agree that our past activities are affecting the planetary system and will likely lead to some level of "global warming."

This is the essence of our contemporary energy crisis. The burning of vast amounts of fossil fuel is emitting carbon dioxide that is altering our planetary climate. Evidence is mounting that global temperatures are rising already. It

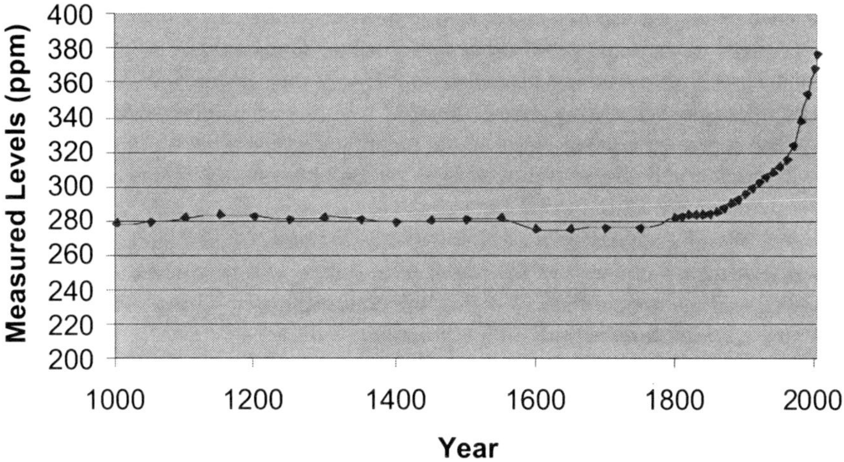

Figure 4.3 Carbon dioxide levels in the atmosphere.
Source: Carbon Dioxide Information Analysis Center, Oak Ridge National Laboratory.

is difficult to prove that this warming trend is solely due to human releases of greenhouse gases. Moreover, it is impossible to predict accurately the future consequences of past and present activities. However, the weight of the evidence and the credibility of the science make a very persuasive case that we are significantly and fundamentally modifying the planetary climate system.

In spells of unseasonably warm weather, I hear frequent mention that "global warming" is the culprit. Given the complexity of our global processes, it is unlikely that a few days of unusually balmy weather results from planetary warming. These processes are neither simple nor straightforward. Instead, the changes are likely to be complex and varied by region and by topography. Most predict that any warming will have a greater impact on winter temperatures than on summer temperatures. In some areas, milder winters will offer increased hospitality to certain pests that currently are eliminated by freezing temperatures. Increased atmospheric temperatures will alter rainfall patterns, causing some regions to become wetter while others will become drier. Hotter temperatures offer increased energy as fuel to more turbulent storms, causing heightened havoc and harm. In some areas, the altered climate will lengthen the growing season and offer a boon to local farmers, while others will see their efforts at eking out an existence made more difficult. Global warming will increase ocean temperatures and therefore raise the sea level, flooding coastal lowlands unprotected from the rising seas. Whatever the specific impact, change will be the constant.

Though the changes predicted by scientists are not threatening to the earth, its resilient processes, or life as we know it, these changes will wreak havoc, or even catastrophe for specific organisms, species, ecosystems, individuals, communities, and even small nations. Changing climate will test the mettle of each biological community as the modified conditions threaten their vitality. Those species that can do so will migrate with the shifting conditions. Other species, unable to migrate, will need to adapt to the new conditions or perish. Certain ecosystems will expand their ranges at the expense of other ecosystems. Areas subject to the threat of tornadoes or hurricanes can expect more frequent and destructive storms in the future. Though such events always generate a boon to the construction industry, they also represent a grave threat to the insurance industry, as it grapples with a rise in number and size of claims without historic precedence. Some regions will witness better growing conditions while other marginal lands will become even stingier, thereby affecting those that depend on them. Coastal areas, including the rich alluvial farmlands of the major river deltas, will be subject to increased flooding and the toxic effects of higher salt concentrations. Rising sea levels will threaten certain island nations with extinction.

Why markets will not resolve this energy crisis

Despite certain parallels, we should expect one key difference between our current and the earlier energy crisis. We cannot expect free markets to respond in ways that will alleviate today's crisis. Even as we continue to burn increasing amounts of fossil fuels, freely operating markets will not respond to help resolve this imbalance, at least not on their own.

Markets emerge spontaneously when providers with clear title offer a product or service deemed valuable by buyers. Human ingenuity and the lure of profits combine to ensure a steady progression of new products and services emerging in new markets. Bottled water, computer dating services, and "natural sounds" CDs represent just a few of these examples. Prices emerge that will balance these markets between the needs of suppliers and buyers. No such market over the use of the atmosphere as a sink for our carbon dioxide emissions can emerge without assistance. This is not because we would not value this service if given cause to consider it. Like anything else we take for granted, we recognize its full value only after we lose it. Just consider how you would react if you were told that you could not run your car, your lawn mower, or your barbecue unless you paid something for your waste disposal.[9] Just as many of us now pay for wastewater treatment for water that leaves our homes, we would be willing to pay some fee to be able to use these products. The problem is not that we do not value the service; rather, it is that no "one" has clear title over the atmosphere to charge for our use of it.

Use of the atmosphere clearly operates as an "open access" good. Each of us can employ the atmosphere as our private dump or "air" fill to dispose of nearly any gaseous waste. In the case of carbon dioxide, there is no limit. While each of us may have a collective interest in protecting the atmosphere from undue emissions, none of us has the means or the title to do so. No one "owns" the atmosphere and the various services that it provides us with. Therefore, no one can charge others for the use of the atmosphere as a dumping ground for carbon dioxide emissions. In the absence of a price, we view this service as "free" and continue to use it without limit. We have no financial incentive to limit our impact on the atmosphere by restricting our use of fossil fuels. Despite our recognition of the larger problem, most of us will not adjust our behaviors to reduce the imbalance, thinking that our actions are too insignificant to make any real difference. In the absence of any public policy measures, we can expect the problem of accumulating carbon dioxide emissions only to worsen.

Conclusion

Too often, environmental policy debates devolve around the simple argument of "free markets" versus government regulation. Environmentalists tend to be suspicious of any market-oriented policy. Worried about how corporate greed can lead to practices that degrade our natural environment, they frequently reject any policy that smacks of financial rewards for environmentally sound behavior. At the same time, free market proponents counsel simply letting markets "do their thing." Citing specific successes, they argue that clearly defined markets can solve nearly every problem we face.

Yet, the story about our earlier and current energy crises reveals a more complicated picture. On the one hand, markets operating with technological ingenuity can offer remarkably flexible and pervasive solutions to specific problems. Markets create substantial financial incentives that encourage many corrective behaviors and decisions. Yet, as this story suggests the effectiveness of markets is not without limits. In the case of the early energy crisis, the market incentives were so effective that they undermined themselves as they solved the initial problem. However, as the contemporary crisis shows, not all environmental problems lend themselves to automatic or easy market solutions. In both cases, supportive public policies can enhance the effectiveness of market institutions.

If enacted, complementary public policies could have encouraged a different development path. For example, as oil prices collapsed in the mid-1980s, their decline could have triggered a partially offsetting increase in government taxes on oil (and fossil fuels more broadly). Such a tax could permit some relief to oil consumers in the form of lower prices, but not so low as to kill the economic appeal of energy conservation. By maintaining moderately high gasoline and oil prices, the tax would have encouraged car buyers to seek fuel-efficient models and manufacturers to pursue more fuel-efficient designs. At the same time, the accumulated tax revenue could have funded investments in mass transportation and alternative energy designs. For sure, we would have paid higher prices on oil-related products, including gasoline, than we actually did. Yet, our resulting investments in energy-efficient technology would have mitigated the subsequent oil shortages through lower consumption as well as providing better protection against surging prices. In essence, the tax would have worked as a collective investment to lower our future energy bills.

To what extent does the tale of our two energy crises corroborate the views of those who argue the Environmental Kuznets view? Certainly, the experience of the supply crises of the 1970s offers strong evidence of their position. Market incentives did work effectively and pervasively to redress the underlying supply shortages. Both market incentives and public policy encouraged new energy-conserving technologies that limit the amount of energy we consume. In fact, our economy in 2007 used 50 percent less energy per dollar of real GDP than we did in 1973 – testimony to the power of markets and technology.[10] On the other hand, the emissions problem that generates our current energy crisis offers less support for the Environmental Kuznets position. The problem of increased CO2 emissions will not generate an automatic market response. Unlike the oil supply shortages that led to higher prices, no such mechanism will emerge in this case. Public pressure can and has led many cities and even some states to limit carbon emissions. These represent important steps. However, without some national public policy that effectively curtails or raises the cost of carbon emissions, no real solution is likely. At this time, the House of Representatives has passed a "cap and trade" bill that would limit carbon emissions and raise energy prices over time. Its eventual form, and even its passage, remains uncertain pending Senate action. It is unclear whether sufficient public pressure exists to encourage the enactment of an effective policy that will act as a tax on our fossil fuel consumption – something for which the American public seems to have little appetite. At this point, the jury is out.

In this and the prior chapter, I have examined those environmental challenges that are susceptible to market incentives and effective resolution as distinguished from those that are not. In the next chapter, I discuss the specific conditions that limit the effectiveness of market incentives. Not all forms of market dysfunction are subject to easy remedy. By making this distinction, we can better discern which environmental challenges we now face are likely to persist and which are susceptible to remedy. Moreover, by understanding the specific circumstances in which market-based institutions are impaired, we can better discern those public policies that can effectively redress the market dysfunction. We can better match policy prescription to the diagnosis. We can design public policy changes that effectively alter the underlying financial incentives to encourage day-to-day decision-making that is more hospitable to our natural environment.

Further reading

Douglas Bohi and Joel Darmstader, 'Twenty Years after the Energy Crisis: What Lessons Have We Learned?', provide a thoughtful analysis of this period.

Energy Information Administration, *Annual Energy Review*, offers a wealth of information on petroleum and related energy markets.

Daniel Yeargin, *The Prize: The Epic Quest for Oil, Money, and Power*, offers a readable and comprehensive history of the oil market.

5 Dysfunctional markets

Swamps become wetlands

As a child, I frequently explored stagnant, waterlogged areas. We called these places swamps, bogs, and marshes. I found these areas fascinating and full of mystery. The rank smells of decay and the wild, tangled overgrowth contrasted sharply with the drier and less fecund lands nearby. Who knew what creatures and insects hid among the dense and unruly growth? What unfamiliar dangers were lurking in these strange places? Stepping into the gooey mud, I was never quite sure that it would let go of my shoes. Images of losing my way in the dense overgrowth or being held forever in the clutching mud filled my head. These swamps, with their strange and mysterious air, offered a source of entertainment for a child at play. However, most grown-ups at the time viewed them quite differently.

Back then, most adults viewed swamps as wasted lands, at best. At worst, they were seen as barriers to the development of more valued, neighboring tracts or even as refuges fit only for disease-carrying mosquitoes and other pests. Drainage was and has been the typical response. Indeed, much of the nation's history and early public policy was devoted to the draining and "improving" of swamplands. Early in the nineteenth century, the federal government began passing laws encouraging their elimination. To stimulate commerce and travel, our forebears drained swamps to increase navigation of rivers and improve the quality of roads. Once dry, the rich soils made fertile and productive farmland. Drainage eliminated the sitting waters that bred mosquitoes and other pests, thereby reducing disease. Thus, our ancestors could transform lands that were idle at best into highly productive and useful lands. As a sterling example of their "can do" accomplishments, they eliminated nearly half of the swamps and bogs found in the continental USA in just over a century.[1] Of the estimated 200 million acres of swamps, bogs, and marshes likely existing before the appearance of Europeans, only about 100 million acres remain.

Today, we refer to these areas as "wetlands," a change that transcends the merely semantic and symbolic. This shift reflects an increased appreciation of the role that wetlands play in the natural landscape, triggering a reversal in our public policies. Throughout the twentieth century, biologists and ecologists slowly began to understand the value of wetlands. Along the coasts, they provide an effective buffer against the eroding power of tides, hurricanes, and tsunamis.

They protect downstream areas from the ravages of flooding as they soak up excess water during floods and later release it in manageable amounts.[2] In calmer times, water flows slowly across these lands, permitting effective water purification that benefits downstream communities; impurities suspended in the waters fall to the sediment where they feed vegetation and are transformed by bacteria.[3] Such areas offer a unique habitat to a diverse set of plants and animals, creating highly productive ecosystems.[4] Coastal wetlands are important havens for shellfish and other commercially valuable fishes and birds.[5] Inland, they offer crucial sanctuaries for migrating birds. In either case, these lands offer a valued resource to their local economies, whether through fishing, hunting, or bird-watching activities that encourage local tourism.[6] These refuges offer an asylum for birds and insects that feed on pests that infuriate us and eat our crops. Far from idle, these areas function at high efficiency and provide us with a bundle of services, *all free*.

As our recognition of their value has grown, so federal policies have switched from open encouragement of "swamp busting" to strict wetland protection. Interestingly, duck hunters, particularly through their relatively powerful and well-funded organization Ducks Unlimited, became early and effective advocates for protecting the dwindling wetlands.[7] Assisted by biologists, they demonstrated that the observable decline in waterfowl was attributable to the massive number of drainage projects already undertaken. In response, the federal government initiated the National Wildlife Refuge System as a way of sustaining the nation's waterfowl populations, causing over 91 million acres to receive some level of protection.[8] Later federal laws such as the Migratory Bird Treaty Act of 1918 and the Migratory Bird Conservation Act of 1929 supported this system. Other federal laws including the Migratory Bird Habitat Stamp Act of 1934 and the Land Water Conservation Act of 1964 authorized the creation of user fees and taxes to finance further wetland acquisitions. In addition, Ducks Unlimited has spent over $1 billion in land purchases to protect another one million acres of wetland.[9] Still, these efforts protected only a small portion of the wetlands existing at the time.

Further federal protection came as scientists and lawmakers recognized the crucial role that our wetlands play in sustaining the quality of our water resources. Federal laws enacted during the 1970s symbolized this recognition. As part of the larger strategy to improve water quality, section 404 of the Clean Water Act of 1977 prohibited further drainage of these lands without permission. At the time, it struck many observers as absurd to give the Army Corps of Engineers the responsibility for issuing permits. Historically, the Army Corps has viewed its primary mission as draining wetlands to facilitate surface water navigation. Many argued that this regulatory change was like placing the fox in charge of the henhouse. In hindsight, it appears that the Army Corps has done a credible job both in supervising the permitting process and in transforming its mission objectives.[10] Subsequently, the Food Security Act of 1985 strengthened wetland protections as it legally defined wetlands for the first time and set punishments for those who drained them without permission.

"No net loss" policy

Starting with the first Bush Administration, recent administrations have observed a "no net loss" policy concerning wetlands. Not quite a singularly conceived policy, "no net loss" represents an informal guide to specific regulations. At its cornerstone is the belief that, at minimum, our historical reduction in our valuable wetland endowment must end. At the same time, the policy recognizes the need for local flexibility. Rather than simply outlaw any further elimination of our wetlands (a move that would place nature herself outside the law, as some wetlands naturally dry out), the policy considers the different ways that a particular parcel of land could serve the public good. As such, the mass of regulations and legislation that comprise the "no net loss" policy have created a flexible, yet complex set of arrangements.

At the heart of the "no net loss" policy is section 404; it requires landowners wanting to transform wetlands to other uses to get a permit. Initially, substantial exceptions exempted many landowners from the requirement of prior approval. Over the years, the Corps has reduced these exemptions. To obtain a permit, one enters a process that makes land-use decisions after consideration of the tract's potential uses. Ideally, the Corps grants a permit to drain a specific wetland only if the project meets some broader, public need. In these cases, the developer is responsible for creating "offsetting" wetland in other areas, thereby ensuring "no net loss." The policy directs a decision-making process in which the Army Corps of Engineers, often with the consultation of the Environment Protection Agency and the Fish and Wildlife Service, provides a forum that evaluates and selects from among competing uses offered by the parcel of land.

Despite the reversal in federal policy, old habits and actual practices remain. Recent estimates suggest that the erosion of our nation's endowment is continuing, though at a diminished rate.[11] To be sure, a variety of definitional and practical problems confound easy measurement of wetland acreage. Wetlands are not simply lands permanently covered with water. Areas subject to frequent and intermittent flooding or to extremely high water tables can generate the changes in soil and vegetation that create wetland habitats, even if the surface appears dry during some periods of the year. One-time visual observations can overlook some wetlands, depending on their timing. Nonetheless, there are credible measures of the extent of wetlands in recent decades that provide us with rough estimates of what is happening to our wetland endowment.

We can get a reasonably clear picture of this from the Department of Interior's own Fish and Wildlife Service Report, entitled *Status and Trends of Wetlands in the Coterminous United States 1986 to 1997*. This report represents the inaugural survey required by Congress in its Emergency Wetlands Resources Act of 1986. I provide a brief summary of the findings in Table 5.1. At first glance, these figures indicate that the federal policies have been quite successful in reducing our wetland losses. Annual wetland losses have declined from 458,000 acres per year to less than 59,000 acres per year, a reduction of almost 90 percent. Although our current losses do not yet match the rhetoric of "no net loss," the reductions are

Table 5.1 Trends in wetland losses

Time period	*Policy regime*	*Annual wetland losses (gains)*
Mid-1950s to mid-1970s	Some wetland acquisition	458,000 acres
Mid-1970s to mid-1980s	Permits required	290,000 acres
1986–97	"No net loss"	59,000 acres
1998–2004	"No net loss"	(+ 32,000 acres)

a significant and welcome consequence of federal policies. A more recent report offers even more encouraging results. During the 1998–2004 period, human-induced declines in wetlands slowed modestly. Newly created wetlands more than offset the declines, causing an annual *net gain* of 32,000 acres during the six-year period.[12] Likely for the first time since Europeans came to this continent, wetland acreage increased.

However, as is so often the case, one cannot solely trust the aggregate numbers. Freshwater wetlands account for over 90 percent of our wetlands inventory and for 98 per cent of the losses that occurred during the period of "no net loss." In most cases, these reported losses in freshwater wetlands were "offset" by increases in acreage labeled "ponds." While naturally occurring ponds do offer most of the functional services mentioned earlier, this classification includes a wide variety of aquatic areas, among them small lakes found in residential developments, fish farms, water traps on golf courses, and open-pit mines. Certainly, not all wetlands are of equal quality nor do they offer similar levels of ecological services. While the increased acreage given to ponds may offset losses in other freshwater wetlands, the quality of the surviving wetlands is a concern. For example, of the wetlands restored as ponds during the 1986–97 period, only 2 percent were classified as vegetative freshwater wetlands.[13] This raises some doubts over the quality of these wetlands and the range of ecosystem services they provide. The data mask other likely declines in the quality of the wetlands, too. When forested wetlands undergo clear-cutting and timber removal, the affected acreage merely changes its category from "freshwater forested" to "freshwater emergent" wetlands. Though the elimination of the forest cover certainly affects the local habitat and its ecological services, this action leaves the aggregate figures unchanged. Though acreage quantity is unchanged, it is unlikely that acreage quality is unaffected.

Apart from these concerns, examining the aggregate numbers offers another insight. Prior to any federal restraints, wetland losses were substantial. Moderate and then more determined federal restraints on wetland losses have substantially staunched the declines, though the erosion continued, at least until the most recent period. Commercial pressures still threaten the remaining wetlands. While legislators have determined that it is in our long-term public interest to observe a "no net loss" policy, private market calculations still drive land-use decisions. These contrary market pressures explain why our wetland resources are still under threat qualitatively, if no longer quantitatively, even with the "no net loss" policy. Turning to these issues now can instruct us on how these land-use decisions threaten not only our remaining wetland resources, but also other forms of natural capital that are similarly vulnerable. As the two previous chapters identified those ecological services that are most at risk of further degradation and decline, we now examine more carefully the underlying circumstances that contribute to their decline. In understanding the specific circumstances that cause markets to function ineffectively, we can better design public policy remedies.

Market failures

Effectively functioning markets operate much like the thermostats found in our homes. We set our thermostats to obtain a comfortable temperature. Whenever the actual temperature varies significantly, the heating or cooling equipment restarts to warm or cool the home as required. As the actual temperature returns to the desired temperature, the equipment stops and remains idle until the actual temperature again sufficiently diverges from the chosen temperature. As long as the variance in temperatures is not too broad, the thermostat keeps us comfortable. At the same time, we know that this system is not foolproof. Defective thermostats permit uncomfortable conditions, either too warm or too cold depending on the malfunction. Even with accurate thermostats, problems can occur. Specific placement of the thermostat within the house can affect comfort and performance. Air temperatures in most homes, especially in structures like my drafty 90-year-old house, will vary from location to location. For example, placing the thermostat in a sunny location will likely cause excessive cooling in the summer and inadequate heating in the winter, at least on clear days. Placement near air vents can lead to comparable problems. In any case, the thermostat can only work as effectively as the information it is given. So is the case with markets. Markets function poorly when the information available to the key decision-makers is incomplete or inaccurate.[14]

Poor information

Ignorance and uncertainty play a substantial role in market decisions that go awry. No doubt, each of us has experienced regret with the purchase of some item or the sale of another. We were unable or unwilling to research fully the desired product and hence were disappointed with its actual level of service. We may have purchased some item based on an expected need only to find that the need never materialized, at least to the extent expected. Or, we may have sold or given away some item, which we later regretted as we recognized its value. In each of these cases, we are likely to experience some level of disappointment and regret. Potentially, we could avoid most, if not all of these decisions if we operated with full information. Unfortunately, we cannot escape the likelihood that we make many of our market decisions with incomplete information.

Throughout much of our history, ignorance has been the primary culprit behind the demise of our dwindling wetland resources. Until recently, most landowners and even scientists viewed wetlands as lands largely without value. Generally seen as valueless in their undeveloped state, such lands were given a market price that hovered around zero. Therefore, any owner suffered no loss of value by draining these lands or filling them with dirt. Indeed, these actions could only create market value by making the lands more suitable for a variety of human activity, including farms, homes, or strip malls. Markets gave landowners strong encouragement to drain their wetlands. As long as the increased value generated by the new uses of land exceeded the cost of drainage or filling the land, landowners were financially encouraged to do so. This rather low bar to development encouraged the elimination of much of the wetland endowment. Consequently, we have lost prime wetlands that provided substantial life-support services due to their location and quality, often in service of some modest and even transitory human venture. We have sold off much of our natural endowment mostly out of ignorance of the valuable ecological services that wetlands provide.

Our historical experience offers us a cautionary tale as well. Though we may now believe that we fully understand the value and services offered by wetlands, it is likely that we will learn yet more about their value and benefits. We can never be certain that we hold all of the key information as we make any given decision. In addition, we must recognize that decisions taken today will influence future generations, albeit with very different effect. Perhaps a particular decision taken today makes full sense given our currently available information. However, we cannot know whether new information or even the altered perspectives of future generations will cause a reconsideration of our decisions in a much dimmer light. Because of this inevitable uncertainty, every decision is subject to the risk of being wrong. Any decision, and this includes the choice of doing nothing, makes us vulnerable to later pangs of regret and dismay.

Recognizing this point need not lead us to the "paralysis of analysis." Most often, the offending decision can rather easily be remedied. If we buy a piece of clothing and later realize that it does not really fit, we can easily buy a more accommodating alternative. If we sell some item that we never expect to need again only to find ourselves desperate for it, we can often buy a replacement that will serve us equally well. Yet, some actions lead to irreversible consequences. The lumbering of an old-growth forest is not a decision that can be undone once implemented. We cannot easily restore wetlands to their prior level of functioning once we have drained the waters and eliminated the biotic residential community. Naturally occurring wetlands include numerous plant and animal species, each adapted to the specific climatic conditions of the area and functioning in a web of interrelationships. Recreating this kind of habitat is currently beyond our understanding and skill. As one knowledgeable scientist has confided, current practices in wetland restoration resemble the "default approach in which we provide certain hydrological conditions, do some planting of hydrophytes that we would like to see established, and hope everything turns out for the best."[15]

Recognizing which decisions may generate irreversible consequences gives rise to the "precautionary principle." As future information and new understandings tarnish the sheen of "smart" decisions taken today, we should avoid making decisions that will generate irreversible outcomes. We should refrain from decisions that further deplete our natural capital, particularly those forms of natural capital that do not have human-created substitutes. I discuss further policies that encourage adherence to this principle in Chapters Nine and Ten.

Incomplete information (1): the "open access" problem

Even if we fully appreciate the substantial benefits offered by wetlands, dependence on markets for land-use decisions poses significant challenges. Virtually all of the ecological services offered by wetlands are subject to the "open access" problem discussed in Chapter Three. This problem allows each of us to benefit fully from some service, regardless of whether we compensate the service provider or not. Under these circumstances, most of us will behave as "free riders" and therefore undermine any who might market these services. The absence of a market means that services provided are done so without charge. A zero price encourages unrestrained use of these services, even as their overuse may lead to their decline. Even worse, as these services generate no revenue to the property owner, we consider the land as valueless. Under these conditions, property owners have no financial incentive to maintain the conditions that provide the service, much less make improvements. Assessing these lands at zero value causes market transactions to ignore these forms of natural capital and the services they provide.

Consequently, any who benefit from the services rendered by a wetland can do so without need to compensate the owner. At issue is the complexity of these ecological services as well as the prevailing social norms and legal precedence facing landowners trying to charge for them. For example, in moderating water flows and by improving water quality, an upstream wetland offers downstream landowners protection against flooding and poor water quality. Since neither service is easily discernible or measurable, they benefit a host of downstream property owners and water users without requirement of any payment or compensation. Attempts by owners of these upstream wetlands to capture some form of payment for these services would generate indifference and even derision. Yet, these services are essentially the same as ones that we duly pay for, such as the regular flow of safe water into our homes. Non-payment for these services generally leads to a "cutoff" notice and then a charge to reinstall the connection. For most of us, the capacity of water officials to cut off the service for non-payment is usually sufficient to ensure regular and reliable payment. The owner of the wetland has no similar recourse. As the downstream beneficiaries, we will continue to receive the same level of services from the owner's land whether we pay for them or not, at least until the owner decides to use the land for a different purpose and to drain the land accordingly. The wetland's owner cannot selectively offer the services to some (payers) and withhold from others (non-payers) as can the local water department. Virtually all of the other valuable services provided by our wetlands suffer the same fate. The storm and tidal water protection offered by coastal wetlands in particular benefit all property owners located inland. Coastal wetlands that provide spawning grounds for commercial fish and shellfish benefit those who catch them. Wetlands support migratory birds and insects that offer different services in regions that span continents. Even local farmers benefit, as the habitats provide cover for different animals that feed on the pests that ravage nearby crops. Directly or indirectly, we benefit from the provision of these services, often without much awareness. In each case, we do so without paying for any of the services.

Though this may sound like a fortunate set of circumstances indeed, it does have a disturbing downside. Since the owners of wetlands are incapable of capturing any income from the services that their land provides, the price (and economic value) of these lands is virtually zero.[16] Due to this disconnect, wetland owners suffer no economic loss by destroying their land and the services it provides. Moreover, landowners have no financial incentive to maintain the quality of the wetland, much less improve, or expand them. Unlike other forms of capital, markets currently offer wetland owners no financial incentives to perform good stewardship of their valuable, if not valued lands. Even worse, as the quality (and quantity) of the wetlands endowment declines, the price of the remaining lands stays at zero. Their market value will not register their increasing value to human society as they become scarcer. Instead, the prevailing economic incentives encourage their further elimination whenever the owners spy an alternative use for their land.

Most economists argue that the problem of "open access" resources is largely one of poorly defined property rights and therefore is solvable by the extension of private property rights. The ocean fishery is an oft-cited example. Extensive evidence indicates that we are catching fish at rates beyond their biological limit, triggering declining fish catches in many fisheries around the world.[17] Most experts attribute this over-fishing to the demand for a relatively cheap source of protein, the desire of all coastal countries to support their fishing communities, and the introduction of new fishing technologies. As no one owns the fish in the oceans, they are available to whoever can catch them first. Under these conditions, boat captains have little incentive to show restraint and permit the regeneration of fish stocks, since such restraint will only benefit others still willing to fish. To mitigate this problem, officials in New Zealand have created a system of fishing licenses and harvest quotas to limit the fish catch. Along with careful monitoring and prevention of unlawful poaching, these officials have created a system that mimics private ownership. Under this system, the fishing boat captains can trust that restraint today – in observing the fishing limits – will benefit them tomorrow by ensuring a reliable supply of fish to catch.

Wetland services offer us a much more complex problem. As individuals or corporations already own most of our freshwater wetlands, the absence of private ownership is not really the problem. In this case, the problem lies with the complex mechanisms through which many ecological services function and our failure to meter these services accurately. Clearly, the water purifying services offered by a given wetland benefit many downstream users. While one can certainly follow downstream water flows, identifying which downstream residents actually benefit and by how much, given their other water sources, is nearly impossible. Downstream landowners who benefit from flood prevention services offered by upstream wetlands do so in ways that defy easy measurement. Exactly how much does each downstream landowner benefit from this service? Does their level of benefits depend on how much rain falls in a given year? For those wetlands that serve as critical havens for migratory birds and insects, exactly which other communities benefit from pest elimination services, recreational services, and the aesthetic value of hearing songbirds? How should these benefits be valued?

Conceptually, it is relatively easy to imagine the metering of benefits when one is considering key resources that provide many of our provisioning services, such as blue fin tuna. Goods are easily measurable and can be subject to close monitoring. Services, however, are much more difficult to measure. The valuable ecological services provided by our wetlands cross our geographical and temporal boundaries in ways that are largely imperceptible. Nature refuses to observe our property lines just as my cat refuses to stay solely on my property to conduct its affairs. The problems described here extend to each life-support service discussed in Chapter Two. The specific benefits of these services are difficult to discern and monitor, thereby discouraging our appreciation for the ecosystems and natural endowment that generate the services.

Under these circumstances, government regulations are poorly equipped to stem the expected decline in wetland quality. Even if the regulations prevent property owners from draining their wetland, many other actions can affect the quality of ecosystem services provided. Wetland owners can engage in a variety of commercial activities that permit them to earn income from their land.[18] Many of these activities can harm or reduce the natural services provided by their lands. Selected coastal estuaries can become sites for fish farming and shellfish beds. Property owners can use certain freshwater lands to grow rice and other water-tolerant crops. Some wetlands naturally support mangroves and cypress while other bottomlands support a variety of hardwoods. Many of these activities can have substantial impacts on the quality of functions provided by the wetland. For example, overt manipulation of the water and nutrient levels can increase the yields from fish farms and conventional farming. While these modifications to the normal flows can increase the value of the harvest, they usually lead to disruptions in the wetland ecology and to reductions in the natural services offered. Both the water purification and water regulation functions provided by the wetland are likely to suffer as a result. Clear-cutting of the local timber can leave the wetland unchanged in its land classification, but it clearly disrupts the wetland's natural functions. The property owners can replace the hardwoods with faster-growing pines that generate quicker profits, though at the expense of a less productive ecosystem. These actions, and so many others, that lead to a reduction in services rendered by the wetlands are avoidable; nonetheless, landowners have little incentive to avoid them.

We can now better understand the mixed results of the "no net loss" policy. As the exemptions to the policy and review process have narrowed, the policy has effectively slowed the loss of our wetland acreage. In the most recent reporting period, we have witnessed a slight gain in our wetland inventory. Yet, the policy does not affect the underlying financial incentives facing wetland property owners. Their lands offer a number of valuable ecological services, none of which generates income. Consequently, the landowners have no financial incentive to use their lands in ways that maintain, much less enhance the level of services provided. The policy does restrict their ability to eliminate unilaterally their wetland and to do so without requiring an offsetting wetland. Though the policy may effectively eliminate the decline in our wetland acreage, it will have only modest impact on the level of services our wetlands provide. Property owners have no financial incentive to use their wetland in ways that maintain their ecological services or to develop an "offsetting" wetland that truly functions effectively. Without such incentives, we can expect the quality and quantity of ecological services to decline even as we maintain and even enhance our wetland acreage. However, designing public policies that modify the current incentives represents our most pressing and intractable set of challenges.

Incomplete information (2): the negative externalities problem

In addition, markets function poorly when significant market externalities, either positive or negative, occur. Recall that these are benefits or damages borne by individuals not privy to the market transaction (either buyer or seller). In the case of negative market externalities, decisions taken by property owners can lead to damages and costs shouldered by others. Under these circumstances, decision-makers are not fully accountable for their decisions. Further, decisions that are uneconomical, when one considers the full range of costs and benefits, are undertaken nonetheless since the market participants bear only a portion of the costs. From personal experience, we know what problems arise when individuals can make decisions for which they are unaccountable. These circumstances encourage a continuation of misinformed decisions, often with disastrous results.

The same can occur in the economic sphere when significant market externalities exist. In search of profits, businesses adapt and respond to the conditions they face. Customer preferences, legal and regulatory constraints, and the prices of related products and services all influence their economic environment. Given these conditions, businesses seek the most efficient, usually least costly manner of meeting their customers' needs. In searching for the least costly method, businesses can lower their prices to compete with their rivals. For this reason, businesses select production methods that permit them to avoid certain costs, even if those costs are borne by others. Historically, businesses and individuals have used the environment as a "free" waste disposal system. We have utilized the waterways and skies as dumping grounds for any liquid or gaseous wastes that we did not want. Since these services are "free," we are encouraged to use them as liberally as needed. We frequently do so, even as we know our actions will adversely affect others downstream or downwind.

As property owners look for ways to gain value from wetlands, their actions may not only reduce the flow of ecological services rendered by the tract, but also generate damage to downstream residents. As most wetlands are naturally nitrogen-deprived, rice farmers will likely add nitrogen and perhaps other key nutrients to increase the yield of their harvest. Although the rice plants will capture some added nutrients, some amount will undoubtedly seep downstream, contributing to excessive nutrients in these surface waters. In severe cases, these conditions can lead to algae blooms, oxygen deprivation, and even fish kills. The declining water quality can affect not only the recreational value of downstream water resources, but also the quality of the water supply. Other practices can encourage soil erosion that can harm downstream navigation, decrease water turbidity, and increase flooding by filling streamwater channels. Though these damages are real enough, they are difficult to monitor and assign to individual actions taken upstream. Moreover, as these adverse consequences rarely affect the offending landowner, they seldom influence land-use decisions. As such, we can expect some decline in the quality and level of services rendered to downstream users, given the current financial incentives.

To remedy negative market externalities, economists generally advocate either emissions taxes or marketable emissions permits.[19] Either policy mechanism requires the property owner to pay some amount for the offending activity that harms others downstream. Emissions taxes require the property owner to pay a "per unit" fee for the offending activity so that increased emissions translate into increased fees. Under a regime of emissions permits, the offender is required to hold a permit to engage in the activity. Similar to the emissions tax, one must hold more permits to generate increased emissions. However they are initially distributed, these marketable permits can be traded among individuals, depending on who is willing to pay the highest for them. However, both schemes require some form of monitoring to ensure compliance. In the case of wetlands, this is difficult given the large numbers of wetland tracts and the difficulty in monitoring the flow of harmful substances. In some cases, this challenge is less daunting than it seems. For example, property owners who use fertilizers to boost their crop yields can be assessed by either paying an emissions tax or permit license as they purchase the chemicals. One can estimate the likely downstream flow of these chemicals and therefore set the levy accordingly. Though this only crudely meters the actual damage, it discourages unrestrained use of chemicals that can create eutrophic conditions downstream. However, not all practices used by wetland property owners can easily be estimated and discouraged.

Taking stock

We can now better understand the mixed results of the "no net loss" policy. As the exemptions to the permit review process have narrowed, the policy has effectively slowed the loss of our wetland acreage. Yet, the policy does not affect the underlying financial incentives facing wetland property owners. Their lands offer valuable ecological services, most of which yield their owner no income. Consequently, they have no financial incentive to use or improve their lands in ways that mitigate harm or increase services to those downstream. "No net loss" may staunch the decline, and even enhance our wetland acreage; however, it will allow a continued erosion of the quality and quantity of ecological services provided. We cannot expect to redress these trends until we modify the economic incentives that currently influence wetland owners.

As this chapter illustrates, each of the three sources of market dysfunction creates different challenges as we look to balance material aspirations with the limits of the natural environment. Out of ignorance, we can make what we believe are well-considered, though irreversible, decisions that we later lament. The problem of "open access" prevents the emergence of markets, causing us to treat indispensable services as if they have no value. In addition, the complexities of natural systems that transcend our property boundaries lead us to behaviors that meet our immediate needs to the detriment of our neighbors. Each of these challenges generates a different problem that requires a different policy remedy. Adding to the difficulty, much of our natural endowment, just like the wetlands discussed in this chapter, is subject to all three of these challenges. Solving these problems will require an understanding of the particulars to ensure a tailoring of solutions that will yield effective results.

Many of the same financial incentives facing owners of wetlands also affect other property owners. Most properties, depending on their developed use, offer a variety of life-support services. My own residential property, small as it is, provides a number of life-support services. My large trees reduce atmospheric carbon dioxide, slow the occasional wind gusts that accompany severe storms, and offer shade on the sultry summer days. The varied landscape offers a host of habitats for a variety of resident animals. My shrubs and fruit trees discourage soil erosion, regulate the water supply, and capture solar energy that serves as a food source for my family and my wild neighbors. Despite all of these valuable services and more, they have never influenced my property value. No matter whether I expand the footprint of my house to create more living space for my family or cultivate a landscape that increases these services, the market value of my property will not reflect any changes in these services. No real estate appraiser will consider the life-support services rendered by either my property or its landscape. To be sure, I can create a landscape that increases the "curb appeal" of my property; nonetheless, the market value will largely ignore the critical life-support services that the property generates.

This problem is extensive indeed. Let us reconsider the local land sale discussed in Chapter Three. As the property came on the market, no doubt a variety of interested buyers, representing a multitude of interests, contemplated the land. These suitors would have considered the various carrier services that the land offered as well as possible provisioning services. Some likely eyed the woods for timber while others considered the tract for crops or grazing animals.[20] Developers wanting to build homes and apartments competed against each other and others interested in building office buildings and shopping centers. Some company employees and nearby residents argued to preserve the parcel to retain its historical and aesthetic attributes. Local officials considered the road needs that any development would require. Local interests likely valued each of the carrier services, with the exception of energy conversion and refugia.[21] At the same time, excluding water runoff issues, I suspect that the project discussions rarely considered the property's life-support services. While we can expect markets to prioritize a variety of social needs, we cannot expect that they will give adequate due to the life-support services offered by a parcel of land. Thus, we cannot blindly assume that markets will always generate desired decisions, particularly if they neglect essential services.

Yet, as the prior chapter illustrated, competitive markets can function effectively and serve us well. Under certain conditions, well-defined property rights and competitive markets can encourage good stewardship of our natural capital and solve some of our environmental challenges. As certain resources and services become scarcer, rising prices will encourage businesses and households to reduce their use. Higher prices will encourage others to find cheaper substitutes. In this way, markets can encourage individual responses that simultaneously meet the common good. Rather than simply attributing our environmental problems to "greed" and markets, we should discern the strengths and weaknesses of markets in resolving our environmental problems.

Recognizing the limits of market institutions in creating socially desirable decisions provides us with two key insights. First, we should distinguish those environmental problems that are subject to functioning market institutions from those that are not. Our discussion of the two "energy crises" makes this point. The prospect of running out of oil created great distress a generation ago, even as it does today. Depleting our "easy" oil reservoirs will seriously disrupt our lives, communities, and economies. Though the damage can be substantial, a market solution will occur, if permitted. Higher oil prices will force changes that will eventually reduce our dependency on oil. Not so for the other "energy crisis." We cannot rely on any emergent market response that will encourage the needed self-correction. Unless we implement different public policies, we will continue to behave in ways that will further promote global climate change without restraint. Recognizing this distinction illuminates the more intractable challenges we face from those that are less challenging.

Our recognition of the strengths and limits of markets leads to a second insight. Many of our current environmental problems do in fact result from markets that function poorly. It takes little imagination to see how our current land-use decisions contribute to the problem of "urban sprawl." Since our land development decisions ignore any value from life-support services, it makes sense that so many of our cities are increasingly devoid of green spaces. Yet, our understanding of these causes permits us to do more than simply complain knowledgeably. Understanding the specific causal link between market dysfunction and environmental problem gives us another advantage. In some cases, rather modest changes in public policy or property rights can enact an effective solution. For example, the imposition of a substantial carbon tax can rather easily and effectively restrain our use of fossil fuels and encourage the search for alternative technologies.[22] This policy change could effectively harness market forces in reducing our current carbon dependency. Not all of our environmental problems could be so easily resolved. Nonetheless, we should move quickly to remedy these less challenging problems.

Looking ahead

Before jumping ahead to offer solutions to many of our environmental challenges, we should pause to examine how natural systems function and how they persist through time. We shall take this slight detour in the next chapter. In particular, we will examine the key elements that appear to sustain natural systems through time and despite changing circumstances and devastating disturbances. Each of the four key elements identified in Chapter Six will then be the focus of the subsequent four chapters. In these chapters, we will apply each key element and identify public policies that will encourage their development in our economy. In this way, we will use nature as a guide to how we may better organize our economy.

Further reading

T. Dahl, *Status and Trends of Wetlands in the Coterminous United States 1998 to 2004*, as well as in any of his earlier reports, offers substantial evidence on the state of wetlands acreage in the USA.

G. Hardin, 'Tragedy of the Commons', offers the classic treatment of the "open access" problem, although he mistakenly labels the problem as one of "common" ownership.

N. Keohane and S. Olmstead, *Markets and the Environment*, give a more comprehensive review of the strengths and sources of market failures.

W. Lewis, Jr., *Wetlands Explained*, offers an instructive account of how wetlands function and our changing attitudes toward them.

6 Nature as guide

The great experiment

In the last third of the nineteenth century, a horde of settlers swept west past the Mississippi River seeking their share of America's prosperity. Discoveries of gold and silver lured some, while land free for the taking attracted others. To encourage settlement of the American West, Congress had passed the Homestead Act of 1862 offering any citizen 160 acres of land if they occupied and developed that parcel of land for five years.[1] As settlers streamed west, they encountered vast expanses of tall grasses, largely devoid of trees, except in the relatively sheltered and watered areas along riverbanks. The grasslands of the Great Plains, the largest of their kind in the world, supported a complex ecosystem that included large herds of bison and a still substantial population of native peoples. Within the space of several decades, both populations were largely annihilated as the immigrants from the east modified the landscape into their vision of the American dream that included neither.

The immigrants found a land covered with thick grasses, often crowned by a bouquet of wild flowers, suggesting the richness the land had to offer while masking its harsher reality. Given adequate rainfall, the rich soil provided ideal conditions for growing corn and wheat for an increasingly hungry population back east. Fortunately, newly developed plows could cut through the tough native grasses. Providence seemingly smiled upon them as the decade from 1878 to 1887 brought years of unusually wet weather.[2] Bumper harvests attracted even more immigrants. Each homesteader removed the native grasses to capture the hidden treasure buried below in the rich soil.

In normal years, the climate of the Great Plains is not an easy one. The land is subject to long, cold winters and dry, hot summers, buffeted throughout by strong winds. When the rain does come, it tends to fall in short, drenching bursts characterized by severe thunderstorms. Sudden downpours pulverize the soils, causing severe erosion if left unprotected. Often, storms bring a different hazard to the land. Hot and dry summers create tinderbox conditions. Storms that bring lightning without the accompanying rainfall can set the land ablaze, igniting vast prairie fires that sweep across the landscape, whipped by the strong winds. Winters offer freezing temperatures and violent snowstorms that often blanket the ground under drifts of snow for weeks at a time.

The perennial native grasses are uniquely suited for this harsh climate. Ninety percent of the plant material resides below ground in the thick matting of roots. While the wintry freezes and occasional summer fires may wreak havoc with the exposed portion, most of the plant lies protected by a layer of soil. Only the uncovered tops are vulnerable to grazing animals. The vast networks of roots enable the plants to replace their damaged crowns and protect the soil from drenching downpours and wrenching winds. Shielded by this plant cover, the soil can slowly accumulate, thereby accommodating a larger underground maze of roots. Farmers expressed astonishment at the topsoil depths, often reaching a dozen feet thick. Not only were the native grasses well suited to the dry conditions, but they depended on it. Hot summers and episodic prairie fires kept the thirstier trees at bay, relegated to the wetter bottomlands that lined the area's streams. Unshaded by their taller rivals, the grasses could capture all the sunlight they needed to flourish.

Removing the native prairie grasses allowed the sodbusters to tap the land's natural capital; it also left the land denuded and unprotected. Planting annual crops left the land bare and vulnerable for much of the year. In the wet seasons, intense thundershowers pummeled the soil and pushed it down the gentle slopes. Given the deep topsoil, these losses to erosion did not cause great concern. However, these withdrawals worsened in years of drought. As is inevitable on the Great Plains, the drought conditions returned during the last decade of the nineteenth century. Crops withered in the heat as farmers looked to the skies for the rains that never came. Even amid such a fertile land, hunger was widespread. Even worse, the winds swept up the topsoil, now loosened by the plow and dried out by the drought. Vast dust storms ravaged the landscape and deposited the silt hundreds of miles downwind. Such dust storms, both during the 1890s and the later Dust Bowl era of the 1930s, exhibited most visibly the cycle of drought and erosion that plague the Great Plains.

Most settlers endured these difficult times hoping for relief. Help came in the pendulum swing of climate and the advance of modern technology. The return of the rains and the high demand for wheat during World War I brought renewed prosperity to the region. Cheap energy in the form of petroleum, along with new drilling and water-pumping technologies, enabled farmers to tap an unseen resource and supplement the region's unreliable rainfall. Much of the Great Plains lies above a vast groundwater reservoir, known as the Ogallala Aquifer. Groundwater withdrawals could offset any shortfalls in precipitation, thereby watering crops reliably as needed. Abundant water along with the fertile soils produced bumper harvests and rising profits.

In areas without locally available water, new technologies permitted the introduction of "dry-land farming." In anticipation of a fortuitous rainfall, farmers could cultivate vast amounts of land with newly developed mechanized equipment. Longer plows that pulverized the soils permitted deeper penetration of rainfall and increased moisture of the soils. Newer strains of drought-resistant wheat imported from Asia flourished in these conditions. In other areas, farmers planted winter wheat in the fall and harvested it the following summer before the heat depleted the soils of all moisture. Strong demand buoyed wheat prices and encouraged farmers to bring more lands under cultivation. "Yankee ingenuity" and modern methods seemingly assured capture of the land's expected bounty.

Such practices allowed some to farm profitably in the region, but each was subject to severe limitations. The easily tapped groundwater encouraged so many users that water withdrawals far exceeded natural renewals. This vast aquifer displayed its limits as early wells went dry, requiring deeper wells to tap the declining water table. The deep tilling needed for dry-land farming left the turned soils more vulnerable to erosion. Winter wheat production required that the land lie fallow for over a year to recuperate from the intensive cropping. Without a cover crop, these soils remained unprotected and subject to erosion. The cycle of drought returned in the 1930s, bringing the memorable dust storms that haunt the region even today.

Once part of the "bread basket" of the world, the Great Plains are experiencing a new migration today – one that rivals the flow of pioneers only several generations earlier. In recent decades, a reverse migration has left rural communities depopulated, especially of young people. The erratic climate and eroded soils are the primary causes of this exodus. Efforts to grow crops and graze animals brought from other lands and climates have not provided many with the prosperity they expected. The natural ecosystem of wild perennial grasses and grazing herds had endured for thousands of years; our modern reconstruction of the landscape has lasted barely a century and a half.

Despite the ingenuity and efforts of millions of farmers and ranchers and the potency of our modern technology, our apparent inability to create a sustained and highly prosperous economy in the Great Plains raises the question of whether it is possible to do so.[3] Perhaps these lands are too dry and too vulnerable to generate the level of prosperity and security that we seek? While this conclusion is highly possible, there is evidence that suggests otherwise. This evidence stems from the experience of the Great Plains prior to the nineteenth-century onslaught. For 10,000 years, the ecology and economy of the Great Plains had offered the Native Indians a rather prosperous and stable lifestyle. The underlying grassland ecosystem, while always in flux, has remained remarkably unchanged in structure over these millennia. An understanding of the underlying ecology offers insights into why our modern attempt to work the land largely has failed. Structuring an economy in ways that undermine the region's natural endowment can only yield a short-lived system. Any new attempts to work the land should incorporate a better understanding of nature's endowment and its limits. More broadly, as we consider ways to restructure our economy to make it more "sustainable," we should look toward nature and its self-sustaining ecosystems as a guide to our efforts.

Nature's model for sustainable systems

Over the past generation, "sustainable (economic) development" has become the catchphrase of our time. No doubt, two underlying currents have encouraged its ascendancy in academic and public policy forums. First is the growing evidence that our current practices are generating substantial stresses on numerous environmental systems. Increased awareness of the litany of environmental problems

– declining fish and animal populations, eroding soils, rising levels of harmful pollutants, increasing numbers of species extinctions, perceptible changes in our climate – gives us pause as we consider where our current development path is taking us. Many of the book titles mentioned in Chapter One reflect this issue. Second, we are increasingly aware of the evidence, often literally beneath our feet, of past human societies that have failed after periods of prosperity and achievement, frequently because they undermined their local ecology. Among many examples, two highly complex and technologically adaptive societies, Sumer and Maya, both suffered eventual societal collapse, in part due to practices that led to local, environmental ruin. Both societies represented the pinnacle of human ingenuity and technological prowess in their day, yet neither could avoid their fate. To be sure, few of us realistically contemplate such an end for our modern society or ourselves. Yet, one suspects that few citizens during the glory days of Sumer or Maya anticipated the outcome that befell their societies.

Like the concepts "liberty" and "justice," "sustainable development" is a term that conjures positive values worth striving. Moreover, just like these more familiar ideas, it is a concept that defies easy definition and means very different things to different people. The contemporary literature on the subject has spawned tens, if not hundreds, of different definitions.[4] Many proponents use the rather pithy definition found in the Brundtland Report, which describes it as "meeting the needs of the present without compromising the needs of the future." This quotable definition clearly articulates one element of the concept: intergenerational equity, or the sharing of our natural endowment across generations. Yet, it ignores a second value also important to the authors of the Brundtland Report: intragenerational equity, or the sharing within generations. The authors argued that any development that neglected either the future consequences or the present (unequal) distribution of benefits is not sustainable. Today, there exists a consensus that sustainability is required in three spheres – economic, social, and ecological – in order to achieve sustainable development.[5] Despite the agreement, this definition gives little guide to policymakers who are interested in following its precepts. What kinds of development projects are sustainable? What kinds are not? How does one tell the difference? As all economies, societies and natural environments are subject to ongoing evolution, which changes are sustainable and which are not? Without clear direction on these issues, how does one move from an unsustainable development path to a more sustainable one?

By looking to nature as our guide, we can identify ingredients that appear crucial to the persistence of natural ecosystems for long periods despite the limitations and changing circumstances that nature imposes. I have identified four such elements. They are the recycling of key nutrients or system inputs, the availability of a plentiful and reliable energy source, a capacity for adaptation, and a capacity for system resiliency. Each is critical to understanding how ecosystems persist over time without undermining essential ecological processes, while adapting to the periodic disturbances and changes in their broader environment. Each attribute offers us insight into how we can design economic structures that meet human well-being over time without undermining the natural endowment. Each of these natural elements can assist us in our efforts to discern more sustainable economic development projects.

Self-regulating cycles of system nutrients

Biological communities must structure themselves in ways that meet the imperative of the First Law of Thermodynamics: matter is neither created nor destroyed; otherwise, the community is short-lived. Every form of life requires a continual supply of key nutrients to survive and flourish. At the same time, every life form must expel certain waste byproducts, which if permitted to accumulate in their local environment can lead to harm or even death of the organism. Since the earth is finite and the First Law suggests that matter is limited, each biological community must structure itself in ways that will recycle both the critical inputs and the harmful waste products that are continually needed and generated.

We are already familiar with the complementary interaction between plants and animals regarding oxygen and carbon dioxide. As part of the process of photosynthesis, plants absorb carbon dioxide from the local environment through their leaves. Along with key nutrients, water, and solar energy, they use the carbon dioxide to fuel the plant processes and produce new growth. They expel oxygen through the leaves as an unwanted byproduct. Animals breathe in that oxygen to burn energy that feeds their bodies. They replenish the carbon dioxide with each exhale. The very oxygen molecules that are critical to animal life are the unwanted byproduct of plant photosynthesis, while our respiration provides a critical ingredient to fuel photosynthesis. The two complementary processes have kept both carbon dioxide and oxygen in relative balance for hundreds of millions of years. In keeping this balance, the two complementary processes create a virtually limitless supply of both critical gases, though they are each finite in actuality.

Such recycling is not the exception, but rather the rule in biological communities. Most plants require some twenty-odd key nutrients, of which carbon, nitrogen, phosphorus, and sulfur constitute the "Big Four." Through a variety of complex processes, each of these key nutrients is slowly recycled through the earth's atmosphere, waters, and landmasses. Due to these functioning bio-geochemical cycles, the finite amount of each of these crucial nutrients is reusable without exhaustion as long as these cycles continue to function. While the specific processes vary for each of the key nutrients, the nitrogen cycle can serve as an illustration.

Nitrogen is critical to all life forms as it bonds those molecules that comprise amino acids, the very building blocks of proteins, DNA, and life itself. It is the most abundant element of our atmosphere, comprising about 79 percent of the air we breathe. Despite this vast reservoir, nearly all life forms are incapable of using this gaseous form of nitrogen. Instead, we depend almost completely on bacteria found in the soil to transform atmospheric nitrogen into usable forms.[6] In a process called nitrogen fixation, soil bacteria transform atmospheric nitrogen into ammonia, which then reacts with water to form ammonium ion. Plants can absorb this ammonium ion through their roots and use it for plant growth. Other bacteria transform this ammonium ion into nitrates, which plants also need to flourish.

As plants decompose, the cycle is continued. Decomposing plants release both ammonia and nitrates back into the soil. The ammonia reacts with water to provide ammonium ion for plants in need. Similarly, the nitrates become available to other plants or are transformed by other bacteria into nitrogen gas and slowly released back into the atmosphere, completing the cycle. Each component of the nitrogen cycle is essential in allowing life to continue. In this way, death and plant decomposition are essential for future plant growth. Nitrogen that either is in the atmosphere or locked up within plant structures is unavailable to support further plant growth.[7] Without this continual recycling process, nature would eventually deplete all usable sources of nitrogen.

Further, these nutrient cycles have self-regulating features that compensate for disruptions that may cause imbalances to occur. For example, increases in gaseous nitrogen could hamper plant production since the nitrogen becomes largely unavailable to plants in this form. Fortunately, increased concentrations of atmospheric nitrogen encourage the growth of bacteria that fix gaseous nitrogen into the soils. In turn, these bacteria furnish more nitrogen into the soil, thereby encouraging increased plant production that transforms the nitrogen into plant structures. Imbalances of nitrogen of one form encourage compensatory changes that restore the balance of nitrogen flows. In this way, nutrient cycling can weather changing conditions and disruptions caused by natural or human forces.

Although our human communities are subject to the same law of thermodynamics, we rarely act accordingly. All economic production of valued goods for human satisfaction draws upon the provisioning services of nature. We use raw food, fibers, ores, and chemicals to make the vast array of commodities that sustain and enrich our lives. At some point, we discard these products. Normally, we simply dispose of these waste products into our watersheds, airsheds, and landfills. Rarely do we recognize that these emissions are the "stuff" of future raw materials. Instead, we have designed our economy based on a simplistic "cradle to grave" worldview, in which natural resources evolve from valued commodities to discarded wastes.[8] Though this linear system serves human convenience, it creates substantial disruptions to the natural cycles.

Many environmental problems result from this misuse of the world. Consider the problem of climate change. As already discussed, our switch to fossil fuels over the past century and a half has caused a growing imbalance of carbon dioxide in our atmosphere. Unlike other examples of pollution, this problem does not result from the production of some "unnatural" or toxic chemical. Instead, we are simply producing a global imbalance, as we extract fossil fuels from the earth and transform them into atmospheric carbon far faster than natural processes can respond. Our modern agricultural system creates a similar problem. Most of our high-yield hybrid crops quickly deplete the soils of their fertility. To compensate, farmers import chemical fertilizers, including nitrogen, to replenish the soil's nutrients. Though much of this nitrogen fuels plant growth, a substantial portion leaches into the adjacent watershed where it can create problems. Excessive nitrogen, called eutrophication, can cause massive fish kills and other disruptions to aquatic habitats. Off the coast of most major rivers of the world are dead zones in which most marine life is absent, largely due to the extreme concentrations of nitrogen and other nutrients. Though essential to life, too much nitrogen in one location has deadly consequences.

Only by correcting the underlying imbalances and disturbances to the natural cycles can we resolve these problems effectively. To limit the damage that our economic systems impose on the natural environment, we must redesign our production and consumption systems to reflect and support these natural cycles. We can mimic nature by reusing and recycling the products and materials that meet our needs while limiting the imbalances and the disruptions they impose on the natural environment. In moving towards full recycling of these critical materials, we strengthen the long-term foundation of our economy as we create replenishing sources that can sustain our communities indefinitely. Although this suggests an optimistic portrait, there exists a looming cloud that requires our attention.

A plentiful and reliable energy source

Nature has created a vast recycling system in which a finite amount of material resources can support life on a continuing basis, virtually limitlessly. Yet, the driving force for each of these cycles, energy, is subject to the Second Law of Thermodynamics, called the Law of Entropy, which places energy in a class by itself. Chemical reactions involving energy leave the *quantity* of energy unchanged (due to the First Law) while the *quality* of energy declines (due to the Second Law). In each transformation, the *overall* usefulness of energy decreases as the energy changes from a more concentrated to a more dispersed form. Thus, the work potential of the available energy must decline with each use. The law concludes that energy ultimately is limited in its usefulness and cannot be endlessly recycled. The reservoir of potential energy thus places a limit on any system, natural or human.

Central to the Second Law is the concept of entropy, or the amount of disorder in a system. Consider the following example. Imagine a construction site for a new home in which all of the building materials (e.g., bricks, cement, lumber, and nails) are onsite and neatly packaged. To create a home, one needs substantial energy, mostly human labor, to place these materials in a specific order in relationship to each other. Only then will the construction materials provide the functions we expect from a home. However, the creation of this orderly home generates new problems. If left unattended, the natural forces of gravity, erosion, and oxidation will eventually reduce this house into a pile of debris. Although this heap contains all of the materials used in building the home, its disorder makes it virtually useless. In this state, the pile of materials would have even more entropy than the original site full of packaged materials. As every homeowner also knows, one requires further energy to defer this process of decline (maintenance) and even greater amounts to correct (repair) any deterioration.

While the Law of Entropy does state that the overall quality of energy must decline with each energy transformation, this does not mean that *all* energy must increase in entropy. In fact, many energy transformations, whether natural or human designed, create *some* lower-entropy (or higher-quality) energy. In photosynthesis, plants transform solar energy into lower-entropy chemical energy in the form of carbohydrates. Though most of the solar energy becomes heat that must be dissipated by the plant, these carbohydrates offer a much more useful and concentrated form of energy. Humans mimic this process (less efficiently) by using photovoltaic cells to create electricity. Alternatively, we can harness the high-entropy, physical energy of wind by using windmills to generate low-entropy electricity. Most of the potential energy contained in the wind is lost as heat, but small portions of it become useful electrical energy. Current dependence on fossil fuels is due to the uniquely high-quality (low-entropy) energy that they contain. Rather small amounts of oil, natural gas, and coal generate sizeable amounts of energy, causing them to be both highly productive and economical.

The house analogy, just discussed, applies to all life forms including microorganisms, plants, mammals, humans, and even economies. Each form of life requires energy to forestall decline and death, and, with each use, the available energy declines in quality. To prevent this degradation, organisms must continually tap new energy sources. At least temporarily, individual organisms can rely on stored energy to power their operations. However, tapping this low-entropy source leaves unusable (high-entropy) energy in its place. Without a reliable source of energy, the organism will die once it depletes its reserves of stored energy. Without additional food sources, humans cannot survive more than a handful of weeks. Similarly, human economies cannot survive without constant sources of energy. Thus each system, natural and human, must rely on continual sources of low-entropy energy to *delay* the inevitable rise in entropy and disorder.

Much of the material prosperity of our modern economy is due to the harnessing of low-entropy energy. We require reliable and plentiful energy to drive our productive machinery, fuel our vast transportation networks, and power our household appliances. We need energy not only to produce more and to add to our existing forms of physical capital, but also to maintain and operate the vast infrastructure already in place. Despite the essential role of energy in our lives, it usually takes the rare power outages and gasoline shortages to remind us of energy's singular importance. Without a stable energy foundation, our economic security is clearly threatened. While the twentieth century witnessed mostly plentiful and rising levels of fossil fuels, we now recognize the limits of this option. Arguably, world reserves of petroleum, coal, and natural gas can accommodate further growth in our use of these energy sources over the next several decades. However, our increased use of these sources exacerbates the daunting challenges posed by climate change. Until we resolve this energy uncertainty and develop new sources of reliable energy, our economic forecast will remain cloudy.

Capacity for adaptation

Mostly, we view nature as a static and unchanging entity. In our yards and gardens, we struggle to capture a "look" – whether it is the green, manicured lawn, a formal, flower garden, or some other regionally inspired model. Capturing that "look" can take much time, effort, and money, while maintaining that "look" can consume even greater quantities of each. Our impulse to "preserve" certain natural areas frequently reflects this view of nature as we attempt to eradicate human influences on the land. In removing our impact, we believe that we can maintain the pristine nature of the area, often for posterity. If nature reflected our static worldview, then the two attributes already discussed would adequately explain the persistence of natural ecosystems. With an ample energy source and self-regulating nutrient cycles, ecosystems could indeed operate in machine-like fashion without limit.

However, contrary to our assumptions, change and disturbance are the defining characteristics of nature, not continuity and stability. Over the period of a century, a particular location can witness a near complete turnover of its resident plant species and a wholesale change in its appearance – a process called *ecological succession*. At one time, scientists believed that each ecosystem was set on a predictable path toward a relatively limited number of destinations, or climax communities.[9] Most now think that this process is far more complicated. Rather than a single climax, ecologists believe that specific areas can evolve toward different climax communities, depending on specific conditions early in the successional process.[10] Unpredictable events like disease and fire can substantially alter the eventual path taken. So can the impact of humans. Further, ecosystems are not homogeneous units, but rather a patchwork of different biotic communities, each reflecting local conditions and recent disturbances. Different parts of a forest may reflect different stages of a successional path, depending on the timing and intensity of the most recent forest fire. Lastly, ecologists no longer view succession as a linear progression that achieves completion, but rather as an ongoing process that responds to relentless changes in external conditions and interspecies dynamics.

This capacity for adaptability is crucial in the face of changing climate, topography, and even location. From extensive research, we know that the earth's landmasses have witnessed tremendous change, due in part to atmospheric changes that have altered temperatures and precipitation patterns, geological pressures that have raised mountains, and moving tectonic plates that have rearranged continents. These changing conditions impose shifting circumstances that require continual adaptation on the part of our natural systems. Further, migrating plant and animal species create new community dynamics within specific ecosystems. In the face of this relentless change, natural systems require adaptability to remain viable. Succession encourages a flexibility that enables natural systems to adjust and persist through changing climatic conditions.

The process of succession "starts" with the creation of new habitats, often the result of declining water levels, retreating glaciers, or cooling lava flows. This altered physical landscape largely denuded of vegetation invites opportunistic plant species. While random forces apparently influence which plant species first colonize the bare landscape, these early colonizers, often called "pioneer" or "r-selected" species, share similar traits.[11] They have developed dispersal strategies that enable them to take rather quick advantage of the naked landscape. Their seeds are light enough to be carried by water or wind to the new location or durable enough to survive the ravages of fire. Once they have immigrated to the new location, they are quick to establish themselves. Characterized by rapid growth, fecund reproduction, and short generation times, these rather simple organisms are ready to spread quickly. However quick they are to dominate the landscape, their dominion is rarely long lasting.

As they cover the denuded area, the pioneering species modify the landscape. In some cases, they anchor the thin soil and allow it to accumulate over time, thereby creating hospitable conditions for competing species. In all cases, their rapid growth quickly diminishes the available sunlight, water, and nutrients, thereby triggering competition for them. Their simple structures make them less suited for this form of competition.[12] Instead, more complex plants and shrubs, better able to use whatever key resource is in short supply, exert their advantage. In deserts, succession will favor plants that are particularly efficient at using and conserving precious water; in wetter environments, succession will encourage species that are more shade tolerant. Slowly, these new species, often called "K-selected" species, emerge and replace the early pioneers. Though less nimble than the pioneer species, their more complex plant structures permit them to slowly replace the pioneer species in resource-challenged conditions. In some habitats, this succession of dominant plant species may occur several times as each stage of succession unfolds. For example, in the southeastern USA, succession may cause a specific piece of land to evolve from weeds and grasses to shrubs to pine forests to an eventual climax stage of hardwood forests over the period of a century.[13]

Succession does more than merely alter the make-up of species that comprise a particular location; it also significantly alters the ecosystem's structure and functioning.[14] Temperature and the availability of sunlight, water, and key plant nutrients influence the composition of plant species that flourish. At the same time, changes in vegetation patterns can influence each of these key variables. As the composition of plant species changes during the phases of succession, so do the key attributes of the ecosystem, including those that drive ecological functioning and determine the level of ecological services provided.[15] Although the changes are myriad, one can grasp them by looking at how ecosystems utilize solar energy and key nutrients over the course of succession.

In the colonizing stage of succession, conditions are ripe for rapid growth. Simple weeds that quickly colonize the area require little energy for plant maintenance and thus devote most of their energy to plant growth and reproduction. Abundant sunlight in a denuded landscape fuels rapid growth in plant biomass. In this stage, a relatively small amount of plant biomass can generate rather large increases in new plant growth. This state of high growth is what modern agriculture attempts to mirror. Farmers sow relatively simple annuals in bare fields with the hope of harvesting a large bounty at season's end. For a relatively small biological investment, often just a seed, farmers can potentially harvest a sizeable amount of commercially valuable plant material.

In later stages of succession, a different set of conditions exists. The competition for declining sunlight (and available nutrients) encourages more complex and efficient plants to dominate. Some plants, like tall shrubs and trees, use their complex structures to tower over others as they grab their share of the available sunlight. Shade-tolerant plants have evolved specific structures to better use the lower-quality sunlight found in shaded areas. The variety of conditions allows different plants to fill different niches, thereby increasing plant diversity, at least in the early and middle stages of succession. As these more efficient plants continue to dominate, they slowly create an increasingly efficient energy system, in which a finite amount of plant inputs support a growing amount of biomass.[16] As these plants devote more energy to simply maintaining their increasingly complex structures and less to continued plant growth, the annual additions to the local biomass slowly decrease, though the aggregate amount continues to rise. Consequently, as the local area evolves toward a larger, more diverse, and more complex plant biomass, the annual increments decline. Somewhat paradoxically, as the wealth of the local biomass increases, at some point, the income or the additional increments begin to decline and head toward zero.[17]

Modern economies are subject to the natural changes just described. Changing climates cause some plant species to flourish while others decline, thereby affecting directly industries based on agriculture and forestry. A warming climate will affect other industries indirectly, such as clothing and leisure, as the changing temperatures influence people's preferences. Further, cultural adaptations generate catalysts for change. Rapid changes in technology encourage the emergence of new industries, along with the demise of existing industries. Expanded knowledge and changing values cause each generation to reinterpret how best to meet their needs. The economy must adapt and respond to the changing preferences. Without the capacity to adapt to changing conditions, our economic institutions would become outmoded and unresponsive to current needs. Fortunately, one of the recognized attributes of market economies is their capacity to adapt to changing circumstances. Market responses to the oil shortages in the 1970s offer a compelling example of this point.

Not only do market economies demonstrate similar flexibility to that shown by natural ecosystems, but they also mimic the process of succession. Two generations ago, during an era of cheap energy, we built structures, cars, and appliances that consumed lots of energy. In response to rising energy costs, we now produce LEED-compliant buildings, hybrid car technology, and Energy Star appliances.[18] As a result, we operate with much greater energy efficiency than did our economy even one generation ago. Similar to maturing natural systems, we are producing more complex structures that use less energy and fewer resources to satisfy human needs. This illustrates one way that our market economy adapts to the changing circumstances.

System resiliency

The longevity of any natural system requires more than a cycle of nutrient replenishment, a reliable energy source, and a capacity to adapt to evolving circumstances. Just as we humans must cope with the "ups and downs of life," so must every natural system be capable of surviving the wrenching disturbances that periodically buffet it. Pestilence, disease, violent storms, avalanches, and fires sporadically sweep through any given location. Between these episodic events, specific locations must contend with periods of drought and flooding. Disturbance and disruption are the inevitable prospect for any natural system. To persist, natural systems must have the capacity to withstand the impact of any unpredictable, episodic disturbances.

Although a somewhat debated term, "system resiliency" refers to the capacity of ecosystems to resist, absorb, and recover from external disturbances, giving it three key elements.[19] Two of these elements are the system's capacity to resist change (resistance) as well as the speed with which it returns to its initial state (elasticity). A simple example can illustrate these two factors. In response to some chemical spill, lakes usually exhibit both weak resistance and low elasticity, as they initially collect and subsequently retain the harmful chemical pollutants. Free-flowing rivers demonstrate a similar weak resistance as they collect the chemicals, but are much more elastic given their ability to flush out the chemicals relatively quickly. The third aspect of resiliency refers to the amount of change that an ecosystem can endure because of a disturbance (amplitude) without undergoing a fundamental shift in its ecological functioning. Some ecosystems exhibit the capacity to absorb significant disturbances without losing their functioning capacity. Temperate forests can absorb substantial timber harvesting and retain their basic ecological processes. Their soils are rich in nutrients and foster new growth as long as they remain undiminished, as they lie unprotected. On the other hand, substantial timber harvesting in tropical forests can devastate their productive capacity. Extensive harvesting in tropical forests removes the system nutrients, leaving the thin and poorly enriched soils unprotected and vulnerable to severe erosion. In this case, the ecosystem undergoes organizational changes that initiate lower levels of ecological functioning and are difficult to reverse. The result is a reduced level of ecological services rendered.

The factors that determine a particular ecosystem's resiliency are indeed complicated. However, there exist strong interconnections between the resiliency of a given ecosystem and the process of succession. For example, succession can affect resiliency as it alters the balance of nutrient flows. During the colonizing phase of succession, key plant nutrients are usually quite abundant. However, as plant growth occurs, the freely available nutrients decline as plants lock them up in their living biomass. The decline in available nutrients favors plants with more efficient structures. The continued increase in biomass means that ever fewer nutrients are locally available. If this process continues long enough, the scarcity of available nutrients can severely inhibit new plant growth and the renewal of local flora. Only well-established plants can compete effectively, thereby encouraging a decline in biodiversity. Nutrient flows wane under these conditions, creating local ecosystems that become "over-connected" and "brittle" and vulnerable to blights and pests.[20] Just like people, natural systems can suffer from aging and maturity.

Disturbance and disruption play a prominent role in the ongoing sustainability of ecosystems. Storms, floods, and fires offer mature systems opportunities for renewal. Not only do natural disruptions weed out the less healthy stock, but they also create opportunities for new growth. The disturbances release stored nutrients from the destroyed plant biomass, thereby fueling new growth and offering opportunities for a variety of species. In cases where a thinning of the existing growth has occurred, the disruptions create favorable conditions for younger trees to compete against their established rivals. Where the damage is more extensive, succession begins anew as pioneering species recover the bared landscape.

According to this view, periodic disturbances are necessary to the renewal of the ecosystem and its underlying functionality. They provide opportunities for the early pioneer species to reassert themselves, assuring their continued presence in the area. Small disturbances can create patches in the larger ecosystem in which each patch is evolving along a different part of the successional path. Such patchiness encourages broader diversity within the ecosystem and ensures the continuation of species that comprise the successional process. This may be particularly critical for an ecosystem in the face of a dramatic disaster. Without small disturbances and the opportunities they afford, pioneer species may decline for want of opportunity. Without their quick recovery of the bare soil, the denuded landscape can degenerate as wind and water erode the natural soils.

As with a diverse stock portfolio, biodiversity buffers ecological disturbance. On the Great Plains, small patches of undisturbed prairie can contain up to fifty species of different grasses and forbs (leafy herbs).[21] That diversity gives the prairie its strength and resiliency. In periods of increased rainfall, the taller, thirstier grasses thrive as they compete with their shorter cousins for available sunlight and nutrients. In subsequent periods of drought, shorter grasses can better withstand a prolonged absence of water. No matter the specific weather, a greater variety of grasses offers better coverage in protecting the underlying topsoil. In addition, increased biodiversity protects the land from devastation caused by disease and pestilence. Though a specific pest or pathogen may ravage a particular type of grass, it will likely leave the neighboring grasses and herbs unaffected.[22] Not only does the mixture of grasses mitigate the damage caused by the disturbance, but it also fosters faster recovery from injury.[23] Some grasses recover more quickly from the devastating effects of a prairie fire, while others rebound more quickly after freezing temperatures. Having both kinds of grasses limits the period of recuperation. More broadly, increased biodiversity offers any ecosystem a greater variety and number of interspecies links that produce essential nutrient flows. While a specific ecological disturbance may disrupt some of these links, others remain unscathed, thereby leaving the ecosystem with some capacity to recuperate more quickly.

Human systems are equally vulnerable to a wide variety of disruptions. Not only are we subject to the natural calamities like flooding, fire, violent storms, and earthquakes, but we have our own, human-caused disturbances like depressions, war, and terrorism. Although the natural disturbances are largely outside our control, we do have some control over the latter. In either case, we must recognize that these disturbances are part of our reality. In recent years, we have witnessed the substantial damage and harm wreaked by hurricanes, whether natural or financial. Given their potential for damage and destruction, they can affect our capacity to meet future needs. Rather than acting surprised when they occur, we should take steps to insulate ourselves from their harm and to anticipate ways that we can assist the recovery and recuperation from their injury.

Applying the lessons learned

For fifty years after the conclusion of the Civil War, waves of immigrants settled on the Great Plains, ready to claim their share of the American dream. To work the land, they demonstrated considerable amounts of determination, ingenuity, and hope. Yet, many of their descendants have abandoned their attempts to farm and ranch this land in favor of other places and pursuits. In most cases, the decision to stop was made neither quickly nor easily. Nor did they reach this decision before applying the best efforts of modern technology. To compensate for the unreliable and stingy rainfall, massive pumping of the underlying Ogallala Aquifer brought needed water. Yet, this vast resource has proved to be finite. Agronomists have developed drought-resistant strains of wheat and barley, giving local farmers additional hope. Vast quantities of petroleum-based fertilizers and pesticides have pumped up yields and battled pests, increasing the commercial viability of farming the land. Yet even these efforts have proved insufficient. The long hours and difficult work, combined with uncertain and often low rewards have encouraged many to forego the effort. The Great Plains experiment, to cultivate the vast grasslands in order to provide a secure and prosperous livelihood to greater numbers of people, has largely failed. Today, we are witnesses to a reverse migration in the region. Young people and families are emigrating, leaving behind an aging population and declining rural communities. Today, in many parts of the Great Plains, the land supports fewer numbers than when the native peoples hunted buffalo across the grassland.

The Great Plains experiment failed not for lack of determination or technological ingenuity. Rather, its failure rests with chosen farming techniques that ignored the principles of sustainable systems just discussed. The intensive cropping of the land and exporting of its harvest to distant cities prevented adequate recycling of nutrients, thereby requiring increasing applications of commercial fertilizers. The shift to modern methods, including mechanization and commercial chemicals, converted farming from its reliance on plentiful energy sources, such as solar and human, to reliance on the ultimately short-lived fossil fuels. Modern technology and economic pressures persuaded farmers to switch to monoculture farming. Though farmers could grow corn and wheat profitably during the wet years, their crops could not adapt to the drier periods that visit the region from time to time. Investments in specialized equipment and accumulated debt raised both the risks and costs associated with switching crops in response to changing conditions. In plowing up the perennial grasses and their thickly matted roots, farmers tapped a deep and fertile reservoir of topsoil. However, the removal of the grass cover left the rich deposit of topsoil, the wealth of the region, vulnerable to theft. Violent storms that brought drenching rain and strong winds eroded the soils, diminishing them in quantity and quality. In essence, farmers were boosting the "income" or yield from the land by the diminishing its underlying "capital" or endowment. No enterprise, whether farm or business, can long survive by depleting is capital.

In recognizing the underlying failures of the nineteenth-century vision for the Great Plains, one should not conclude that the land is inhospitable and barren.

Rather, hope springs from recognizing the region's special qualities and developing ways to utilize these qualities in a sustainable fashion. In the driest areas, proponents are encouraging a new "crop" to farm as well as an old form of ranching. A bane to farmers past, the steady wind that blows across the land offers itself as a source of income. Wind farming is sprouting up throughout the Great Plains as entrepreneurs seek to capture this dependable and free source of energy. Wind turbines can transform this renewable source into electricity that can power factories, businesses, and homes hundreds of miles away. Wind farms offer a long-term investment in a durable energy source that imposes limited harm to the local environment.

Others argue for returning the land to perennial grasses. Since 1976, Wes Jackson and the Land Institute have been promoting "natural systems agriculture" as a way of meeting human food needs while recognizing the ecological attributes of the prairie system. In particular, researchers have been developing perennial strains of various grain crops as a means of achieving a farming system that is both durable and economical. The use of perennial grasses mimics the natural ecology of the region while producing food crops available for human consumption.[24] Others have argued for a return of native, prairie grasses and to herds of buffalo that feed on them. Raising cattle has not worked, in large part because the short-horned cattle imported to the region had evolved in a wetter and more hospitable climate. Unlike bison that tend to graze on all grasses and forbs, cattle are much more selective. As cattle graze on the local grasses, their choosy eating changes the plant community, usually for the worse.[25] Bison have evolved on the Great Plains and their eating habits sustain the plant community, rather than undermine it. During winter snowfalls, bison know to sweep away snow to graze on nutritious grasses lying underneath, while cattle frequently starve even if the same grasses are inches from their nose. Restoring the native perennial grasses could anchor and slowly replenish the remaining topsoil. Ranchers could avoid expensive feed and supplements to boost weight gain; instead, they could rely on the natural grasses that nature provides freely. Ranchers could restore an ecosystem that is both productive and sustainable in place of one that is neither.

In ways similar to what happened on the Great Plains, we have created an economy that neither fully understands nor appreciates our natural bounty. Our market-based institutions are effective in preserving certain parts of our natural capital while neglectful and even abusive of other elements. We have an economy that largely neglects the recycling of key resources. As such, we face a multitude of environmental problems that are largely attributable to growing imbalances in natural substances. We have an economy that is addicted to an energy source whose continued use is problematic on several grounds. Although our economy does exhibit adroit adaptability in many areas, we continue to ignore the likelihood of episodic disturbances and fail to anticipate both their occurrence and likely impact. Consequently, we leave ourselves unnecessarily vulnerable to their harm. Continuing on this path will eventually lead to stark choices, similar to those facing families and businesses struggling to survive on the Great Plains. Yet, in recognizing and adapting those characteristics that convey durability to natural systems, we can foster an economy that is both responsive to human needs and respectful of natural limits.

The next four chapters examine public policies that can foster each attribute in our economy. Rather than ignore the strength and limits of our natural capital, we should learn from and apply this knowledge to create new structures and incentives for more informed decisions.

Further readings

Thomas Cox *et al.*, 'Prospects for Developing Perennial Grain Crops', give a careful discussion of the key issues relating to the development of perennial grain crops.

Nicolas Georgescu-Roegen, 'The Entropy Law and the Economic Problem', provides an early and classic understanding of how the entropy law limits our economic options.

Dale Lott, *American Bison: A Natural History*, offers a comprehensive understanding of the American bison in relationship with its grassland habitat and neighbors.

Richard Manning, *Grassland: The History, Biology, Politics, and Promise of the American Prairie*, examines the Great Plains ecosystem as it has evolved under natural selection and human selection in recent centuries.

Eugene Odum, *Ecology and Our Endangered Life-Support Systems*, offers a readable book on ecology, particularly as it relates to human affairs.

7 Closing the materials loop

Kalundborg

Seventy-five miles west of Copenhagen along the Danish coast lies a medium-sized harbor town named Kalundborg. Living amid buildings that date back to the twelfth century, the residents of Kalundborg are not simply good stewards of their past, but they nurture the futures of their children and grandchildren. Over the past thirty years, the city's inhabitants have witnessed a remarkable transformation, resulting from many individual steps taken without some master plan. With a nose for profit and an eye on the future, the city's economic leaders have fashioned an intricate network of the area's key, economic actors. Rather than simply dispose of "waste" materials and energy, the area's businesses are recovering and selling waste byproducts to limit disposal costs and increase revenues. This expanding web of relationships creates an industrial system that mimics the interdependent relationships among members of any biotic community found in nature. It is a story that can and no doubt will be replicated in the future.

At the center of the Kalundborg network is the Asnaes Power Station, a typical 1,500-megawatt generator of electricity. Burning coal, the plant generates steam to drive huge turbines that produce the region's electricity. As in photosynthesis, much of the potential energy released by burning coal is lost as high-entropy heat. As it cools, the steam can no longer drive the turbines and normally is vented into the air. However, the steam is still hot enough to serve other purposes. In a series of bilateral agreements, the power station began selling this unused resource to two neighboring plants, Novo Nordisk, a producer of pharmaceuticals and industrial enzymes, and Statoil Refinery, a large oil refinery. Both companies use "waste" steam to heat their pipes to increase pressure needed to drive their chemical processes. Later, the power station began selling steam to the city of Kalundborg as a source of space heating for residential and commercial buildings. As this source of heating became available, residents no longer needed their highly polluting, oil-burning heaters, thereby reducing smoke and fumes.[1] Early success led to the heating of 4,500 homes.[2] In using its "waste" heat in this way, the power station is working to improve its thermal efficiency as it reduces by 80 percent the heat emissions it simply discards.[3] In tapping its waste heat stream, the power plant has substantially increased its revenues – a primary reason for its innovative measures.

The plant's management did not stop there. They installed a desulfurization unit to remove the sulfur from the flue gases. In doing so, they removed a key ingredient of "acid rain." They did so not simply because they treasure a clean environment; they also recognized that they were effectively burning "money" up in the smoke. With sulfur, they could now produce calcium sulfate, or gypsum, the primary material used in construction wallboard. They began selling gypsum to the local producer of plasterboard, Gyproc. In 1998, the power station produced nearly 200,000 tons, replacing much of the natural gypsum that Gyproc had imported from faraway Spain.[4] In addition, the power plant managers began selling the fly ash, the residue from burning coal, to a local cement manufacturer. In each case, the management converted parts of the waste stream into commercial byproducts. In doing so, they simultaneously increased their revenues and reduced disposal costs.

This network of cooperation and integration spawned other links as well. As part of its oil-refining operation, Statoil Refinery had typically burned off excess fuel gases. Now, it sends these gases through a desulfurization process. Liquid sulfur is captured and sold to the Kemira Acid Plant, while they sell the sulfur-free gases to Gyproc and the power station.[5] These gases provide nearly all of Gyproc's current power needs, replacing more polluting energy sources. As part of its operations, Novo Nordisk produces vast amounts of nitrogen-rich sludge that serves local farmers as fertilizer. Even without charging for the sludge, this disposal method is cheaper than shipping it to the local landfill.

The commercial network also limits water consumption. Local concerns about dwindling fresh water supplies encouraged Asnaes Power Station to use seawater in meeting some of its substantial water requirements. Rather than disposing the heated salt water back into the fjord, where it could harm the local ecosystem, the plant uses the water to heat its fish farms, providing yet another source of income. To meet 75 percent of its remaining freshwater requirements, it uses recycled water from the Statoil Refinery. The oil refinery sends its cooling water to the Asnaes Power Station as its source of water for its boilers. In an unrelated transfer, Novo Nordisk is proposing to send its treated wastewater to Gyproc for use in making plasterboard. In each case, the parties reduce their need for local water, decrease their costs, and increase their revenues.

Each of these linkages resulted from private negotiations among the parties. They did not require some grand vision or far-sighted public policy; rather, they resulted from a willingness of management to review operations with a discerning eye. No doubt, "good intentions" encouraged these exchanges. Nonetheless, the desire to reduce operating costs or to exploit profit opportunities assured their fruition. Finding commercial uses for previously considered "waste" products offers the producing firm the dual benefits of avoiding disposal fees and gaining additional income. The receiving firm gains access to a local, reliable, and lower-cost source. While these relationships often require some capital investment to improve the quality of the waste materials or to construct delivery facilities, these investments are justified by the resulting revenue stream. Close proximity to each other certainly reduces the needed infrastructure and delivery costs. Geographic proximity is important for another reason as well. It encourages professional contacts among the different managers, leading to increased communication of potential opportunities. Personal relationships also provide the trust needed to complete such agreements. It probably helps that the firms operate in different industries and serve different markets; they are more prone to cooperation if they do not view themselves as rivals.

Though these agreements reflect actual conditions facing the businesses and are not the result of government regulations, public policy can encourage similar networks. Government policies that discourage free dumping of industrial wastes – whether gaseous, heat, solid, or liquid wastes – are encouraging firms to seek innovative ways to reduce disposal fees. Without such financial incentives, firms searching to reduce their operating costs can simply vent their wastes into the local environment. More stringent disposal regulations and higher costs can only encourage businesses to identify new processes and likely partners who can use their "waste" products. The experience of Kalundborg offers the lesson that public policy may best serve by creating the conditions and incentives that encourage bilateral agreements rather than by simply coercing the behavior.

Extending the experience of Kalundborg

There are remarkable similarities between the ecology of plants and animals in their natural habitats and the ecology of commercial businesses in a capitalist system. In each ecosystem, plants and animals must garner key nutrients and expel waste byproducts in a complex tangle of links. In an economy, businesses and households interact in a similar fashion. As Figure 7.1 illustrates, the production of economic goods (and services) are the result of a multi-stage product stream. Provided by nature in raw form, these goods are initially "extracted" by some firms, subsequently "manufactured" by others, "merchandised" by still other firms, and finally consumed by households. Each step requires energy and possibly additional provisioning resources from nature that supplement the initial raw materials. The solid lines in Figure 7.1 illustrate these flows from nature. At each stage, businesses disperse waste byproducts into our air, waters, and ground. The dotted lines in Figure 7.1 illustrate these flows. At whatever point we deem the product no longer

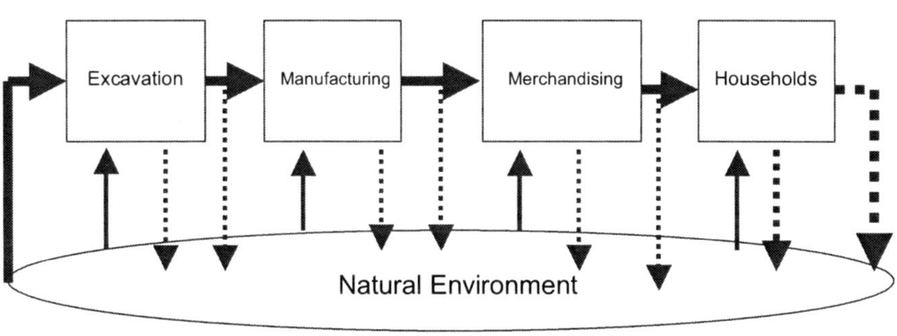

Figure 7.1 Provisioning services and waste emission flows.

useful, we return it to the environment as a waste byproduct. One key difference from natural systems, however, is the imbalance in these material flows. Many waste byproducts are accumulating in our airsheds, watersheds, and land much faster than natural processes can assimilate them.

Just as plants and animals compete for scarce resources to survive, so do businesses struggle for scarce consumer dollars to meet payrolls, suppliers' invoices, and other ongoing costs. Natural selection encourages better-adapted plants and animals to flourish at the expense of their rivals. The same often holds true in business. Companies seek new ways to meet customer needs more effectively and with fewer resources. In both worlds, change is constant, creating new opportunities for members to exploit and adapt. In forests, the growth of large trees creates new opportunities for shade-tolerant plants that function effectively in their understory. Understory plants attract insects and animals seeking a source of food or safe refuge. Similarly, changes in the business community continually create new opportunities. In recent decades, the grocery business has shifted to huge warehouse stores that have displaced the "mom and pop" stores that once predominated. While hugely successful, these megastores have created a new niche for "convenience" stores, which emerged to serve those with short shopping lists and little interest in wandering the long aisles of the large stores.

Lastly, natural communities reflect and adapt to the underlying conditions that give rise to them. Forests emerge in landscapes that afford ample amounts of precipitation and a moderate climate. In regions with more arid conditions, grassland systems will evolve instead. In the same way, the emergence of specific businesses and their web of connections largely reflect the underlying conditions. Since the advent of the Industrial Revolution, textile firms have sought locations that offered both abundant energy and cheap labor. Steelmaking has largely located in areas proximate to the key ingredients of steel as well as accessible to efficient transportation networks. To understand why the experience of Kalundborg is so unusual, we simply need to consider the underlying conditions, or climate, in which our business communities currently operate. Pervasive throughout our economy and culture is the belief that the natural world can serve as a limitless sink to remove all of our unwanted wastes. Businesses traditionally have paid little attention to waste-reduction processes, technologies, and contracts, though this is changing. To alter this underlying climate and encourage more of the linkages found in Kalundborg requires implementing two related concepts: the *polluter-pays principle* and the *principle of full-cost pricing.*

Two principal solutions

As discussed in Chapter Four, market incentives can serve as powerful tools in promoting environmental stewardship. Markets can encourage individuals to safeguard their resources as they maintain, and even improve, their natural capital. Yet, markets do not function effectively if the substantial costs of using our environmental capital are ignored. In these instances, markets require modification to alter the incentives they generate. Two relatively simple rules provide our guide here. They are the polluter-pays principle and the principle of full-cost pricing. Though simple in concept, implementing these guidelines is much more difficult. Nonetheless, they offer us clear and effective guidelines in creating market incentives that can promote environmentally benign behavior.

The polluter-pays principle requires that those who contribute to the waste stream should fully pay for safe disposal. Polluters should not be able to transfer some or all of these costs onto others, as is currently the case. Instead, this principle requires that we pay directly for these costs to insure a clear financial link between our behavior and the waste generation that it produces. By implementing the polluter-pays principle, we tangibly recognize that our ecological systems are not limitless, especially given our modern capacity for waste generation. We pay directly for the use of these services, giving us a constant reminder of their value. Paying these fees will temper the use of natural systems, thereby offering them some measure of protection. In these ways, implementing the polluter-pays principle fundamentally alters our relationship with the natural environment.

An example can illustrate this point more sharply. Like many communities across our country, my own community pays for trash pick-up and waste-disposal services through local property taxes. Though each household pays approximately $15 per month to cover the city's solid waste-disposal costs,[6] this payment structure does not meet the polluter-pays principle on two counts. First, payment for trash pick-up is part of a larger tax levy for all city services, thereby masking the actual costs of the disposal services. Second, no direct link exists between my use of these services and the fee I pay. Households that minimize their wastes by composting food and garden wastes and recycling glass, plastics, and paper pay the same amount as households that engage in none of these activities. The waste-disposal levy offers no reward to households that limit their wastes, even at higher personal costs. Moreover, there are no financial penalties for households that contribute more to the solid waste stream, despite the higher costs and increased toll on the local environment.

What would happen if my community moved to a levy system in which households and businesses pay fully for the solid wastes they generate? Simply answered, a lot. By measuring the amount of solid waste by volume or by weight, each household would receive a monthly bill clearly stating the amount of trash generated and the resultant fee. Households and businesses would then have a financial incentive to minimize the amount of trash they generate. To save money, some would increase recycling in order to avoid pick-up and disposal charges. Others would turn to composting.[7] Moreover, this novel billing system would trigger a proliferation of outcomes. When shopping, residents would recognize the disposal costs of product packaging, creating a preference for products using less packaging. Quickly, retailers and manufacturers would get the message and reduce their product packaging to offer increased value to their customers. If sufficiently widespread, this novel fee system would encourage broad innovations in packaging to minimize or even eliminate the disposal costs. Throughout the community, businesses, manufacturers, and builders would all be under similar pressure to limit their wastes in order to reduce their disposal costs. Direct disposal fees would encourage a variety of waste-reduction practices, including those found in Kalundborg. All of these changes in behaviors and practices would result from modifying the way we assess our solid waste-disposal services. This policy would not just reduce our need for future landfills, but also lower energy costs and waste emissions that result from the manufacture and transportation of product packaging. This is quite a lot for such a small change.

Applying the polluter-pays principle to other forms of effluents, including air and water emissions, would offer similar benefits. To avoid excessive disposal costs, polluters would seek new ways to reduce their emissions, whether by changing production methods, seeking markets for "wastes," or altering purchases. Suppliers and related businesses would offer less polluting alternatives to help their customers avoid these costs. Such fees would encourage innovation and the emergence of pollution-abatement technologies. Moreover, such direct levies would encourage all, whether households or businesses, to seek ways to limit their impact on our natural systems as they reduce their disposal costs. All this could be accomplished without the heavy hand of government.

Implementing the polluter-pays principle takes an important step toward the broader principle of full-cost pricing for all products and services. This broader principle functions to insure that the full production, environmental, and social costs are included in the price of each product. In this way, rival products truly operate on a level playing field. Ignoring "external" costs causes products to be underpriced and undervalued. Artificially low prices then encourage greater consumption, thereby exacerbating damage done to the natural environment. Further, market externalities stunt the development of "greener" alternatives, whose concern for the environment often leads to a higher purchase price. In some cases, greener alternatives are cheaper if one considers the full cost of manufacturing (and using) these products. By implementing this principle, the prices of all competing products reflect their full cost, both actual production costs and any emissions costs of producing or using the products. With such a level playing field, the market would show a preference to those manufacturers and products that minimize environmental damage as well as production costs.

While enforcing the polluter-pays principle would provide steady improvement in meeting the broader full-cost principle, we must take other steps to achieve this goal. In particular, we must curtail, if not eliminate, public subsidies for resource development and end subsidies to firms that purchase natural resources from public lands. In many cases, these subsidies stem from a nineteenth-century vision that encouraged the settling and development of the west. As the federal government owned extensive land in the west, our federal officials deliberately offered low prices for timber, water, mineral, and grazing rights to these lands to stimulate settlement and development. Many of these public subsidies continue today, protected and maintained by federal laws that have been unchanged for over a century.

For example, mining companies continue today to prospect on public lands, often paying negligible royalties to the government for the privilege. Set by an 1873 law, the payments ignore the market value of the mined ores and the increasing value of these dwindling resources. The artificially low royalty payments discourage reuse and recycling, as it is often cheaper and easier simply to mine more material. When the royalty payments reflect market value, the price of new minerals better reflects their actual value and rewards those who reuse and recycle materials.

Policy prescriptions

We can replicate an economy like the one in Kalundborg in which natural materials are reused and recycled while the waste stream and adverse impact on the environment is minimized. Through the development of resource auctions, emissions taxes, and marketable emissions permits, we can encourage economic decisions that respect the endowment of natural capital rather than ignore it. With these policy tools, we can create markets for key ecological services or remedy currently dysfunctional markets. While these market-based policies have some problems, they offer several key advantages over more administrative and regulatory methods of environmental protection. Most importantly, market incentives offer flexibility and self-correction not possible with administrative regulations. Market incentives allow prices for ecological products to adjust over time as circumstances change. Changes in the economy that make some ecological product or service more valuable will automatically raise its price and thereby encourage consumers to limit their use. In this way, prices continually reflect actual conditions and encourage appropriate behaviors. This organic and ongoing adjustment capacity of markets mimics how natural systems respond and adapt to changing circumstances.

In remedying the current imbalances, Herman Daly's simple guide to sustainable material flows offers a useful model to follow. In recognition of natural processes, Daly argues that we should consider our impacts in three areas: our use of renewable resources, of non-renewable resources, and of natural "sinks" that assimilate our waste emissions. In the case of naturally replenished resources, Daly argues that we can consume these resources up to their natural replenishment rate. Exceeding this rate signals that we are jeopardizing the underlying biological stocks that produce this resource. In a similar vein, Daly argues that we should not produce waste emissions in levels that exceed their natural rate of assimilation. To do so means that we are placing ever-greater stresses on natural systems, as these imbalances lead to mounting problems. Lastly, Daly identifies circumstances under which the consumption of non-renewable resources is prudent, if not technically sustainable.[8] Specifically, Daly argues that the consumption of non-renewable resources is sustainable as long as we are investing in renewable substitute resources that will eventually replace our reliance on the non-renewable resource. Daly believes that, in following each of these rules, we can mimic the nutrient and materials recycling that occur in natural systems.

Emissions taxes

Conceptually, the easiest method of enforcing the polluter-pays principle is by levying waste-emissions taxes. Properly designed, these taxes should assess directly and visibly actual use of waste-disposal services. In essence, these taxes should mimic how we pay for private-sector services. In many cases, households and businesses would receive monthly billing statements that detail their level of emissions as well as their tax burden. In this way, residents could recognize how their practices affect their tax liability. Not only could this system work effectively for solid waste disposal as discussed earlier, but also for wastewater disposal. Government officials should design these tax levies so that they fully pay for the transport and disposal costs required to prevent any harm's being done by these emissions.[9]

Although "taxation" is a dirty word to many, emissions taxes represent an effective way to reduce harm done to the natural environment. Part of their effectiveness is due to the way they imitate other aspects of our economic system. We are used to paying private companies for any services that we use. We are also familiar with various user fees to access public accommodations and services, including toll roads, public recreational facilities, and campgrounds. Once we recognize that our actions threaten our physical environment, learning the habit of paying emissions taxes should not be a difficult stretch.

Yet, there are technical challenges in implementing and maintaining emissions taxes.[10] Often, assessing the actual harm caused by some emissions is very difficult. For example, gauging the cost of increased sulfur dioxide emissions is a complicated and contentious issue that has created broad divisions among experts regarding their actual harm. We should be concerned about setting the emissions levies to reflect the actual costs of any harm done. However, we also should avoid the danger of inaction in controversies about measuring "true cost." Just moving from a regime of no cost to some cost, even if imperfect, will affect behavior and encourage movement toward full-cost pricing. As our understanding of the actual harm improves, we can adjust the tax accordingly. In other cases, direct metering of emissions is either very costly or technically infeasible. This is particularly the problem in non-point sources of emissions. For example, both farmers and suburban households use commercial pesticides and herbicides. Metering actual use of each buyer is clearly infeasible. Yet, by moving upstream in the product stream, one can design an effective emissions tax by levying the fee at the point of sale. The higher purchase price will limit the use of these chemicals, though it will not affect how the chemicals are used, whether appropriately or not.[11]

One further difficulty with emissions taxes is their static nature. The per-unit emissions tax should reflect either the per-unit harm done by the specific pollutant or the per-unit disposal costs that make the substance environmentally innocuous. However, circumstances will change that could either raise or lower these costs. Yet, once set, tax levies tend to languish undisturbed as legislators avoid modifying taxes, particularly if the levy requires an increase. In contrast, fluctuations in actual emissions will likely influence either environmental harm or actual disposal costs. For example, the amount of wastewater generated would likely affect the wastewater treatment costs. To determine a per-unit emissions levy, one would need to know not only the expected costs, but also the amount of wastewater generated. Higher fees would likely encourage households and businesses to generate less wastewater. Reduced wastewater flows and their accompanying fees would likely decline below what is sufficient to cover the full disposal costs. In response, water officials would need to raise the per-unit levy, which would only further encourage practices that limit wastewater emissions. If officials failed to respond, the water levy would not reflect the full costs of using the environment as a sink. As administered prices, emissions taxes do not respond automatically to changing circumstances and therefore will eventually diverge from meeting the full-cost principle. This particular problem is avoidable if one uses an alternative policy tool, marketable emissions permits, as discussed next.

Marketable emissions permits

Marketable emissions permits offer an alternative method to achieving many of the same objectives attained by emissions taxes. They confer value on our natural assets, discourage profligate pollution, encourage pollution-abatement technologies, and potentially raise funds to remedy and restore damage done to our natural capital. They function in the following way. A government agency distributes emissions permits that allow the bearer to discharge certain amounts of the specified substance. To emit that substance, one must have a permit or be subject to prosecution or fine. No longer can we consider pollution as our personal entitlement; rather, it is now an option that must be paid for. Freely marketable, one can buy or sell these permits on open markets, thereby giving them a price that serves as a deterrent to polluters. To limit their expenditures on emissions permits, polluters will seek various ways to reduce emissions, including changing operations and adopting pollution-abatement technologies. As circumstances change, so will the permit prices.

Marketable emissions permits offer two key improvements over emissions taxes. First, they offer public officials direct control over pollution levels. By limiting the number of permits, local authorities can determine the level of emissions that occur. As with emissions taxes, effective regulation and enforcement are required to prevent unauthorized pollution. Enforcement costs will likely vary from one pollutant to another. Some emissions are largely the result of *point source pollution*, in which the sources of pollution are fixed, identifiable, and few in number. In these circumstances, enforcement costs are relatively manageable. In the case of *non-point source pollution*, the sources of pollution are far more diffuse, making enforcement much more challenging. However, like the emissions tax, these permits can be attached to the substance at the point of sale. For example, any homeowner wishing to purchase a specific herbicide at the local nursery would also buy a permit to use the chemical(s). Alternatively, manufacturers could only produce as much of the chemical(s) as their permits allow them to produce. In either case, the permit price would raise the purchase price and insure that the user/polluter pays for the consequences.

In most cases, public officials should target an emissions level that reflects the expected assimilative capacity of the local environment. In other words, in the case of non-toxic materials, the level of permitted emissions should not exceed the capacity of the local environment to assimilate that substance. Under these circumstances, ambient levels of the substance should not increase in the environment.[12] Two exceptions might cause policymakers to diverge from this standard. First, policymakers may argue that the current pollution level is already too high and that there are strong grounds for reducing the ambient levels. In this case, they might set the acceptable emissions level below the current assimilative capacity with the expectation that pollution levels need an opportunity to decline. Second, shifting immediately from current levels of emissions to the standard of assimilative capacity might impose too much hardship on households and industry. In this case, policymakers might choose slowly declining levels that give households and businesses some period to adjust to the long-run standard imposed by current assimilative capacity.

Marketable permits offer a second advantage, since their price will adjust over time as circumstances warrant. Suppose the authorities decide to phase in the policy by slowly reducing the number of permits each year; assuming a constant demand, the permit prices would slowly rise. In this way, businesses and households would have time to adjust to the new policy. Yet, demand is not likely to stay constant. As households and businesses discovered ways to reduce their need to emit the substance, the value or price of permits would naturally decline. Permit prices would continue to fall as new pollution-abatement technologies further reduced emissions. In some cases, permit prices could drop to zero as the need to pollute fell below the assimilative capacity, ending this substance's status as a problem pollutant, at least temporarily. On the other hand, an increasing need to emit this substance would cause households and businesses to compete for scarce permits, driving up the price. Higher permit prices would further reward producers who could limit their emissions or innovators who could develop pollution-abatement technologies. Obviously, decisions to raise or lower the number of permits, based on new information regarding assimilative capacity or other environmental factors, would affect their price. Nonetheless, permit prices would signal their relative value to potential users and convey worth to those natural systems that assimilate the offending pollutant.

Implementing a system of marketable emissions permits is not without its challenges. One particular difficulty is how to design a scheme to distribute the permits to their potential users. Under one system, officials can simply auction off permits to the highest bidders. Presumably, those individuals with the highest need would outbid those whose need is lower. The funds from the auction could finance any disposal costs or environmental remediation costs that might be necessary. Under some circumstances, such a shift in "how business is done" could create substantial financial hardship on businesses and households. Resistance to this new "tax" could be considerable. To mollify this resistance, public officials could distribute the permits *without charge*, based on past use.[13] This method would reduce the financial shock of the new program and share the sacrifice of reduced emission levels proportionately. It would also generate no government funds for any disposal or remediation costs. Although this distribution method would not require an auction (and therefore no primary market) for permits, a secondary or resale market would emerge anyway. Assuming the number of permits is below current emission levels, each polluter would need to make some adjustments. Some would find it easier to reduce their emissions and therefore have excess permits for sale, while others who find it more difficult to limit their emissions could purchase permits. Each year, public officials could distribute fewer permits without charge and increase those allocated through the open auction. Shifting toward the open auction method would give new businesses the same opportunity to obtain permits and it would insure that polluters increasingly faced the full cost of their emitting behavior.

Implementing either emissions taxes or emissions permits to insure that polluters pay for their behavior generates one additional problem. Both function to discourage behaviors that lead to pollution by raising the price of such practices. Households and businesses can choose to purchase products and services that are highly polluting, but they will do so at the expense of their checkbooks. This in itself is not a problem. However, given the current income disparities among our nation's households, the burden of paying higher prices is not equitably shared. Rising prices for goods and services due to the imposition of these "green taxes" would disproportionately affect lower-income households, since they spend disproportionately more on these items. The imposition of these policies would impose a significant financial hardship on those who live on modest, fixed incomes. To redress this problem, public officials could make certain allowances. Local officials could provide each household with a modest level of permits to generate trash, without charge. For emissions that exceed the modest thresholds, households would need to purchase additional permits at the market rate. In this way, households would be sheltered from the full brunt of the new taxes while effectively being discouraged from generating unnecessary trash. Policymakers could design similar arrangements for emissions taxes as well. Each household could generate modest amounts of trash before any per-unit tax on solid waste became effective. Taxing authorities could offer further help through tax shifting. As local and regional governments implemented these green taxes, they would generate additional revenues that would allow them to lower taxes in other areas.[14] Taxing authorities could take advantage of the revenue windfall by targeting lower-income households for tax relief. These adjustments could soften the financial blow imposed by the "green taxes" without undermining their effectiveness.

Lastly, there are jurisdictional issues to consider. Some forms of pollution are largely sedentary in nature and their impact is solely local. Non-hazardous solid waste, or trash, offers us a clear example. Most garbage is generated and disposed of locally, usually in landfills.[15] In these cases, local authorities could use either emissions taxes or permit systems to protect the community from unnecessary use of natural sinks. Other forms of pollution, like sources of water pollution, are more mobile and their impact is regional. Pollutants carried from our streets, neighborhoods, and farms into local creeks flow downstream through watersheds until they reach the oceans. Lastly, trade winds sweep many forms of air pollution across continents and even oceans, creating global consequences. The migratory nature of many water and air pollutants limits the effectiveness of purely local efforts to protect the environment. Actions taken upstream or upwind do influence the quality of local environments. In these cases, local efforts would be largely ineffective. These circumstances require the agreement and implementation of regional, national, or even international policies to accomplish the desired outcomes.

"Upstream" production issues

Implementing either emissions taxes or emissions permit systems for each significant source of pollution would do much to fulfill the principle of full-cost pricing as consumers and manufacturers pay the full cost of using our environment as a natural sink. Though these policies focus on the "downstream" portion of our production stream, where waste byproducts are returned to the environment, they also affect the "upstream" portion where the provisioning resources are taken initially. Most mining operations today require huge amounts of rock ores to collect moderate amounts of the desired mineral, as caustic chemicals are applied to the ores to leach out the desired mineral. These modern processes create large amounts of waste rock and toxic chemicals; enforcing the polluter-pays principle would have substantial impact. The imposed cost burden would generate higher prices for mined minerals and thereby dampen industrial demand for them. Higher prices for mined materials would encourage more reuse and recycling of used materials, less wasteful production technologies, and the introduction of substitute materials. The result would be a lower depletion rate of these minerals.

Even in those cases where the extraction of new materials generates minimal waste, the impact of downstream policies are felt nonetheless. As customers would need to pay for hefty disposal fees, they would seek alternative products and methods to avoid or limit their payment. In response, manufacturers might offer to repossess the product, so that their customers could avoid the disposal fee. Repossession would encourage manufacturers to reuse the materials as fully as possible and even to redesign the product so that reuse could be more economical. For example, car manufacturers might offer to repurchase the vehicle at the end of its useful life. Car companies could revamp their designs to reuse the more durable parts, say the chassis. In this way, end-use emissions taxes or permits could revamp the initial production process as manufacturers redesigned products to reduce the full life-cycle costs.

As discussed in prior chapters, markets function more effectively in insuring a reliable and prudent use of our provisioning resources than in protecting our natural systems from the burden of waste emissions. Nonetheless, it makes sense to consider this point more carefully. As we do, we should recognize a key distinction among provisioning resources: those that result from essentially non-renewable processes, as opposed to those that result from renewable processes. Regarding non-renewable resources, the total amount available is fixed. Strictly speaking, any use of that raw stock depletes it, making less available for the future. Fortunately, most non-renewables are reusable and recyclable, thereby making the finite stock infinitely available, at least potentially. The notable exception to this rule is non-renewable energy sources, which justifies the solitary focus given to them in the next chapter. Renewable resources also offer us a continual supply, as long as we avoid undermining the production processes. Such harm can occur either by consuming these resources at a rate that exceeds their replenishment rate or by harming the underlying ecosystems that produce these resources.

Under normal conditions, markets encourage private landowners whose lands offer non-renewable resources to act as stewards of their natural assets. Let us return to mining as an example. For many reasons, mining companies tend to exploit first the most accessible and richest deposits of ores. As these deposits dwindle, the price of the ore must rise to cover the costs of mining less economical deposits. Higher prices encourage users of this material to switch to substitute products (including recycled metals) and to practice other forms of conservation. As even the moderately economical mines begin to fade, prices must continue to rise, encouraging even more conservation by users of this resource. As such, increasing scarcity of the richer mineral deposits drives up the price of new metals, thereby discouraging future consumption. Given that most minerals reside in very low concentrations, the cost of mining will encourage alternative uses before the resource is fully exhausted.

Other market incentives discourage excessive depletion of these reserves. If circumstances lead to unwarranted mining of a specific mineral, the excessive supply would dampen price and raise concern regarding future shortages, offering some mine owners substantial encouragement to withhold supply today in expectation of higher profits tomorrow.[16] As non-renewable resources are non-perishable, their owners are not discouraged from patiently withholding them from current use. In this way, markets conserve valuable reserves and preserve them for the future. Some argue persuasively that the market restraint is not sufficient.[17] As mentioned, Herman Daly argues that the use of non-renewable resources is prudent only if their depletion does not exceed the investment in a renewable substitute. In this way, as the non-renewable resource is exhausted, the alternative renewable resource can offer a lasting means of meeting the same need. For example, our use of fossil fuels should include some payment toward the creation of alternative, renewable energy sources that will fully replace our diminishing non-renewable reserves. This represents a prudent, though stringent standard. Whether corporations emphasize their long-term interests sufficiently is debatable, though as we see more "oil" companies convert into "energy" firms, one is heartened by their recognition that their long-term interests require new ventures.

Many of the same market incentives function to encourage good stewardship among landowners who offer renewable provisioning services. Under normal circumstances, landowners are encouraged to protect and invest in their natural assets to insure a reliable and productive supply of resources. Farmers certainly have a financial interest in using technologies and methods that encourage the long-term vitality of their lands. Yet, some concerns do emerge. Most notably, certain practices that yield greater harvests might have undesired consequences not captured by any emissions levy. Once they have harvested the natural growth, many woodland owners have replaced their woodlands with plantation forestry. In replanting the land with fast-growing softwood trees, the owners have selected species that will generate increased future yields. Yet, these homogenous forests will lead to a decline in many of the life-support and cultural services discussed in Chapter

Two. Uniform food and habitats will undoubtedly reduce the biodiversity of the wildlife community and thereby lead to a reduction in some ecological functions. An emissions levy will mitigate the use of chemicals that may harm neighboring areas. However, just as we saw in the prior chapter, the multifaceted functions of a given property mean that multiple challenges can occur. We cannot expect a single policy to meet all of the challenges equally effectively.

Despite these concerns, it does seem that the implementation of extensive emissions levies will encourage generally prudent use of our provisioning services. Markets will function so that the prices of resources reflect their full cost, including all production and distribution, as well as any environmental costs. Higher costs will yield higher prices that will dampen consumption rates. Nonetheless, we must consider two remaining practices that cause prices to diverge from their full cost. I turn to these issues now.

Resource auctions

To attain full-cost pricing, all commercial resources and services provided by the use of public lands should be subject to a resource auction that prevents the emergence of "sweetheart" deals that underprice their true value. This includes all lumber sales on federal and state lands as well as any mining operation that takes place on public lands. It also includes the leasing of government lands for grazing and other commercial activities. In each case, specific resource auctions should function to capture the fair market value of each of these products and services. With these auctions implemented, firms will face increased economic incentives to recycle and reuse materials to mitigate the burden of higher prices.

To insure a sustainable supply of material resources, public officials must determine the sustainable yield of each resource, or the amount that can be continuously provided through time. Though determining these amounts is rarely easy, one can derive rough estimates, particularly given Daly's guidelines previously mentioned. Regarding renewable resources, the harvesting rate from public lands should not exceed the replenishing rates occurring on those lands.[18] Using ecological models and field studies, public officials can refine these harvesting rates over time.[19] Assessing the sustainable yield is much more challenging, given the variety of factors that can affect its estimation. For example, new discoveries of mineral deposits along with more effective extraction technologies could substantially alter the sustainable yield. Further, new technologies in creating renewable substitutes would also alter the calculations. Despite these challenges, implementing resource auctions of mineral deposits on public lands would reduce the current depletion rates and encourage a variety of behaviors that would limit our dependence on quickly depleting resources.

Mineral depletion allowances

Given current property laws, resource auctions could feasibly occur only on public lands where government officials have clear title to the material resources that are harvested from these lands. Mining, farming, grazing, and lumbering that occur on private lands are exempt from these policies. Yet, the government still has wide influence on private lands and can exert a substantial impact on their use and harvesting rates. In particular, the government can undo policies that have long outlived their day and that encourage behaviors that are now clearly against the public interest.

Lawmakers should end favorable tax laws that encourage contemporary mining of natural resources. To ease the transition on current mining operations and local communities, the elimination of these tax credit and depletion allowances could occur over a decade. With their removal, the prices of newly mined minerals would slowly rise to their full-cost price. As these materials rise to their full-cost price, new efforts to curb their consumption will be encouraged as businesses look toward recycled sources and new, less scarce substitute products.

Conclusion

Each of the policy tools mentioned above offers us ways to restructure our economy to implement both the polluter-pays principle and the principle of full-cost pricing. With these changes, markets will offer more accurate signals based on the actual costs and benefits of specific behaviors. Certain decisions, previously made without thoughtl by households or businesses, will now involve accountability and responsibility. Just as we now shop for the products and services that best meet our needs, we will increasingly consider our actions as they affect the environment. As consumers, we will seek the real bargains, those products that meet our needs with the least harm to our pocketbooks and to the environment. Businesses will use the full range of their technological and commercial acumen to find new markets and opportunities for products they once considered "waste." Failing this, they will engineer new processes and adopt new practices to minimize the increasing costs of disposing of unwanted products. In this way, we will encourage and support the practices that have emerged in Kalundborg.

Once implemented, each of the policy tools will cause a cascade of changes throughout the economy. Imposing disposal costs upon households will encourage new choices and behaviors as householders seek to reduce their impact. Shoppers will view alternative products differently as they consider not only price but also any disposal costs. Shifting customer preferences will cause manufacturers to reconsider their product line as they revisit ways to capture larger market shares. Ultimately, each of these decisions will affect those businesses that provide the provisioning materials needed to make the product. Some primary producers will lose substantial portions of their market while less harmful substitutes garner increased sales. At each stage of excavation, manufacturing, and merchandising, businesses will rethink their materials use, production processes, chosen technology, and business strategies, as they scramble to respond to new circumstances.

The likely changes are myriad and not always anticipated. Moreover, the adjustments to a Kalundborg-style economy will not be easy, no matter how pleasant

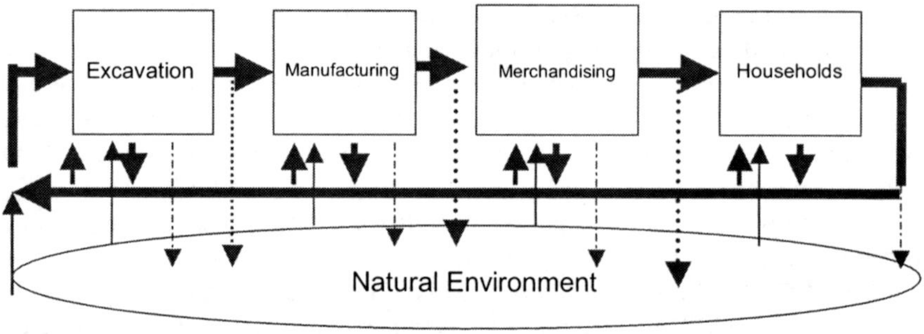

Figure 7.2 Post-policy relationships.

the result appears. The likely changes will severely disrupt some industries and challenge some regions of the country. By phasing in these policies, we can ameliorate some of the transitional pain. Public officials can implement emissions taxes and emissions permits slowly, to provide households and businesses time to adjust to the new circumstances. The earlier these policies are implemented the more time we have in phasing them, thereby easing the transitional difficulties. Procrastination can defer the pain, but it will neither reduce nor prevent it.

No doubt, other localities will make decisions similar to those made in Kalundborg, even if none of these recommended policies is implemented. The specific circumstances that gave rise to the changes witnessed in Kalundborg do exist elsewhere and they will likely lead to similar results. Pressures on our natural systems will create conditions that will foster such changes in different places, regardless of whether we act or not. Yet, implementing the polices just discussed will foster the kinds of decisions taken in Kalundborg and insure their replication. In placing values on the use of the natural environment, we will reward behaviors that minimize their harm and encourage decisions that are benign or even benevolent. Taking these steps will encourage changes in our economy in which the key materials provided by nature's provisioning services will be part of a cycle rather than a one-way path from farm to landfill. As Figure 7.2 shows, much more of the "stuff" that comprises our economy will be reused and recycled, limiting our further depletion of new sources and the harm that our wastes inflict. In the next chapter, we turn to the related issue of energy policies.

Further reading

Herman Daly, 'The Steady State Economy: Towards a Political Economy of Biophysical Equilibrium and Moral Growth', examines many of the issues raised in this chapter using a broader, more conceptual framework.

John Ehrenfeld and Nicholas Gertler, 'Industrial Ecology in Practice: The Evolution of Interdependence at Kalundborg', offer a more extensive examination of the Kalundborg network and its place in industrial ecology.

W. McDonough and M. Braungart, *Cradle to Cradle: Remaking the Way We Make Things*, discuss the many benefits and challenges of creating industrial systems that truly recycle materials as found in the natural world.

Thomas Sterner, *Policy Instruments for Environmental and Natural Resource Management*, provides an excellent discussion of the range of policy options, including marketable emissions permits and emissions taxes.

8 Shifting back to renewable energy sources

Throughout history, gold and silver have held a special attraction. In recent centuries, the discoveries have lured waves of immigrants to cross formidable oceans and daunting continents to stake claims. Regions, previously remote and thinly populated, have experienced extensive settlement and development. Towns have sprung up as businesses emerged to meet the needs of newcomers. Native peoples found in the way were killed or forcibly removed in fits of genocide. Rich veins of ore fueled new commerce as prospectors gained the financial means to satiate expanding appetites. Coined into currency, the mined ores provided needed credit and fostered commerce.[1] To follow the veins deep underground, miners developed new methods of excavation and encouraged new industry. The immense natural wealth brought great prosperity and eventually respectability to some and funded great cities like San Francisco. It brought new wealth to governments, which could then spend it on needed improvements in roads and infrastructure. Far beyond its mining operations, the gold and silver stimulated human energy and economic vitality like few other sources.

That certainly is the story of the Comstock Lode of Nevada. The discovery of gold in 1859 marked what is arguably the richest find in North America. Virtually overnight, waves of prospectors seeking their fortune transformed the remote and sleepy community of Virginia City. During its heyday in the 1870s, Virginia City counted nearly 25,000 residents, making it one of the largest cities west of the Mississippi.[2] A multitude of bars, brothels, and dry goods stores emerged to serve the hordes of miners searching for their fortune. All told, estimates place the value of gold and silver found in the area in excess of $400 million. Beyond being a magnet to new immigrants and entrepreneurs, the discovery sped the inclusion of Nevada as a state in 1864 as President Lincoln sought new funds to finance the Civil War.

From the beginning, this discovery was an unusual one. The bluish clay soil clogged the machinery, thereby thwarting early efforts to extract gold nuggets. Working on a hunch, one miner scooped up some clay and took it to a nearby assessor's office; it contained an astonishing amount of finely ground silver and gold ores. Despite its richness, this find was no friend of the common prospector. At claim after claim, miners realized that the richest veins were deep underground, requiring a vast outlay of capital, machinery, and time. Unlike the California strike, this discovery would prove to be a "corporate" bonanza – one beyond the capabilities of the typical prospector. Yet, that fact brought benefits to Virginia City. Between the richness of the mineral deposits and the engineering challenges posed to those trying to extract them, Virginia City became a veritable industrial center as foundries, machine shops, and carpentry yards blossomed.

The wealth and technical expertise that flowed through Virginia City gave it a sophistication unrivaled in the other mining towns dotting the west. Considered the most important city between Denver and San Francisco, its opera house welcomed the major performers of the day, including Edwin Booth. Its six-story hotel had the first "rising room" or elevator in the west. Initially attracted to the mines, one immigrant quickly signed on with the local newspaper and began his illustrious writing career under the pseudonym Mark Twain. At its height, Virginia City had twenty music halls and theaters and supported Shakespearean plays. Undoubtedly, few observers during its heyday could have accurately foretold what was in store for Virginia City.

Despite its fabulous wealth, the Comstock Lode was finite and began to fade during the 1880s. As one mine after another closed down, the town slowly declined and shuttered. By 1900, fewer than 4,000 residents lived in the county and thirty years later, the number had fallen below 1,000. Like many communities across the west, Virginia City was well on its way to becoming a ghost town. All that remained were the moribund buildings that corroborated fading memories of an illustrious past. During the town's decline, residents and city boosters likely suggested new directions in order to stem the town's fall and regain its past prosperity. However, nothing quite worked and the area continued to lose residents and opportunities. The source of its economic vitality, though dazzling in its abundance and wealth, was temporary. As such, Virginia City offers a powerful lesson to other communities that anchor their economies on sources of wealth with short lifespans. Moreover, given the role of energy as the wellspring of wealth in our modern industrial economy, we also should consider the lessons that Virginia City holds for our economy.

Curbing our addiction

In a moment of candor, President George W. Bush confided to the nation in his 2006 State of the Union Address that "we have a serious problem: America is addicted to oil, which is often imported from unstable parts of the world."[3] Coming from a Texas oilman, this admission on the national stage should have signaled a turning point in our public policies. Unfortunately, President Bush understated the gravity of the problem in a variety of ways. Our addiction is not simply to oil, but also to other non-renewable fossil fuels including coal and natural gas. In addition, our difficulties go beyond securing reliable energy supplies. Among other problems, our overwhelming and unrelenting reliance upon fossil fuels contributes to the threat of climate change. Further, the President suggested that we simply needed to fund and adopt new technologies to wean ourselves from this addiction. He listed a number of projects that he predicted would reduce our imported oil from the Middle East by 75 percent in 2025.[4] None of these policies suggested a whiff of pain or sacrifice, usually necessary in behavioral changes required to end an addiction. Nonetheless, President Bush should receive credit for raising the issue.

There exists ample evidence of our addiction. Though Americans constitute about 5 percent of world's population, we consume 21 percent of its commercial energy.[5] On a per capita basis, we guzzle energy at a rate that is largely unmatched around the world. Among other industrialized nations, only in the colder climates of Canada, Iceland, Norway and Luxembourg do their citizens consume more energy per capita than do Americans.[6] To be sure, our economy is becoming more energy efficient; we have halved the energy requirements per dollar of GDP produced since the 1970s. Nonetheless, industrial rivals like Japan, Germany, and the United Kingdom use between 20 to 50 percent less energy per dollar of GDP than we do. Not only does this make them more energy efficient, but it also insulates them better from price shocks.

We consume lots of energy and most of it is from non-renewable sources. Currently, over 80 percent of our energy comes from fossil fuels, while another 8 percent comes from nuclear power.[7] Renewable energy sources account for only 7 percent of our energy needs.[8] Energy forecasts predict that these figures will not change much over the next two decades. Under the Energy Information Adminstration (EIA) Reference Case,[9] our energy needs are expected to grow by 10 percent by 2030; to meet this growing demand, our dependence on fossil fuels will remain largely unchanged.[10] The EIA forecast predicts that nuclear energy's share will remain at 8 percent, while alternative sources will rise only to 10 per cent. Perhaps, we can take some solace from the fact that the rest of world, collectively, is even more dependent on non-renewable sources. According to EIA estimates, nearly 86 percent of the world's current commercial energy requirements come from fossil fuels while less than 8 percent are from renewable sources.[11] Yet, this only compounds the risks to our economy. Substantial dependence on energy to fuel our way of life, along with reliance upon non-renewables from unreliable sources, makes our problem of addiction unique around the world. More than other countries, we have built our economy and way of life on precarious ground.

As with any addiction, changing our behaviors and weaning ourselves from a fossil fuel-based economy will be neither easy nor pleasant. Given the pivotal role that petroleum plays in our economy, curtailing its use will be both slow and painful. The cure for this addiction is rather clear and straightforward. Indeed, the sooner we act to reduce our need for fossil fuels, the longer we can make the adjustment period. Our inability to confront effectively this addiction is more a problem of will than of imagination. In addition, I suspect, like the elimination of most addictive behaviors and bad habits, the result will yield some surprising and unintended benefits.

Reducing our dependence on non-renewable energy sources will require reforming and strengthening our nation's energy markets. Since energy sources fall into the category of provisioning services, most of the discussion in the prior chapter will apply here as well. As provisioning services, our energy resources lend themselves well to market institutions that can function effectively. Thus, we should encourage energy markets that meet both the polluter-pays principle and the principle of full-cost pricing. However, since energy is unique within both the natural and policymaking worlds, the solutions must reflect its distinctive place. As such, the strategy for weaning ourselves off non-renewable energy sources should focus around three fronts. First, we need to eliminate all tax subsidies that encourage the exploration, extraction, or refining of non-renewable energy sources. Second, we must examine and end remaining infrastructure subsidies that benefit non-renewable sources. Third, we must add specific emissions levies to internalize any external costs that arise from the use of these sources. Taken collectively, these measures should ensure a level playing field among the various energy options. Further, these policies will provide financial incentives that will generate a cascade of economic decisions and behaviors that will, in turn, end our current addiction. In addition to the pain and higher prices, these policies will simultaneously create new opportunities and rewards.

Relying on market incentives offers us a powerful and effective method for changing individual and organizational behaviors. Yet, this change does not come without costs or challenges. Increasing reliance upon market incentives forces us to consider the *distributional* impact of these changes on different individuals and sectors of the economy. We must consider these impacts particularly in light of the substantial and growing disparities that currently exist, whether one considers income or wealth. At minimum, we should offset any increase in economic disparities that these policies may create. Beyond that, we should frankly discuss the merits and challenges that such disparities create for our communities and our economy.

Entering the energy subsidy thicket

Given the importance of harnessing cheap and reliable energy sources for our modern economy, the federal government has enacted a variety of public policies to foster new energy supplies. As a result, the oil, natural gas, coal, and nuclear industries receive government help, tax credits, and preferential treatment, all aimed at providing cheap and abundant energy. Whether this assistance takes the form of cash payments that increase company income, preferential tax treatment that lowers corporate tax payments, or federal regulations that effectively lower business costs, the result is lowered production costs and cheaper energy. Discounted energy prices from non-renewable sources encourage their consumption at the expense of less- subsidized renewables. Ignoring the issue of whether these policies ever made sense, little justification exists for continuing them today. Not only do they encourage the depletion of dwindling energy resources, but they compound other problems as well. Policies that encourage the use of fossil fuels, particularly coal, only add to the alarming problem of global climate change. They undermine national security, as they encourage dependence on foreign oil and gas sources that are located in politically volatile areas of the world. In addition, subsidies to the nuclear power industry encourage the creation of dangerous and long-lived wastes that are still without a permanently secure storage site.

Given the variety of ways that public policies benefit and shelter these industries, measuring the importance and value of these subsidies can be extremely challenging. However, this is not always the case. A recent Department of Energy study assessed federal support of energy by examining federal programs that offered direct cash payment, specifically designed tax reduction, or targeted funding for research and development. The study estimated the value of federal subsidies supporting energy as exceeding $16 billion in 2007 – a doubling of the largesse provided in 1999.[12] According to the authors, nearly one-fourth of this amount in 2007 funded energy conservation or energy research and development (R&D); however, most of the remaining support targeted energy production, particularly non-renewable energy sources. Approximately $12 billion annually supports the extraction, production, and consumption of our non-renewable energy sources.

Other studies have considered a more expansive understanding of benefits and subsidies. A 1992 study conducted by Douglas Koplow for the Alliance to Save Energy calculated a range of estimates of energy subsidies, from a low figure of $27 billion to a high figure of $46 billion annually.[13] He included a larger number of federal programs, taking in specific subsidies to housing and transportation sectors that had direct impacts on energy use. As his estimates were for 1989, his figures include about $12 billion in tax reductions for programs that have ended under the Tax Reform Act of 1986.[14] Yet, even subtracting this amount, Koplow's lower estimate attaches a markedly greater value to these subsidies, particularly adjusted for inflation. In another study, Wahl argues that subsidies to the petroleum industry alone could be valued as high as $87 billion annually, when one considers indirect subsidies.[15] He reasons that dependence on petroleum requires a defense-related presence in the Persian Gulf to stabilize crude oil markets; this represents an unrealized expense of $52 billion annually that benefits the industry.[16] He estimates that the industry is shielded from an additional $31 billion of external environmental health costs resulting from air pollution. Though these specific figures are subject to intense debate, they suggest some of the external costs that energy producers are not required to bear, therefore indicating significant ways in which current energy prices do not fully reflect their true cost.

Leveling the playing field (1): eliminating current subsidies to non-renewables

Despite the complexities and controversies over how much current policies subsidize energy markets, we can make significant headway in leveling the playing field among the various energy sources by eliminating several key programs. Regarding programs that unduly encourage the exploration and extraction of fossil fuels, perhaps the worst offender is the Alternative Fuel Production Credit. Initiated during the Carter Administration as a way of encouraging "alternative" fuels, this tax credit has largely benefited the natural gas industry. In particular, this program has encouraged drilling for natural gas in coal seams, tight sands, and shale oil, as well as drilling for coal bed methane, as each is defined as "alternative energy." In many cases, the tax credit has encouraged drilling that otherwise would not be economical. In 2007, the credit was worth over $2.3 billion dollars. Though the tax credit is scheduled to expire in 2009, it has been renewed several times in its lifetime.[17]

Two other tax breaks directly encourage the exploration and drilling for oil. First, oil drillers get preferential tax treatment as they can quickly write off exploration and site development costs. While most businesses must amortize capital equipment costs over the effective life of the equipment, oil companies can deduct these costs much more quickly against current income. For example, large oil companies can deduct 70 percent of exploration and development costs in the first year of operations and then expense the remaining 30 percent over the next five years. Smaller oil drilling companies can deduct 100 percent of their expenses in the first year. Although the oil drillers must eventually pay their income taxes, this provision of Expensing Exploration and Development Costs allows them to defer payments, and thereby encourages further exploration and quicker depletion of gas and oil reserves. As this tax deferment is available only to new exploration, its significance is somewhat limited in scope.

A more generous and widely available tax provision is the Excess of Percentage Over Cost of Depletion. Not only can owners of oil and gas wells rapidly write off exploration and development costs, but they also can write off depletion of their mineral wealth by deducting the diminishing value of their mineral assets against their current income. Annually, these owners can take a set percentage of their gross revenues (10 percent for coal, 15 percent for gas and oil, and 25 percent for nuclear), and deduct this amount from their taxable income. True, all businesses can expect to deduct any "depreciation" of their productive assets against their income; this is a cornerstone of current tax policy. However, the value of these mineral assets is not the result of sweat and personal investment, but rather the bounty of nature. As such, this preferential treatment enables the owners to capture tax benefits that are unrelated to any developmental costs. Even worse, the more rapidly owners deplete the mineral resource, the more quickly they receive the tax benefits. In this way, the American taxpayer is subsidizing faster depletion of energy assets; in 2007, the subsidy was valued at nearly $800 million for the year.[18]

Though the percentage depletion allowance benefits the nuclear power industry, this industry's most generous source of benefits stems from the Price Anderson Act. Enacted in 1957 during the birth of the commercial nuclear power industry, this law limits the total amount of damages that any nuclear plant operator is liable for in the event of an accident. Initially capped at $560 million, the ceiling has risen several times to its current cap of $9.26 billion.[19] Given the proximity of many reactors to adjacent metropolitan areas, most experts believe that the damages would likely be far higher. In limiting the operator liability, the Act limits the cost of insurance that every nuclear plant operator needs in order to operate. Two different studies have estimated that this provision saves each power plant operator between $2.32 million and $21.72 million in 1985 dollars.[20] When adjusted to 2007 dollars, the liability cap could save the nuclear power producers somewhere between $400 million to $3.9 billion per year.[21] The analyses that generated these estimates are somewhat dated, but one would expect the savings to be higher today given the increased insurance rates and rising real estate prices. While it is quite likely that this liability cap was necessary for the development of the commercial nuclear power industry during its infancy, that argument rings hollow today. Phasing out this liability protection would place nuclear power on a more level competitive playing field with other energy alternatives to fossil fuels.

These four policies form the most visible tip of the subsidy iceberg; many other policies promote conventional energy sources in less direct ways. For example, governments at all levels provide facilities and promote services that encourage private car transportation. Communities offer subsidized parking, whether in parking garages or on-street spaces, to encourage car drivers to patronize downtown businesses. Governments have constructed a vast network of roads, highways, and interstate freeways to accommodate the private automobile and commercial truck. While gasoline taxes and other fees finance a substantial portion of the current road construction and maintenance costs, one study suggests that 40% of our current road building and related services come from other revenue sources.[22] Simply requiring that all road building and maintenance costs come from dedicated funds generated by gasoline taxes and other transportation-related user fees would eliminate this subsidy. Doing so at the federal level would add approximately 22 cents per gallon of gasoline to the current federal gas tax.[23] State and local contributions to road construction and maintenance should come from similar funds, too. As well, governments subsidize the air transport industry through public funding of airports and air safety programs that relieve the private airlines and air traveler from a major source of costs. In some cases, public support is largely an unintentional consequence.[24] At each level of government, public policies need review to consider how they unduly encourage the use of non-renewable fuels, either directly or indirectly.

By ending certain subsidies, we can solve several problems simultaneously. Elimination will reduce current depletion rates as prices rise to reflect the full cost of supplying these energy sources. Reduced consumption of fossil fuels will curb greenhouse gas emissions as we take more seriously the threat of climate change. Higher prices for conventional fuels will encourage increased investment in renewable sources and energy-saving technologies, as energy customers look for ways to cut their energy bills. Lastly, the elimination of the tax subsidies will swell federal revenues. Such proceeds can provide tax relief to households and businesses coping with higher energy bills.

Leveling the playing field (2): internalizing the externalities

Though their impacts are quite different, using fossil and nuclear fuels create significant environmental harm. Burning fossil fuels not only contributes to climate change, but also adds significantly to urban smog, atmospheric particulates, and toxic gases like nitrogen and sulfuric oxides. These effluents harm human health, especially as they exacerbate respiratory diseases and damage nearby agricultural yields, causing decreased profits for growers. As we foul the air in our cities, more and more residents move to the suburbs to find less polluted environs. This demographic shift has led to longer commutes, increased road congestion, and greater need for electrical generation capacity, all further polluting the air. Fuels with high sulfur content generate highly acidic emissions that accumulate in lakes and ponds, harming wildlife in these aquatic habitats. Acidic emissions harm buildings and homes, such that they require more frequent repainting and other maintenance. The damages caused by our heavy reliance on fossil fuels are complex, varied, and widespread. For the most part, they are costs that neither the fuel provider nor the fuel user is required to pay.

Many energy experts hail nuclear power as the key to solving our energy dilemma, as it generates negligible air emissions, particularly climate-changing gases. Nonetheless, it is an overstatement to claim it as a "clean" alternative to fossil fuels. The excavation, processing, transportation, and burning of nuclear materials create waste storage and disposal problems of monumental proportions. Each year, the industry creates thousands of barrels of low-level and high-level radioactive liquid wastes as well as hundreds of tons of spent fuel. The industry generates additional waste from all the equipment exposed to radioactive materials. Due to the high toxicity of contaminated materials, they must be isolated from most forms of life for decades or centuries, to prevent tragic results. Even fifty years after the start of the commercial nuclear industry, we do not have a satisfactory waste-disposal plan. While many argue that Yucca Mountain in Nevada will provide this site, we still must hurdle many scientific, political, and economic obstacles blocking its operation. Even then, the backlog of wastes would quickly exhaust Yucca's storage capacity. Further, the horrific consequences of any nuclear accident could operate as a magnet to any terrorist group with designs for attention and impact. Only through a heavy layer of spending on intelligence, security, and vigilance can we even begin to hope to avoid such a calamity. Many of these costs and their underlying risks are borne by the public and not by the producers and users of nuclear-generated electricity.

Applying the polluter-pays principle to eliminate these external costs is a complex and challenging venture. Computing some of these costs is relatively easy; others defy simple or unassailable assessment. We must develop better methods in evaluating these costs. Yet, action on internalizing these costs cannot wait universal acceptance of the estimated harm. Instead, we should enact policies where the principle is clearly applicable. For example, a tax on nuclear power should fully cover the cost of nuclear waste storage, so that the users of these services directly pay for them. This step requires little more than political will. In cases where the costs are more nebulous, we should nonetheless implement policies that internalize these costs, even in approximate terms. As better estimates are developed, we can modify the policies accordingly.

A carbon tax

Although there are several ways to internalize the emissions costs of burning fossil fuels, I recommend the introduction of a "carbon tax."[25] Under this scheme, each fuel would be taxed on the amount of carbon dioxide it generates; thus, the tax internalizes the external costs that are specific to burning fossil fuels. In addition, as the carbon content of different fuels varies, the tax selectively discourages each fuel differently. Coal has the highest carbon content, followed by petroleum, and lastly natural gas.[26] Since coal has nearly twice the carbon content as compared to natural gas, it would receive nearly twice the tax burden. Not only would the tax discourage the use of fossil fuels, but it would also affect the choice among these fuels. One very important problem with this tax would be its impact on those communities that are particularly dependent upon coal as an employment or energy source. However, as will be subsequently discussed, this problem is solvable by using some of the tax revenues to offset the harm.

Given the central role of energy in our industrial and urban economy, it would be important to phase in any such tax slowly and incrementally. Throughout the economy, energy purchases take a significant portion of any budget, whether household, business, or governmental agency. Significant increases in energy bills would threaten low-income households and preclude spending on non-energy products and services, thereby threatening businesses and employment. Further, many energy choices are the result of past investment decisions that were made under different energy circumstances. Families buy cars and purchase homes, businesses build offices and expand workplaces, and governments construct schools and offices, with some future price of energy in mind. Many made these decisions with the expectation that energy prices would remain low. Yet, these investments frequently offer poor choices when energy prices do rise. To mitigate these inevitable challenges, the tax increase should be predictable and incremental. In this way, families, businesses, and government agencies could absorb rising energy bills more easily. More significantly, they could plan longer-term investments with the expectation that energy prices would rise in the future.

One carbon tax proposal would initiate at $5 per ton of carbon that would subsequently be raised annually over an eight-year period. According to estimates, such a levy would modestly impact on gasoline, heating oil and natural gas prices, while having a more substantial impact on coal. The estimates of the annual levy are given in Table 8.1.[27] As the figures suggest, the annual tax would raise natural gas, gasoline, and home heating oil prices by amounts that are far less than the price swings experienced by each of these energy sources in recent years. Still, these increases would injure low-income households. Only coal, with its extremely high carbon content, would suffer significantly from the levy, causing electricity rates to rise substantially as well. Areas of the country that rely significantly on

Table 8.1 Impact of a $5/ton carbon tax on selected fuels

Fuel source	*Price increase*	*Percentage increase*
Bituminous coal ($/ton)	$11.19	21.7%
Gasoline ($/gallon)	$0.05	1.7%
Heating oil ($/gallon)	$0.06	2.3%
Natural gas ($/mcf)	$0.27	2.9%

coal as their primary source of electrical generation would experience even greater price increases. Nonetheless, phasing in this tax could make the adjustments much more manageable.

The benefits of this phased tax increase are many. Assured of price hikes to come, households, businesses, and governments could make decisions now to weather higher prices in the future. Families could purchase more fuel-efficient cars and energy-efficient appliances and even move to neighborhoods closer to their workplace. Businesses and government agencies could invest in energy-efficient equipment and patronize local suppliers to limit transportation costs; they could also modify their operations, networks, and energy requirements. Government agencies could help communities by encouraging more energy-efficient construction, fostering public and alternative transportation, and assisting the development of new start-up businesses. Higher energy prices would encourage appliance manufactures to seek energy savings from new designs and materials. Consumers would give increasing attention to the operating or energy costs of a given appliance, not simply its purchase price. Higher energy prices would not only encourage energy consumers to conserve, but would also foster further development of alternative sources, particularly wind and solar power. Given the huge potential of this market, the financial incentives to any company that could offer economical power using alternative and renewable sources would be substantial. Further, the expectation of higher conventional energy prices would reduce the risk of investing in new and alternative technologies. Increased spending on new technologies and designs would generate new jobs and business opportunities. Rather than sending our energy dollars to oil producers around the world, our spending would support local businesses and workers. Lastly, the steady tax increases on fossil fuels would reduce the latter's contribution to our climate-change problem. Though these substantial changes offer substantial challenges, they also offer new opportunities as we reduce our dependence on non-renewables and transition toward more sustainable energy sources.

The carbon tax would be relatively easy to implement and administer. Rather than meter the carbon emissions as they leave tailpipes and smokestacks, it makes much more sense to tax it "upstream" on those businesses that either import fuels or extract them domestically. Since there are about 2,000 businesses that provide our fossil fuels, focusing the tax at this level minimizes collection and administration costs, while assuring equal treatment of both domestic and foreign sources. To offset the tax burden, firms would pass along to customers as much of the tax increase as they could, thereby causing fossil fuels to rise in price. In this way, industry and the final consumer would share the tax burden. Interestingly, states have the authority to impose such a tax in the absence of any federal action or even in addition to it; some states are expressing interest in this tax idea.

Redressing distributional impacts

Eliminating public subsidies and implementing a carbon tax would redress the distortions that currently favor conventional, non-renewable energy sources.

Encouraging energy prices that reflect the principle of full-cost pricing would offer many benefits. However, these changes would generate substantial pain as households and businesses confronted some difficult choices. Adjusting the burden of a new energy regime would be neither easy nor equally shared. Some groups, including low-income households, coal-based and energy-intensive businesses, and some energy-reliant public agencies would suffer disproportionate harm from higher energy prices. Our energy policy should consider these groups and communities and offer specific remedies.

Implementing these policies would yield a substantial financial windfall to government, particularly the federal government. According to one study, the $5 per ton levy imposed would raise $8 billion in the first year and $75 billion annually, once the full levy of $40 per ton was attained.[28] Those revenues would fall to the federal government. Increasing federal and state gas taxes to fund fully all road building and maintenance projects would bring billions more annually. Ending tax subsidies on fossil fuels would generate further savings, mostly to the federal government. For the most part, this financial boon would be unaccompanied by specific mandates for new expenditures.[29] Given the projected federal budget deficits, it is reasonable to expect that a sizeable portion of this windfall would go toward reducing these deficits. Nonetheless, some portion should provide general and targeted tax relief to offset the burdens of these proposals.

Some needed assistance would come automatically. For example, rising energy prices would trigger increases in annual cost-of-living adjustments (COLAs) added to Social Security payments, thereby cushioning many retirees from their worst impact. Yet, some Social Security retirees as well as other low-income households would need additional help. The Low Income Heating Assistance Program (LHEAP) currently offers direct grants toward home heating to those households that demonstrate need. Even today, this program lacks sufficient funding to ensure that all who are entitled to benefits actually receive them. In 2005, only 15 percent of eligible households actually collected LHEAP benefits.[30] Fully funding this program to meet current and anticipated needs could offset the worst harm wrought by higher energy prices. Further, changes in the tax code could offer more generalized assistance. Increasing the Earned Income Tax Credit could assist the working poor as they struggle with the impact of higher energy and gas prices. Raising the income threshold for eligibility for this tax credit would aid additional households with modest incomes. Lastly, general tax relief for all households and businesses could help these groups to survive the challenges of higher energy bills. These changes would need to anticipate the carbon tax increases. Since these programs would offer financial assistance without lowering energy prices that households and businesses had to pay, they would not undermine the financial incentives of higher energy prices. Yet, adequate assistance should prevent circumstances that might lead to draconian choices, such as between heating homes and getting adequate medical treatment.

Providing this assistance should require only a portion of the revenues likely raised by the carbon tax and subsidy cuts. Some of the remaining funds should assist those businesses and communities disproportionately harmed by the energy transition. As the carbon tax would adversely affect businesses and communities that are deeply dependent on coal, they deserve particular assistance. Communities in coal-rich Appalachia as well as in many western states should receive funds to assist in economic redevelopment as well as job training and relocating costs. Surely, the shift in energy prices would affect many other business and communities. Just as the Trade Adjustment Assistance Program attempts to assist individuals and businesses affected by shifts in global trade, so new funds could assist businesses and communities that show hardship due to these policies. Additional income tax relief and increased employment credits could mitigate the burden of higher energy prices and encourage increased employment and business development.

Lastly, some of the new revenues should fund local efforts that make infrastructure investments in energy efficiency. For example, many communities have weatherization programs in which they offer grants and subsidized loans to homeowners and renters who live in poorly insulated structures. Rental housing, in particular, can suffer from poor market incentives. Renters who might benefit from lower energy bills usually do not have adequate incentives to make substantial improvements. While property owners ultimately benefit from any building improvements, they may not see the immediate financial benefits of doing so. Local programs could encourage investment in home weatherization that lowers energy bills and improves the local housing stock. Already the LHEAP program offers weatherization grants; additional funding could simply be added to current levels. Further, federal grants could support local communities that invest in alternative transportation systems, whether better public transportation, new bike lanes, or pedestrian-friendly improvements. By assisting communities in fostering alternative transportation, tax dollars could help to provide more choices for individuals, households, and businesses in avoiding higher energy prices.

Virginia City's new "bonanza"

The vast and rich veins of silver and gold found beneath its ground gave Virginia City an unrivaled bonanza lasting over twenty-five years. Even this largesse of nature reached its limits. Once a glittering and frenetic magnet, Virginia City slowly lost its energy, luster, and attraction. For most of the twentieth century, the population of Storey County hovered around 1,000 souls. Only the persistent mining of the vastly depleted ores kept Virginia City from becoming another ghost town. Even with modern technology, efforts to capture the natural bounty did not bring a return of the town's past prosperity and rarely generated profits for the mine owners themselves. In recent decades, the city's fortunes have improved, largely to the realization of a new "bonanza" – one from an unexpected quarter. In the 1960s, the hit TV series *Bonanza* featured Virginia City. It mattered little that the show portrayed the city as a hub of ranching rather than as a mining town. Drawing upon this unlikely publicity, the city slowly transformed itself into a significant tourist destination. As it grew in popularity, local investors refurbished more buildings and added new facilities and services.[31] Today, two million tourists visit Virginia City annually and the county's population has reached 4,000.

Virginia City today has a steadier, if less spectacular, economy. As its economic base, tourism provides the residents of Storey County with a more reliable and potentially renewable source of employment, income, and opportunities. That is, as long as people are fascinated with the Wild West and connect that fascination to Virginia City. No doubt, city officials and business interests must continue to foster and adapt as each new generation of tourists brings new expectations as to what is attractive entertainment. Yet, the current boom already has surpassed the length of the first bonanza that brought fame and prosperity to this city nearly 150 years ago.

Throughout the mountains of the west, ghost towns serve as reminders of what happens when local communities base their economies on mining, a depletable resource. They also provide us with a warning today as we continue to base our modern economy on non-renewable fossil fuels. Any parallel between the temporary prosperity of Virginia City during its boom years and our current prosperity may be illusionary. Unlike nineteenth-century Virginia City, we may find a substitute energy source that fully replaces our diminishing non-renewable sources. While different energy sources have their advocates, none of the alternatives is without significant liability. Just as most of us give little thought to what will happen as our oil and natural gas reserves reveal their limits, I suspect that most citizens of Virginia City during its golden era gave little thought to what would happen when the ores ran out.

Whatever future we face by continuing down our current energy path, it certainly will lead to significant disruptions and challenges. The world's insatiable appetite for fossil fuels will generate supply disruptions and oil prices that will pierce the $200 per barrel figure – something unthinkable until recently. Even if we discover new energy sources to offset the dwindling reserves of fossil fuels, we face problems on the emissions side. Our continually rising use of fossil fuels will exacerbate climate changes that will buffet and in some cases stimulate our communities and economies. Little will be "business as usual" as each region will need to adapt to the changing circumstances. New patterns of drought, flooding, hotter temperatures, rising sea levels and more violent weather systems will all impose significant costs. By taking the commonsense steps outlined in this chapter, we can forestall or mitigate some of the changes and disturbances that we will otherwise experience. By implementing these steps sooner rather than later, we can use markets and their capacity to adapt to changing circumstances more fully. I turn to this issue in the next chapter.

Further reading

Energy Information Administration, *Federal Financial Interventions and Subsidies in Energy Markets 2007*, gives a detailed analysis of the current energy programs and their support of different energy sources.

Ronald James, *The Roar and the Silence: A History of Virginia City and the Comstock Lode*, offers a comprehensive history of the area.

N. Myers and J. Kent, *Perverse Subsidies: How Tax Dollars Can Undercut the Environment and the Economy*, discuss the range of current government subsidies and the various ways they impair both the environment and the economy.

9 Economic succession

Evolving systems

Thirty minutes drive from my home, a golf course sat adjacent to the interstate highway that I regularly travel. Several fairways ran along the highway, permitting me to briefly observe play as I sped by. A decade ago, unfavorable economic circumstances closed the course. The regular mowing, watering, and fertilizing needed to maintain the course stopped. Without human doting, the verdant fairways and manicured greens disappeared, long since turned to hues of brown. In the absence of human resistance, the forces of nature are reasserting themselves upon the landscape. Even just a few years removed, few vestiges of the golf course remain. Out of familiarity, I can still see the rough outlines of the old fairways along with the distinctive "yardage marker" trees and bunkers surrounding the disappeared greens. As nature has reclaimed this land, few others would likely recognize its past existence without help.

The fairways were the first areas to disclose the golf course's demise. The foliage grew to its natural, unkempt height as native grasses, wildflowers, and shrubs previously cut low thrived without threat. They quickly replaced the hybrid grasses developed specially for their color and resiliency to duffers and golf carts. Although beyond my observational powers as I whizzed by in a speeding car, the taller plants would have offered protection and food for local birds and rodents, I suspect. Venturing from nearby pine forests, these animals would have inadvertently dispersed the seeds of shrubs and trees from the nearby woods. Slowly, these migrating plants are establishing themselves, further blurring the distinctions among rough, fairways, and greens. Better able to compete against their simpler grassy rivals, they will likely dominate the landscape in the years to come. Given more time and further human neglect, this landscape will revert eventually to pine forests as more animals and plants make it home.

Though largely imperceptible to the eye, these changes are occurring continually. Equally difficult to discern is the eventual form that these changes will take. It is simplistic to assume that the outcome will resemble what stood here before humans refashioned the land. Simply invoking the "circle of life" is naïve and inaccurate. Though resembling the nearby woods, what evolves will have important differences. Proximity to the interstate highway will bring additional light as well as noise and air pollution. Each will likely affect the particular species of flora and fauna that populate the space. Proximity to the freeway will also lead to a redoubling of efforts by local fire officials to suppress any natural or human-caused fires. Taken collectively, these different circumstances will affect the inhabitants and underlying structures that embody this particular location. It is this flexibility and adaptability in the face of changing conditions that permit natural ecosystems to persist over time.

More recently, fresh evidence reminds me of a different set of development patterns that affect this and other tracts of land. Bulldozers and other earth-moving equipment have appeared on site and are creating the outlines of streets across its face. Just like nature, humans have the capacity to reshape the land substantially, generating new pressures. Although more episodic than nature, our impact on the land has historically resulted from changes in culture and technology. In contemporary times, these pressures result most from economic imperatives that arise from market transactions that influence the use (carrier functions) of a given parcel of land. Forces of economic development affect the land and require change and adaptability in ways similar to the forces of nature. We turn now to understanding how our changing uses have affected the land.

We cannot know with precision the past uses of this parcel of land, but we can surmise likely histories. Local archaeological evidence, including Clovis and Hardaway arrow points, suggest that humans have inhabited the area for approximately 11,000 years.[1] Few specifics are known about these early inhabitants; however, it is likely they hunted for game, fished, and gathered wild fruits and vegetables. Perhaps they used fire at times to thin the forests and promote new plant growth to attract game. Otherwise, the ancient peoples left untouched their environment or its ecological services. Several centuries before the appearance of Europeans, Siouan Indians from the midwest migrated into the area, displacing the woodland peoples already here. The Siouan built villages along tributaries and supplemented game and forage with swidden or "slash and burn" farming. Perhaps, the sloping hills that later became fairways served as their garden. Clearing the land with fire, they would plant crops for several years until its declining fertility forced them to clear new plots. As they moved on, nature would reclaim the used plot and restore its natural fertility. At the same time, the Siouan people engaged in a trading network that extended along the east coast. They used a system of paths that later guided the roads and highways that now cross the region. The future golf course's proximity to these paths became a significant factor in its development.

As waves of European immigrants reached this area in the mid-eighteenth century, most of the Siouan peoples died or scattered as disease, alcohol, and violence accompanied the white immigrants. Bringing their own customs and practices, the white colonists settled the land as yeoman farmers, or as private landholders; they initially met their household needs and later produced surpluses for local markets. They raised a variety of grains, including corn and wheat, along with flax and tobacco. Normally, crop surpluses would stimulate an expanding economy, much like role of gold and silver in Virginia City. The surpluses could be sold in local towns for desired, store-bought goods not easily manufactured on the farm.

Local demand for these goods could encourage small manufacturing that would further whet the farmers' appetites. Increased crop yields would permit even greater opportunity to purchase goods, completing a synergistic cycle of interests. Instead, this area languished, in both population and prosperity. Relative isolation from markets and poor farming practices were the likely culprits. Contemporary and later observers commented on the wasteful farming practices that led to soil erosion and declining soil fertility.[2]

A different bounty of nature triggered economic development in the area. Blessed with regular and substantial water flows, the area's local streams were used by one entrepreneur after another to power cotton mills. Cotton goods sold throughout the country generated low wages for the workers and profits for mill owners. Growing incomes encouraged the expansion of small towns in the region. Local demand for food gave local farmers reason to consider new farming methods to improve yields, causing harvests to rise. The increased incomes gave them more spending money, further supporting commercial activity in town. Increased prosperity fueled local interest in improved transportation, including roads and railroads. Better transportation further encouraged trade and exchange, creating opportunities and attracting more people. Those farming this parcel of land benefited from their proximity to several mills and small factories.

The decision to transform local farmland into a golf course during the 1940s gives witness to the increased prosperity of the area. Only an area with sufficient discretionary income and leisure time can support such an expensive recreational activity as golf. With sufficient demand, the course offered a higher-valued use of the land. At the same time, its transformation from multi-cropping farm to golf course meant a further reduction in life-support services provided by the land. Uniform grasses and chemical applications required for appearances certainly reduced habitat cover and disrupted certain of the land's ecological services.

Expanding prosperity, a steady flow of immigrants, and an interstate highway brought new pressures to bear. The local community was transformed from small mill town to bedroom community to nearby Durham and Greensboro. The freeway's impact of easy transportation ended the area's historic isolation. The golf course's location adjacent to the interstate highway and one of its valued interchanges bestowed new value to the land. No longer is a golf course, with its extensive land requirements, the most valued use. Now, the land is undergoing transformation once again. New commercial developments featuring retail opportunities are under construction. The local hospital is adding a medical facility to assist this relatively underserved portion of the county. Roads are emerging to permit new housing to accommodate those households whose inhabitants work in different cities. The aging golf course could no longer offer the same value to its owners. Yet, the impact of these new developments arguably will be the most significant to date.

With each stage of economic development that the land has undergone – from swidden agriculture to modern cropping to recreational golfing to intensive commercial and residential development – the land's capacity to provide life-support services has declined. First by removing the land's natural cover and subsequently by replacing it with pavement and buildings, we are undermining the natural processes that provide these essential services. The disturbance regulation, waste treatment, and biological control functions are lost by felling the trees on site, while the impervious surfaces eradicate the water regulation, water quality, nutrient recycling, and fixation of solar energy services. Though these losses are incremental and therefore largely imperceptible, they have occurred nonetheless.

Some losses in ecological services are inevitable. Some land uses impose greater harm than do others on the natural ecosystems and the services they generate. Clearly, areas needed for human habitation, industry, and transportation impose greater damage than areas devoted to refugia and some forms of recreation. Yet, we need homes and we value hospitals. Fortunately, given nature's generosity and resiliency, some of our uses are quite affordable. The more important point is to examine what kind of development we pursue to meet different carrier needs. Agricultural practices that ignore their impact on these life-support services will eventually bear the cost. Residential and commercial development that ignores its impact on natural processes and environmental services will squander our precious endowment. As long as our economic development decisions ignore the value of these declining services, lavish misuse will continue and haunt our descendants.

Complex, adaptive systems

We should not ignore the value of market-based systems, even as they leave their fingerprints on many of our environmental problems. Much of my faith results from recognizing powerful similarities between natural systems and market systems. The enduring nature of ecosystems stems in large part from their capacity to adapt to incessantly changing circumstances. For instance, variations in local climate create a host of challenges and opportunities for any ecosystem's biotic residents. The changing conditions cause a cascading set of changes within the ecosystem as different species adapt to new circumstances. Although altered and sometimes severely degraded as a result, the ecosystem usually endures the change in conditions. Without this capacity to adapt, our natural systems and even life itself would be doomed to short lifespans. Market systems in human affairs function with remarkable similarity. Both share the characteristics of what many label *complex adaptive systems.*

Complex adaptive systems are networks that can respond and adapt to changes in their environments and thereby sustain their basic structures. Our natural world is composed of a web of interlinking ecosystems, interwoven both horizontally and vertically. Each local ecosystem influences the natural systems that border it. Changing conditions in one area inevitably will affect neighboring areas. For example, increased plant growth along a stream offers shade that cools the water, favoring some aquatic species over others and modifying key biochemical processes in the water. Changes in the riverine system will then influence the flora and fauna residing along the banks. At the same time, more regional systems vertically influence local ecosystems. For instance, increased rainfall will encourage plant growth, leading to more shade, while swelling water runoff and creating stronger and swifter currents. Some plant and animal species favored by the slower current will diminish in preference to species that thrive in the faster waters. Swifter currents can erode stream banks and undercut the increased plant growth causing the shading. Warmer water temperatures may return as a result. In the reverse direction, changes in local systems can influence the regional systems as well. New plant growth fostered by the rainfall will augment moisture in the air through increased evapotranspiration. The increased moisture will further feed rainfall patterns in the region. Within a complex web of relationships, the different ecosystems continually adapt to external changes, which requires other linked systems to do the same.

Economic markets respond and adapt in similar ways. Each community serves as the local market boundary for specific goods and services. This explains why the prices for haircuts, vegetables, or plumbing services can vary from one city to another. Though distinct from each other, these markets are horizontally linked. Changes in one local market affect the circumstances in another. One can observe this web of linkages in the aftermath of any significant natural disaster. After Hurricane Katrina struck the Gulf Coast, local supplies of plywood and tarpaulins disappeared as survivors acted to protect their damaged structures. Even areas unaffected by the storm soon saw building supplies vanish as they were rushed to areas of need. Plywood prices rose in countless markets, some hundreds of miles from the ravaged Gulf Coast. Outside the storm-devastated areas, depleted stocks and higher prices were a temporary circumstance as plywood mills increased production to meet rising demand.

Similar to natural systems, circumstances in regional markets limit the conditions found in local markets. Federal timber policies not only affect the forests but also the manner in which lumber companies can cut new plywood. More stringent restrictions and reduced access to federal forests translate into lowered production runs and higher plywood prices. Higher wholesale prices for plywood affect each local plywood market, encouraging builders to seek substitute materials, like particleboard. Building designs may change, thereby influencing local and even national markets for plywood. Markets and market prices reflect circumstances that often are in continual flux. As prices change, they initiate new decisions and economic behaviors.

This chapter makes policy recommendations that aim to implement full-cost pricing, so that the prices of goods and services reflect their full economic cost. Doing so will trigger a multitude of adjustments throughout our economy. Businesses will change production methods to avoid paying the higher costs of materials and energy. Households will reduce purchases and shift buying patterns to meet lifestyle needs in a less costly manner. As conditions continue to change in the future, market prices will adjust accordingly, thereby providing new incentives to households and businesses. The economy will continue to evolve and adapt in ways that will mitigate adverse impacts on our natural endowments.

Yet, the challenges discussed in this chapter are far more difficult to meet than those discussed in the prior two chapters. Recall the argument in Chapter Three and the varied effectiveness of market institutions in accurately reflecting different ecological services. While markets are relatively capable in valuing provisioning services (the focus of the past two chapters), they usually fail in valuing nature's life-support services. This blind spot is significant as we consider that market pressures determine much of our economic development. To be sure, real estate markets effectively weigh different potential uses, particularly among the human-centric carrier services. Higher-value uses for a given piece of land will generally translate into higher offers for that land. However, real estate markets function poorly in capturing the benefits offered by refugia carrier services.[3] Markets in general and real estate markets in particular largely ignore the value of leaving land undeveloped. Typical real estate transactions rarely consider the tract's life support services.[4] Just as importantly, project designs seldom take into account these services. In most cases, the cheapest and most profitable development design, no matter the specific land use, is the one that wins out. Though the sellers of any parcel of land are likely to consider all land-use options, whether residential housing, commercial development, or even a windmill farm, they are not very likely to weigh the impact on the land's life-support services. Nor is the eventual buyer likely to do so. Remedying this failure is no easy task.

Recommended policies

I recommend three policies to redress the current neglect of our life-support services shown by our real estate markets and economic development decisions. First, many communities already make use of conservation easements, or legal covenants that encourage property owners, often farmers, to forgo the financial benefits of developing their property. Increasing awareness and offering additional economic incentives could enhance the appeal of this public policy tool. Second, local communities can alter their uniform property tax system by creating a split-rate system. In doing so, they can encourage local economic development that limits loss of life-support services. Third, governments could require environmental assurance bonds. Such bonds would limit taxpayer liability from environmental damages that may result from development, and they would reward developers who implement environmentally sensitive designs. Taken collectively, these three policies would give due weight to life-support services in our economic development decisions, and mitigate future losses.

Conservation easements

Unlike the previously discussed polices, conservation easements offer local officials and planners a policy tool to achieve more environmentally benign decisions. Title to any property comprises a bundle of rights, some of which are divisible. Easements can reconcile the different interests of property owners, usually by separating the different rights to the land. They sever the existing property owner's right to use the land as it is from the right to develop the land sometime in the future. According to the traditions of common law, these easements are transferable along with the title to the property, precluding any development in perpetuity. At the same time, the property owner and heirs retain all of the remaining rights to the land not specifically excluded by the easement. Conservation easements offer local planners a tool to preserve critical green space along the outskirts of the community and to discourage development encroaching on adjacent farmland.

Moreover, these easements reduce the financial burden of preserving the land. Rather than purchase land outright, local communities and land conservancy groups can simply purchase land development rights. In this way, local planners can insure land use that meets the public interest without having to pay full freight. The land can continue to offer an economic livelihood to the residing household and their heirs. Nevertheless, conservation easements rarely come without a price. Since the value of any parcel of land reflects in part its development potential, restricting or eliminating developmental rights lowers its value. Property owners usually demand reimbursement to offset the potential losses of the easement. Even this requirement poses an unassailable obstacle to communities without ample funds. Fortunately, some landowners, with altruistic motivations, donate their land's development rights in order to preserve the character and use of their land.

Beyond making the option better known, public officials can take steps to encourage increased use of easements. First, public officials should make certain that easements lower the property's tax value. While easements do reduce the property's market value, this change is not always reflected in its tax value. Any property owner will view a potential easement with greater interest if they can expect some relief in property taxes. Second, government officials should insure favorable tax treatment for those property owners willing to donate their development rights. Under federal income tax law, property owners can have their donation recognised as a charitable donation as long as it meets certain criteria, including conservation and education benefits. Similarly, conservation easements that are included in the estates of deceased individuals receive favorable treatment. State and local tax authorities should offer similar benefits in their income and estate tax systems.

Split-rate property tax system

Local public officials have a second tool at their disposal to influence local economic development and land use. By shifting their local property tax from a uniform basis to a split-rate tax system, local officials can limit "urban sprawl" and minimize the loss of ecological services, *even if the changes are revenue neutral*. Two factors influence real property values: the value of the land itself, as well as the value of any improvements made (or deterioration allowed) to the land or buildings. The value of the parcel itself largely reflects its natural features and the specific development of surrounding tracts. Neither attribute stems from the owner's sweat or initiative. On the other hand, improvements made to the property directly result from the owner's effort and investment. Under normal practice, both values, though frequently assessed separately, are taxed identically. Higher property values, whether caused by one's labor or by fortuitous changes in the surrounding area, receive similar tax treatment. Under a split-rate system, the two components are taxed at different rates. By taxing improvements made to the property less severely than windfall increases in the value of the land, local authorities can redirect local economic development and achieve several benefits.

Shifting to a split-rate system better fits our sense of fairness. As is often said, three factors determine the underlying value of land: location, location, and location. Land values are the consequence of what surrounds it. The creation of a nearby park, the building of an interchange to the highway or terminal to the subway, and countless other changes all convey increased value to a given piece of property. Conversely, the construction of a noisy factory or the siting of a nearby landfill can substantially reduce land values. Nearly all of these changes are fortuitous for the property owner. On the other hand, improvements made to buildings and structures are the result of the property owner's effort, funds, and risk-taking. To tax these improvements at the same rate as the windfalls that result from the actions of others is contrary to our sense of fairness.

Shifting to a split-rate system would do more than produce a more equitable tax system. The modified tax structure would create new financial incentives that initiate a cascade of altered decisions. The two-tiered tax structure actually encourages increased building and development by reducing the tax rate on building improvements. Lowering the tax rate on improvements would mean that property owners keep more of the income generated by these improvements, giving them more financial encouragement. Raising the tax rate on land values would encourage further development as well. Facing higher property taxes whether they make improvements or not, property owners would feel greater financial pressure to develop their land. This development could generate increased revenues for the property owner while only modestly boosting their property tax.

The reader may be puzzled by my support for a split-rate system on the basis that it *encourages* economic development. Yes, this tax change encourages more economic development, but development that is less damaging to the environment. It does so for two reasons. First, this change would encourage higher-quality development. By decoupling property tax bills from the value of improvements, the split-rate property tax would offer developers increased financial incentives to use better building designs and more durable materials. Quality improvements would generate more income without unduly affecting their property taxes. Conversely, property owners would have less incentive to let their buildings deteriorate since such neglect would affect revenues much more than their tax bills. The more valuable the location, the more financial pressure the property owner would feel.

Second, the split-rate structure would redirect development from the outskirts to a city's interior. Property located near the city center is more valued normally than a comparable parcel on the periphery, thereby generating higher tax bills whether the property is fully used or not. This financial pressure would encourage property owners in city centers to develop their tracts more intensively to defray higher property taxes. Idle parcels found on the outskirts would have much lower property tax assessments, reducing the pressure to develop them. Intensive development in the city centers would better utilize existing municipal infrastructures, including water and sewer, gas and electricity, and transportation networks. Strengthening the city cores would enable cities to save on infrastructure costs that accompany development along their boundaries. While the intensive development might reduce life-support services generated by these center city parcels, the losses would likely be less than the alternative (and more land-intensive) development on the outskirts. Moving to this tax system should reduce the "urban sprawl" that is bedeviling so many communities.

In addition, moving to a split-rate tax system would improve the local community's fiscal health by stabilizing the tax base.[5] Virtually all taxes produce behavioral distortions in the name of tax avoidance. For instance, substantial income tax rates can discourage individuals from seeking additional income or higher sales taxes can depress local retail activity. Similarly, higher tax rates on building improvements can discourage local investment. The tax on land is uniquely different. Since land is largely fixed by nature, one cannot avoid this tax by limiting one's activity.[6] Rather than "destroy" land to avoid the tax, property owners would more likely sell it as long as the tax rate was not too onerous.[7] Unlike all other taxes, the tax on land does not effectively discourage the very behavior that leads to the tax revenues. In this way, it offers local officials a more predictable and stable tax base upon which to finance local government.

Shifting to a split-rate system would encourage "good government" as well. Much investment, whether private or public, spawns positive market externalities that increase the market values of nearby land. For example, community investment in parks, greenways, or even public education can improve the quality of life and frequently raise property values, even if property owners make no improvements on their own. Under the split-rate system, rising property values would swell the public coffers and thereby fund these or future improvements. Just as in the private sector, local government officials would be "rewarded" for making intelligent and progressive improvements through investments that increase property values and government revenues. On the other hand, poorly designed investments would neither raise property values nor trigger higher tax bills.[8] Property owners would still benefit from appreciating property values resulting from public investment, though more slowly than under the current arrangements.

An interesting case study can illustrate this point. In 1999, the London Underground extended its Jubilee line as it added ten new stations. This extension brought the convenience of public transportation to ten new areas of London, adding to local property values. According to a private study, this transport extension increased the value of properties within 800 yards of newly opened stations by £13 billion.[9] The taxpayer investment in the expanded system was only £3.5 billion. A split-rate property tax system could have "recycled" more of this benefit back to the government coffers and thereby funded additional public investments as needed.

Other experiences with the split-rate property tax corroborate benefits already discussed. Pittsburgh, Pennsylvania, adopted the split-rate property tax in 1913. Today, the local government is taxing land more than six times the rate on building improvements.[10] A recent study showed that the value of building permits increased by 70 percent following a rate adjustment in 1979–80.[11] Though the authors readily admit that the tax structure was not wholly responsible for the building boom, they conclude that the tax structure clearly contributed to it. Across the globe, Melbourne,

Australia, provides another interesting case study. Half of the fifty-six districts that comprise the larger metropolitan region dropped the building portion of local property taxes between 1918 and 1986. The districts that eliminated the tax on building experienced a much greater gain in commercial and residential development. These districts experience population and building densities that are 50 percent greater than those districts that stayed with the conventional tax system, even allowing for distance from city center, industry, and other key factors.[12] Both experiences, Pittsburgh's and Melbourne's, corroborate what economic analysis suggests.

Shifting property taxes to a split-rate structure does generate some problems. Transferring tax assessments away from buildings and improvements onto land values encourages landowners to seek the highest value from their property, not always the most desirable result for the community. In the absence of zoning restrictions, having higher property taxes on land values encourages landowners to shift from residential to commercial uses as they pursue higher income. These changes can undermine the quality of certain older, residential neighborhoods that reside near city centers. Thus, local planners should stand ready to use zoning restrictions, land-use planning, city purchases of land for greenways, and other development tools to insure that the pattern of development preserves key features and improves the quality of life. Similarly, local officials should consider issues surrounding affordable housing. Since much of our stock of affordable housing for low-income households is concentrated in declining areas that are adjacent to city centers, the shift to a split-rate tax structure could easily spawn a burst of "gentrification" that would displace these long-time residents. While reduced property tax rates on new construction should encourage additional affordable housing, this may not be sufficient. Again, local housing and community planners should anticipate such problems and use zoning restrictions to insure minimal displacement or create additional funds for affordable housing.

Implementing the shift toward a split-rate structure creates an even more vexing problem. The property tax bills of a revenue-neutral tax shift would inevitably rise for some property owners and fall for others, depending on location. Older sections near the city center would likely experience higher tax bills while outlying areas would get tax breaks. In some cases, fixed-income households might find the elevated tax payments beyond their means, requiring the sale of their home to avoid undue hardship. Further, when they did sell they would discover a second problem. Their property's higher tax liability under the new system would lower, perhaps modestly, the market value of their property. Changing the tax structure would inevitably generate some turmoil in local real estate market as property values readjusted to the new circumstances. This shift in property prices would not only create some hardship for those who are dependent on their home equity, but also encourage broader resistance to the change.

To mitigate these problems, local officials should implement the shift to a split-rate tax slowly and incrementally. In this way, households and businesses have time to adjust to the changes while city planners can anticipate and remedy any of the problems that may arise. One rule of thumb is to not shift more than 10 percent from buildings to land in a given year.[13] In this way, the shifting burdens would occur over a ten-year period, easing some of the transition pains. To ease the burden on fixed-income households, the use of tax deferments might help.[14] For example, tax officials could exempt certain households from paying the increment in their tax bills until they decide to sell their home. At that point, they or their estate could settle with the local tax authorities.

Flexible environmental assurance bonds

Although both policy tools already discussed can ameliorate the impact of economic development decisions upon the natural environment, neither directly nor broadly addresses the problem. To do so, I now turn to environmental assurance bonds. Used regularly in the construction industry, assurance bonds protect taxpayers from future liabilities due to actions or decisions taken today. To this end, the Miller Act of 1935 required performance bonds on all major federal construction projects. These bonds assure that the actual construction meets the basic standards outlined in the contract agreement. In addition, landfill operators are required to commit funds in the event that their landfill leaks into local groundwater supplies. Mining companies are required to post assurance bonds in the event that mine reclamation efforts fall short and cause harm. Most recently, operators of underground gas tanks are required to post assurance bonds in the event that tanks fail and leak toxic chemicals into local water supplies. Although useful in these instances, the value of assurance bonds as a broader policy tool is even greater. If widely applied and effectively designed, environmental assurance bonds can encourage economic development decisions that take into account any loss of ecological services. They offer us an effective mechanism by which the market failures discussed at the outset of this chapter can be remedied.

Though it can take many forms, a flexible environmental assurance bond should work in the following manner. Any company engaged in a significant development project must conduct an environmental impact statement outlining the project's possible harm. To proceed, the company would post an assurance bond equal to the harm of the "worst case scenario." Normally, that would mean contracting with a separate assurance company.[15] For an annual premium, this assurance company would be liable for paying any or all damages up to the bonded amount, if harm did happen and the developer was unable to make full payment. Under this option, the market would determine the relative risk and cost of the assurance bond. The potential environmental risk of the development project would thus be included as part of its original cost. Given its liability, the independent assurance company would clearly scrutinize both the development plans as well as the financial health of the developer to assess their risk in paying a claim. The assurance company would be responsible for any unpaid claim, even if the development company stopped paying premiums. To insure the financial soundness of the assurance company, state or federal governing bodies should supervise and certify which companies have sufficient financial strength to fulfill this function.

Initially, the bond should cover all known losses of ecological services, along with the potential costs associated with a worst case scenario. Under circumstances of uncertainty, the value of the bond should be sufficient to cover all likely costs and damages. Only in this way will the development decision truly incorporate the polluter-pays principle. As new knowledge or experience determines that this worst case scenario is exaggerated, the amount of the bond should fall. In this way, the bond should be flexible and responsive to increased understanding of the project's likely impacts on the natural environment.

Use of assurance bonds creates several critical incentives that will insure better treatment of our natural assets. They provide greater certainty that those who engage in environmentally damaging behaviors will pay for having done so. However, these bonds do more than satisfy our sense of retribution; they can influence the offending behaviors that give rise to environmental harm. By factoring the potential environmental injury into development decisions, assurance bonds can influence these decisions in two key ways. First, development decisions with excessive worst case scenarios would be avoided as being too expensive. The costs of the assurance bond could make decisions that once looked profitable no longer desirable. Environmentally risky decisions would be discouraged, as they should be.

Second, developers would consider specific designs that clearly limit damage to the local environment in order to lower their annual bond payments. Lower potential damage would translate into lower bond premiums. The bonds would give firms additional motivation to take measures that mitigate the possibility of environmental damage. Since bond premiums would be influenced by past business practices and experience, the bonds would give developers additional motive to pursue environmentally considerate practices. In competitive settings, this point is substantial. Requiring assurance bonds shifts the advantage from companies that currently pay scant attention to the environment to those that consider it respectfully.

The flexible assurance bond offers another intriguing benefit. As the bond amount is determined by estimating the worst case scenario, its costs reflect the current level of uncertainty regarding possible harm. If the firm can demonstrate the improbability of this scenario, the size of the bond and its cost should fall. In some cases, actual experience would provide this demonstration. In other cases, further research could lead to a better understanding of actual damages and prompt a reduction in the bonded amount; this would give businesses a reason to fund targeted research in the hope that increased understanding of our impact on the natural systems could lead to lowered costs. Some caution is advisable, since there are obvious concerns that can arise from "research" funded by those with an economic agenda. However, contemporary models like the Underwriter's Laboratory (UL) and other independent research organizations can offer a reasonable solution to this problem.

Two challenges posed by using assurance bonds are worth discussing. One concern is that the bonds would generate enough added costs to inhibit most development projects. Though some projects would lapse, the broader concern is unlikely. Historical experience with assurance bonds suggests that their costs are not prohibitive.[16] A recent government study concluded that the annual cost of environmental assurance bonds ranged between 1 percent and 1.5 percent of the bonded liability.[17] The report contended that larger firms with solid environmental records could get bonds at rates below 1 percent of the bonded amount. Undoubtedly, using assurance bonds more widely would generate higher rates for many projects. These costs would not likely stop all development in its tracks, though they would eliminate those projects that pose significant risks to the natural environment. While these bonds would require developers to pay additional costs, most of these costs are *redistributed costs*; that is, they are currently borne by society, either in the form of a degraded environment or in actual clean-up costs funded by taxpayers. The cost-shifting would implement the polluter-pays principle, ensuring the inclusion of these costs in development decisions.

Others argue that assurance bonds tilt the playing field of competition against small businesses and favor larger, more capitalized rivals. No doubt, larger companies would find it easier to find the cash to post the bonds. Moreover, larger companies would benefit from any design changes needed to limit environmental damage, as they could apply these changes over several development projects. Larger, better-financed businesses would find it easier to meet the higher development thresholds that assurance bonds would require. To some extent, this is a desirable outcome, as many environmental problems result when undercapitalized businesses adopt cost-cutting practices that lead to unfunded disasters. Nonetheless, the fear that assurance bonds would effectively eliminate all small business wherever they are applied has not been borne out in practice. Similar outcries emerged in response to new federal rules requiring assurance bonds for underground gasoline tanks. The actual costs of getting the needed assurance bond for each tank has been only $400 – a sum clearly within the means of most healthy businesses, large or small.[18] Broader implementation of environmental assurance bonds would likely prune some undercapitalized businesses; this consequence might actually be beneficial.

Summary

While market institutions effectively encourage individuals and decision-makers to consider the full range of commercial opportunities, they are rarely, if ever, expected to account for the loss of ecological services that their decisions may cause. Each of the three proposals discussed in this chapter functions to redress this neglect. Each serves to value more fully the life-support services provided by a parcel of land and therefore to discourage the most harmful forms of economic development. By separating development rights from other property rights, conservation easements in essence give a negotiated value to retaining these life-support services. Requiring environmental assurance bonds will have the same effect, though with a more flexible stance regarding development. On the other hand, split-rate property taxes only inadvertently value life-support services as they discourage the suburban, low-density development that consumes life-support services. Though each of these policies raises the costs of development, only conservation easements prevent further development. Rather, they alter the underlying economic incentives and therefore encourage different and less environmentally damaging development. The requirement of environmental assurance bonds would encourage developers to consider designs that limit the potential harm to the environment. Environmentally friendly designs, heretofore considered too costly, would be more competitive and appealing. At the same time, split-rate property taxation would encourage more "infill" development, making better use of the city's public infrastructure of roads, sewers, and other utility lines. Not aiming to stifle development, these recommendations would rather guide and redirect the economic development that does continue.

Applying these policy recommendations to our golf course example illustrates their mixed effectiveness. What would have happened to this parcel of land if each of these policy tools were available? Presumably, the option of conservation easements was available as an option and, if selected, could have prevented the development. Yet, too many factors were working against that. Given its proximity to the interstate highway and the valued interchange, the development rights to this land were valuable indeed. At the same time, its proximity to the same interstate highway and non-unique natural features limited its value as a provider of life-support services, as compared to other land in the area. Likely, the disparity in values was too vast to bridge under normal circumstances; this option was viable only in the case of a highly motivated landowner with a strong interest in preserving the land as is. Nonetheless, it could have served as a fully effective option in precluding any further development.

A split-rate property tax may actually have encouraged even faster development. Given its proximity to the interstate interchange, the land gained immediate value that only rose as more people migrated to the region. Under a split-rate system, the property would generate higher tax liabilities even as it lay idle over the past decade. This heavier tax burden would have further fueled the desire of the landowner to make sure that the land paid for itself. Likely, development would have come sooner, not later, and without any real consideration for the lost natural services. On the other hand, less accessible lands may stay undeveloped longer due to their tax bills being lower. Nonetheless, one can hardly argue that merely switching to a split-rate system would staunch ecological losses that result from ongoing development.

Lastly, how would the requirement of a flexible environmental assurance bond have affected the development project? The answer relies on how inclusive and extensive the assurance bond is. Certainly, the bond would cover the possibility of some sort of wastewater spill, either from commercial or residential units that soon will dot the landscape.[19] The paving of soils with roads and building foundations will reduce the natural water regulation and waste treatment services. Some estimate for the resultant increases in flooding and declining water quality downstream of the property would be required. The inclusion of these possible losses might encourage developers to change the development design to mitigate these problems in order to lower their bond payments. However, what about the loss of trees that are cut to permit the new construction? How would one evaluate the lost services in biological control, climate change, and even disturbance regulation that these trees provide? What about the lost services in nutrient cycling, solar fixation, and lower biological diversity that will accompany the reduction of green space and the introduction of uniform landscapes that dress so many of our suburban developments? How will the bond account for these losses? To the extent that they escape our attention due to their complexity, we have merely prolonged our neglect of ecological services. Until we are able to better measure the lost services and their value, even these bonds will not prevent the squandering of these services. How to solve this problem represents the biggest unanswered challenge raised by this book.

Further reading

James Boyd, *Financial Responsibility for Environmental Obligations: Are Bonding and Assurance Rules Fulfilling Their Promise?*, gives an excellent analysis of the potential benefits and actual performance of assurance bonds to date.

J. Cohen and C. Coughlin, 'An Introduction to Two-Rate Taxation of Land and Buildings', provides a thorough review of both the theory and practice of split-rate taxation.

Seth Reice, *The Silver Lining: The Benefits of Natural Disasters*, offers a more comprehensive examination of the role of ecological succession and natural disturbances in the natural world.

C. Troxler and W. Vincent, *Shuttle and Plow: A History of Alamance County, North Carolina*, offers an excellent historical narrative of this part of the Piedmont region of North Carolina.

10 Economic resiliency

Many Americans, even those without Gaelic blood, are aware of the Great Potato Famine that befell the Irish during the 1840s as they experienced starvation, eviction, forced migration, and death. Today, we hear still of this suffering in the sorrowful words of countless Irish ballads. Yet, as evocative as these songs are, they seem to speak about a distant past. Even the cause, a rapid and utterly thorough blight that destroyed their staple food, appears to have little connection to our lives. History can provide us with hindsight, but only if we fully recall the past and do not simply recollect mere glimpses.

Native to South America, the potato came to Europe on ships returning from the New World. Largely shunned throughout Europe for being a tuber, or ground-growing vegetable, the potato received a more hospitable welcome in Irish soils and cottages. Much of the island's wet, rocky soils were inhospitable to cereal crops, particularly wheat, the preferred grain. Viewing this land as worthless, the English overlords left it to the Irish peasantry while retaining the island's fertile farmland. The Irish climate and marginal soils favored the potato. On even a small plot of land, an Irish family could easily grow enough potatoes to survive.[1] The Irish peasantry viewed the potato as a blessing, a source of hope for a desperate population.

The unlikely potato offered benefits that went far beyond its prolific nature. A valuable source of nutrition, the potato is rich in protein, carbohydrates, minerals, and vitamins like niacin and Vitamin C. Potatoes are so nutritious and well balanced that an adult can survive solely upon a diet of potatoes, along with occasional cow's milk. Further, the potato can be raised with relatively little labor. In the "lazy bed" method, Irish farmers used a spade to create beds of dirt surrounded by trenches to drain the excess water. Within these beds, they placed manure and crushed seashells to fertilize the soil. They inserted potato seeds into this fertile bed and covered them with dirt dug from the trenches. Growing below ground, the seeds would push up a tangle of vines that required little weeding or attention through the growing season. In the fall, one need only dig up the mature tubers that were easily stored until the next harvest. Without peer, the potato offered maximum nutrition with minimal effort.

The potato offered the Irish peasant some relief from the crushing social structure of that time. Even as they were pushed onto marginal lands, the Irish peasantry found some comfort from the potato. Low labor requirements gave the peasants time to make and sell their local crafts or work for nearby English lords, though English laws increasingly restricted those opportunities. Unlike grain crops, the potato required no milling or refining by price-gouging millers. The potato provided further independence from middlemen since each harvest generated sufficient seeds for next year's crop. Even under difficult circumstances, the potato allowed much of the rural Irish peasantry to thrive, fueling a doubling of the island's population to eight million prior to the Famine.[2] To feed this growing population, the Irish simply devoted more land to potatoes. While the poor throughout Europe were unduly harmed by the rising wheat and corn prices that resulted from periodically poor harvests, the Irish poor were largely unaffected by these disturbances in the emerging market economy.

However, this dependence on the potato created an Irish experiment with a monoculture economy that would become a hellish nightmare. Not only had the potato become the sole source of livelihood among the rural Irish, but also a single variety, the Lumper, dominated the Irish countryside. Worse still, the potato was a genetic time bomb. Like apples, potatoes are clones of each other so that each potato is genetically identical to any of its offspring. Thus, any disease that finds little resistance in one plant will overwhelm all those plants that stem from a common ancestor. Most likely, ships returning from North America in the summer of 1845 ferried such a blight, *Phytophthora infestans*. Carried by the wind, the fungus found the cool, moist climate and the defenseless plants a perfect place to summer. Within days of contact, the fungus would wither both plant and potato, creating a noxious stench from the rotting vines. A single diseased plant could infect thousands of its neighbors over a span of several days. Thus, in a matter of weeks, the fungus spread across the Irish countryside, destroying the food which the Irish were expecting to eat for the next year.

The resulting calamity bears witness to stories and experiences that are painful to hear. Though other crops grown on the Anglo-Irish estates were unaffected by the blight, one needed cash to purchase them. Without any source of income, the Irish peasantry was effectively denied food. Desperately hoping for a quick change of luck, families sold whatever meager possessions they had for small amounts of food. Some parents even resorted to selling their children in order to raise funds to fend off starvation. As a bitter paradox, corn and other crops sat on the Irish docks, waiting for export to places where people could pay top dollar. Many peasants begged for food, in the hope of gaining some charity from others more well off. Few were. Weak from hunger, many succumbed to a variety of diseases, some along the roadside as they searched for relief. Other families disintegrated as a whole generation left the island in a desperate search for food and work elsewhere. Estimates suggest that over a million died and another million emigrated from the island during the peak Famine years of 1845–50.[3]

The culprit of this sad history is not the potato. Other societies, most particularly the Incas, have flourished for centuries on an economy largely based on the potato. Unlike the Irish, the Incas did not rely on a single, or even a few varieties of potatoes. Instead, they developed and produced hundreds of different types, each with its own adaptability to specific growing conditions and resistance to pests. In this way, weather or blight could harm the harvest, but would rarely lead to widespread hunger. This diverse potato portfolio, much like our modern mutual funds, helped Incan society avoid the Irish experience. The real culprit in the Irish Famine was the underlying economic and political system that encouraged a monoculture economy. Just as in finance, too little diversity in natural systems carries higher levels of risk. Though not to the extent reached by Ireland 150 years ago, our modern economies have proceeded down a similar path, exposing ourselves and our children to unnecessary risk.

Calamity and disturbances in our contemporary world

Although we like to think otherwise, calamity and disturbance are part of our experience; hurricanes, tornadoes, tsunamis, earthquakes, floods, droughts, or blizzards periodically disrupt our lives. Not only do these natural disasters damage people's homes and businesses, but they frequently wreak havoc with transportation, communication, and power networks that are critical to modern economies. The damage to local and regional economies can be substantial and long lasting.[4] Similarly, we face the specter of a worldwide pandemic fueled by influenza viruses that could debilitate tens of millions of humans. Though the virus's direct health threat would pass relatively quickly, its impact on our public health systems, communities, and economies would likely be far more enduring and devastating. At the same time, human forces undermine local, regional, and even international economies, usually in more subtle and less physically scarring ways. The business cycle produces an ebb and flow of circumstances that buffet modern economies. Recessions periodically contract commerce and create higher unemployment as people, businesses, and governments cope with their declining fortunes. The increased mobility of capital, technology, and labor across regional and national borders makes local economies increasingly vulnerable to changing circumstances abroad. Emerging technologies that create new products, businesses, and opportunities inevitably shrink the revenues of businesses producing rival products.[5] Changing circumstances, whether due to shifts in technology, consumer tastes, or global resources, all affect local economies and require adaptation. Equally important, we must recognize that disturbances are frequently symptoms of broader cycles that will likely recur. Change and disturbance are clearly endemic to modern, industrial economies.

Curiously, both mainstream economics and ecology have long neglected the importance of disturbances, whether natural or human caused, in their respective areas of study. In each discipline, research emphasized the underlying stability or equilibrium operating in their respective, self-regulating systems. Each viewed disturbances as unusual and interesting tests to monitor the return to equilibrium. Granted, both disciplines had investigators who examined the dynamic properties of their respective systems. Charles Elton's work on succession led many ecologists to examine how natural systems evolved over time. Yet, this view of natural change maintained stability as the norm, predicting that ecosystems would evolve toward a "climax" stage. In economics, growth theorists similarly examined the circumstances of "balanced" growth, again with the focus on stability and equilibrium. One notable exception was Joseph Schumpeter, who argued that economic slumps were crucial to the economy's vitality since they encouraged the transfer of resources from declining to expanding sectors. Schumpeter realized that, like the periodic fire that releases scarce nutrients to fuel growth in natural systems, there is periodic "creative destruction" in economies, too. During such periods, characterized by rising unemployment and business bankruptcies, scarce labor and capital are released to industries poised to prosper in the next expansion.[6] Indeed, there exists a remarkable similarity between Schumpeter's ideas and those of ecologist E.S. Holling, on the critical role that disturbances play in maintaining vital systems.

In economics, our neglect of the role and significance of disturbances in human affairs leads to some worrisome results. In overlooking their significance, we avoid taking steps to minimize their harm. Anybody who has worked with young adults is familiar with their perceptions of risk and their attitudes towards commodities like health insurance. Convinced that they are invincible, many engage in risky behaviors and shun costly insurance premiums. The rest of us are not immune to this phenomenon. Each of us is susceptible to the argument that we can avoid some insurance premium by being careful – or by denying that a risk exists. In my state, auto insurance is required and yet I still pay an uninsured motorist premium, because many of my peers feel that they cannot or will not pay for insurance. Given the uncertainties of assessing risk, many businesses prune their operating overheads by avoiding costly activities that could insulate them against unpredictable havoc.

Yet the problem goes beyond our reluctance to insure adequately against potential risks. Since Adam Smith, economists have recognized the value of increased specialization. Specialization usually permits greater productivity and efficiency in times of stability; therefore, it is strongly encouraged in our competitive economy. College graduates with specialized training usually receive higher starting salaries than their more generalist peers with liberal arts degrees. Doctors with specialized training command higher salaries than do general practitioners. While specialization is advantageous, it becomes a liability during times of crisis and instability. New technologies can make some specializations obsolete, practically overnight. Highly specialized systems are often inflexible in the face of change and disruption and can easily fracture in the absence of system redundancies. Yet, these redundancies are often deemed uneconomical.

Further, the economies that we gain from large-scale operations offer us a double-edged sword, particularly during times of instability. Large-scale operations, whether in manufacturing or distribution, usually offer substantial cost savings. The huge volumes of operations permit producers to use expensive, yet highly productive, methods and facilities to achieve the cost reductions. At the same time, certain tradeoffs do exist. The efficiencies are dependent on large production runs of essentially standardized products. Any significant changes in the product require expensive retooling of the production process. Diversity of product choice is necessarily sacrificed. Since the market is rarely elastic enough to meet the expanding production potential of each rival manufacturer, a winnowing process reduces the number of competing firms. Having fewer firms further reduces product heterogeneity. Under normalcy, this system provides a plentitude of cheap, uniform products. In times of change and disruption, it offers limited flexibility and adaptability.

We can view these forces at work throughout our economy. In agriculture, these changes lead to fewer, but much larger farms that favor monoculture farming. Focusing on one particular variety offers extensive experience as one learns the specific water and nutrient needs of the chosen strain. Different farms frequently use the same seed to meet the preferences of millers or consumers for a uniform harvest. The inherent risks of monoculture farming are either ignored or presumed to have been managed by chemical pesticides. In the media industry, it is far more cost-effective to use fewer sources and reuse programming extensively than to continually offer additional choices. Local newspapers find it far more cost-effective to rely on the same wire services than to send reporters to state capitals and to Washington, DC. Commercial radio is replacing locally produced programming with national programs, while Hollywood is focused as much on foreign audiences as on domestic. In manufacturing, "just-in-time" supply networks are restructuring industries. Rather than tie up scarce resources in large inventories of spare parts, manufacturers are requiring their suppliers to deliver their products as needed. Though inventories have acted as a buffer against unforeseen disruptions in the past, their elimination has permitted businesses to prune unwanted costs. Yet, this evolving system is much more susceptible to any disruptions of the critical communication or transportation networks. The need for close coordination also encourages fewer suppliers, each focused more attentively on fewer customers.

We have not strayed as far down the path as in nineteenth-century Ireland, but modern society has followed a similar course to an alarming degree. Competitive pressures, along with the dictates of conventional economics regarding specialization and economies of scale, have encouraged the standardization of materials, methods, and products. Mass production, distribution, and marketing of homogeneous products and services offer the surest way to prune costs and increase market share. Globalization increasingly means that the seeds, technologies, and products used in one location are adopted around the world. The ensuing losses in economic and cultural diversity are nearly as worrisome as the more publicized concerns regarding biodiversity losses. Further, there exists the specter of rising disparities in income and wealth, both in the USA as well as throughout the world. Mounting disparities prevent an increasing portion of the population from participating in the market-based solutions that can mitigate the suffering that frequently accompanies natural and economic disruptions. Comparable to nineteenth-century Ireland, we are sacrificing resiliency and flexibility for increased prosperity – potentially a devil's bargain.

Economic system resiliency

As the bumper sticker states with uncommon pithiness, "#**# happens!". Though we rarely predict when or where calamities will strike, we do know that natural and human-caused catastrophes will continue to torment. Natural calamities are frequently location specific, but human-caused disruptions can strike anywhere, often with national and even global impact. Rather than react with surprise when they occur, we can prepare for their inevitable appearance. By limiting their occurrence, mitigating their impact, and reducing the recovery period, we can improve our future well-being. Already we take certain steps to diminish the impact of these disturbances, including emergency preparedness, Federal Emergency Management Agency (FEMA) and Red Cross disaster assistance, and unemployment insurance. Yet, there is much, much more that we can and should do to prepare, plan, and limit these future traumas. These efforts should take two complementary strategies: to shrink the likely damages that will result and to improve our recovery from the damages that do occur. The remaining portion of this chapter examines policies that pursue both strategies.

Strategies that mitigate the physical harms caused by disruptions

Discouraging development in high-risk areas

Thin strands of sand dunes called barrier islands protect most of our country's east and Gulf coasts from the force of storms and tides. Due to their beauty and recreational appeal, these islands have attracted intensive development. Despite their apparent calm and remarkable views, they offer neither a safe nor secure haven. While shielding the inland areas from the surge of storms and waves that periodically pound our coasts – the reason they are called "barrier islands" – they are frequently battered by wind and overcome by swelling seas. In most cases, these islands are not permanently anchored. Changing water currents and eroding sand frequently shift their location and size. In North Carolina, a normally imperceptible westward creep is evident as "ocean front" homes are threatened and lost to encroaching seas. "Second row" homes, once relegated to inferior status due to their blocked views of the ocean, are getting an unexpected promotion. Less predictably, but no less importantly, the islands are highly vulnerable to the hurricanes that frequent the region. The powerful winds and storm surges wreak unimaginable havoc on the island communities. Unimaginable, that is, until one recalls the last time a storm hit the area. Yet, the residents and commercial businesses are encouraged to rebuild, as if the event is unlikely to recur.

A variety of federal and state policies encourage redevelopment in these highly vulnerable areas. Federal disaster relief provides residents with loans and even grants to repair and rebuild lost structures. Federally subsidized flood insurance is offered to property owners who build with the ocean lying mere feet away. With each program, the government encourages building in high-risk locations. Such programs should be ended or redesigned to offer aid, but not to assist with rebuilding. While some individuals are willing to take risks with their homes and businesses, we should neither encourage nor pay for their losses. As a further deterrent, state and federal governments should require a minimum amount of flood or storm insurance to accompany any physical developments in these areas.[7] Certainly, this insurance will be expensive, as it reflects the full exposure of the property to likely damage. Undoubtedly, property owners will pass along the higher insurance costs onto their renters or customers. Going to the beach will be more expensive, but collectively we will spend less when rebuilding costs are considered.

Other areas are susceptible to periodic damage and destruction, too. Low-lying areas, along either our coasts or our rivers and lakes, are subject to episodic flooding. Drier lands in the west are similarly prone to periodic fires. Both of these natural forces provide necessary rejuvenating benefits to their local ecosystem, helping to sustain the natural productivity and flow of ecological services.[8] We should phase out federally subsidized flood insurance for flood-prone areas. Similarly, landowners in these areas should be required to demonstrate that their property is fully insured, including full rebuilding costs and some transitory allowance. In this way, much of the disaster relief money that often follows in the wake of these natural occurrences would be minimized and taxpayer exposure reduced. More importantly, landowners would face the full measure of their decision to locate in high-risk areas. This requirement would limit and direct development in such areas. Flood and fire-resistant structures would reduce insurance premiums, thereby encouraging their use. Of course, local officials could use their zoning powers to prevent building in these high-risk areas.

Locally appropriate zoning and minimum building codes

Every community is vulnerable to some natural disaster. California has its earthquakes, the west its forest fires, the midwest its tornadoes, and the east its blizzards. While the risks posed by these natural calamites are real indeed, they do not have the location-specific risks that flood-prone areas face. To be sure, who would want to live on top of the San Andreas Faultline? However, given the incredible force of earthquakes, how much safer, really, is someone who lives ten, twenty, or fifty miles away? Rather than attempt to prevent individuals from living in earthquake-prone areas, which would is not practicable in any case, we should seek to create structures that are likely to survive the earthquake with minimal damage. Local and state officials should strengthen zoning and building codes to mitigate the likely damage caused by area-specific natural disturbances.

Stricter zoning restrictions and stronger building codes are needed because markets do not always adequately account for risk. Homebuyers new to a region may not fully appreciate the risks involved in buying cheaper homes without key safety features or designs. Even long-time residents may find it difficult to assess accurately the risks associated with erratic disturbances. For too many of us, it is simply much easier to ignore the costs of a possible calamity in favor of immediate "savings" offered by a cheaper design. Moreover, some housing designs may generate external costs that affect nearby property owners. For example, wood shingle roofs in the west have long been a highly popular and attractive housing design, despite their expense. While esthetically attractive, wood roofs may become infernos once lit. In areas vulnerable to fire, they represent a major source of fuel and pose a danger to surrounding homes. Such risks to neighboring homes suggest the presence of market externalities and that market incentives may be insufficient. For that reason, communities have enacted local building codes that eliminate wood-shingled roofs or require that they be treated with fire-retardant materials. Local officials should develop building-code restrictions that ensure cost-effective features to resist the likely risks faced in the area. By instituting and enforcing minimum building codes, local officials can mitigate the future damages caused by natural forces that are regrettable but inevitable. Without question, these enhanced building codes will increase the cost of new construction; however, they will reduce the lifecycle building costs and limit the loss of life.

Diversity and system resiliency

Usually, the harm caused by some natural disaster extends beyond the immediate and visible damage. Since we are all part of larger, interrelated systems, damage in one location usually reverberates far beyond. Injury to specific telecommunications and energy facilities, either generating plants or transmissions lines, can wreak widespread havoc as essential functions are disrupted. Destruction of key transportation facilities – whether highway, rail, or airport – can impede normal transportation and business commerce for days, or even months. Harm visited on specific businesses can hurt "downstream" businesses that rely on "just-in-time" deliveries, causing them to reduce operations and thereby widen the injury. Destruction that solely affects residential areas can affect local business and commerce, as workers are either unable or unwilling to report to work. Human-caused disturbances reverberate through these same networks in similar ways. Plant and military base closings cause injury that extends beyond the immediate employment losses. Financial panics and recessions sweep through whole economies as the difficulties faced in one location echo across related businesses. Product scares and terrorist attacks feed fear and panic that further reverberate through our economy.

Natural systems suffer from the same challenges. Fires that periodically sweep through areas not only burn the overgrowth and accumulated brush but also those animals unable to escape. Other animals able to flee lose their food source, their habitat, or both. Whether the animals migrate or perish, their fate affects other species as well. Some natural disturbances generate widening injury as well. Human-caused disturbances, like the paving of natural areas, trigger direct impacts that echo across the local landscape. The capacity of natural systems to withstand and recuperate from these varied disturbances depends in large part on the functional biodiversity and the system redundancies that are available.[9] Since not all species or essential processes are equally affected by a specific disturbance, the existence of duplicity often permits the ravaged area to persist and recuperate.

In a similar way, certain characteristics make our economies more resilient to disturbances, whether natural or human-caused. Economies with greater diversity will likely weather disturbances better than less diverse economies. Not all firms suffer equally during adverse circumstances. During economic recessions, most companies suffer together as households and businesses restrict their purchases; yet, some businesses actually thrive in these challenging conditions. Higher education and "resale" businesses like used-car lots often experience greater demand during hard times, while health-care companies remain largely unaffected. Such employers provide buoyancy to a local economy depressed by external circumstances as they add jobs and supplement incomes. Some new businesses that offer novel products or services can sustain their growth even during depressed periods. Further, not all economic downturns are the same nor do they harm all businesses equally. Oil price shocks that severely injure energy-intensive industries will harm other businesses more mildly, thereby mitigating the overall damage. Increased economic diversity will also buffer government tax revenues from the fluctuations of the business cycle. The same economic conditions that bring hardship to local communities also reduce the government's revenues and capacity to help. Just as any prudent investor reduces risk by having a diversified portfolio, so can a community or nation reduce its risks by encouraging a diversity of businesses, both within and across different industries.

In nature, as in human affairs, size often confers advantage. Larger shrubs can generate broader and deeper-penetrating root systems that can capture scarce water or nutrients. Taller trees can better compete for scarce sunlight as they reach above the canopy of rivals. In the animal world, increased size usually confers speed and strength, two attributes particularly useful in preying on other animals and competing for food and mates. In both plants and animals, size permits organisms to develop complex systems, whether sensory, vascular, or other. Size also gives both animals and plants increased storage capacity (based on their volume) to endure ebbs and flows of key nutrients while creating less exposure (based on their surface area) to the external world. Yet, size is not without tradeoffs in nature. Larger shrubs are more visible to browsing herbivores. Larger size in animals also makes them more appealing, as well as more visible, to predators. Larger size usually entails fewer offspring, making the species more vulnerable to calamity. Increased size can further limit flexibility and agility. While grasses can easily bend with the wind, trees cannot.

Size confers advantage in economic affairs as well. Larger businesses experience advantages over their smaller rivals in raising capital, adopting new technologies, assuming risks, and cultivating broad consumer recognition through marketing and merchandising. Economists give much significance to this concept of economies of scale. They argue, quite rightly, that both consumers and society benefit extensively from the efficiencies of large-scale production. Yet, larger organizations also lose the agility and flexibility of their smaller rivals, just as in the natural world. Reliance upon centralized technologies entails increased risks. To compete effectively, bigger companies need to serve wider areas, broader markets, and more customers. In reaching more broadly dispersed customers, large businesses require extensive transportation, distribution, and communication networks. Damage either to the central production facilities or to these networks will adversely affect a greater number of customers. Just as the forest is affected more acutely by the collapse of a mighty tree versus a handful of saplings, so will a local or regional economy be harmed by the collapse of a major business. Many communities have suffered through the experience of losing a large, local employer. Such a closure wreaks havoc as the lost employment and incomes cause local sales and related jobs to evaporate as well.

Very early on in the history of spaceflight, NASA engineers recognized the critical importance of system redundancy to astronaut safety. In any system, human or natural, circumstances arise in which certain functions are prone to failure. Depending on their importance, individual failures can lead to overall system failure. Sustainable systems survive such circumstances through system redundancies, alternative means of providing essential functions. Thus, spacecraft have back-up and further back-up systems to the primary system. System redundancies permit the craft to survive failure in some critical operation.

Natural systems incorporate such system redundancies in a variety of ways. Different species provide the same functional niche, often by feeding on the same food source. Circumstances that decimate one predator will frequently leave another untouched. In this way, one predator survives to prevent an explosive growth in the prey's population. Without this redundant restraint, the prey species can deplete its food source, leading to deforestation, soil erosion, and a decline in ecological services. Redundancies can serve other functions. For example, rodents may support trees by dispersing their seeds in nearby soils. Birds may serve a similar function, though their dispersal services may extend over many miles. Each offers the trees a different avenue for procreation. Other system redundancies can operate along different time scales as well. In dropping their leaves each fall, deciduous trees create the litter and nutrients for next year's growth. Periodic fires, say every ten to twenty-five years, may sweep through the same forests killing trees and creating a bonanza of nutrients for a whole new generation of flora. Both processes offer different means for forest renewal and growth.

System redundancy is equally important to economic systems as they respond to unexpected disasters. Alternative transportation routes and networks are critical when events shut down the primary system. As an island, Manhattan is particularly vulnerable to closure of one of its major bridges or tunnels. Yet, the existence of rail and subway links mitigates the potential traffic nightmare. Even more critical is redundancy in energy systems. Without back-up systems, disruptions in electrical service or petroleum supplies can cripple vast sectors of our economy. Similarly, disruptions in telecommunications networks can also wreak havoc. As essential as these services are, providing adequate system redundancy can be very expensive. In pruning business costs, competitive firms will avoid such outlays, particularly as they see them as unnecessary. Indeed, the drive to restrict costs is fueling the trend toward less resilient systems with fewer redundancies.

Excess inventory, whether of key materials or marketable merchandise, represents a costly addition to any company's budget. Not only do these inventories tie up funds and require expensive debt, but they also necessitate expensive storage facilities. To limit such costs, businesses have moved to "just-in-time" inventory systems. Key parts and materials arrive at the plant just in time for their use, while production responds to specific customer orders.

Such a system has evolved around a complex set of communication, distribution, and transportation networks. Under normal conditions, these networks function effectively. However, their interdependency makes the larger system more vulnerable to unforeseen shocks. Circumstances that prevent one supplier from meeting its obligations can trigger cascading reactions, as each subsequent partner in the product stream is deprived of key materials. In the past, the larger onsite inventories would have allowed each manufacturer to better weather any disruptions in the supply chain. Now, as each business prunes its inventory costs, we have created a larger collective risk, a classic market externality.

Policies that encourage system resiliency

Most local government officials and economic development promoters recognize the value of a diversified local economy. Yet, devising effective public policies that encourage local diversification is no easy task. Similar businesses are drawn to certain locations. Sometimes climate or a locally available resource lures them. At other times, widely available business opportunities and networking benefits attract related businesses. As ambitious employees leave existing businesses to start their own, they frequently remain in the local area to exploit their regional contacts. Area colleges may offer specialized training programs, and local governments may provide tailored services and a congenial business climate. This indigenous experience and industry-specific knowledge can convey further advantages as these businesses compete with others across the region. Along emerging transportation and communication networks, businesses can expand at the expense of others in less favored locations, further contributing to their entrenchment. While all of this is largely positive, it frequently leaves local economies insufficiently diversified. Local officials have limited tools to combat these trends.

Fortunately, several policies already discussed can provide assistance in this area. In particular, the energy policies discussed in Chapter Eight would raise energy prices and subsequently encourage increased diversification. Higher energy costs significantly elevate transportation costs, making goods shipped over longer distances less price competitive. Higher shipping costs would limit the advantages of large-scale production. Smaller production facilities that are closer to primary suppliers and customers would find rising transportation costs less threatening. In these ways, full-cost energy pricing would discourage long-distance trade and encourage more localized and diversified production. In addition, levying emissions taxes on material wastes would encourage further diversification. Local reuse and recycling of materials would be cheaper than shipping the materials to some distant site. As a result, local firms would emerge to offer services that enable local customers to avoid emissions fees. Both full-cost energy pricing and waste emissions fees would restrain the economic specialization that is encouraged by global competition as they each encouraged more, small businesses in a greater number of locations.

Enhance locally-based business incubators

Just as in the natural world, birth and death is the norm in the business community. New businesses are constantly opening their doors as other businesses shutter theirs. Communities that actively promote new businesses will experience a stronger and healthier economy in the future. Two sources exist for the addition of new businesses to any economy: established businesses relocating from outside and start-ups. Though business promoters frequently focus on the former due to their visibility, promoting new businesses offers the surest method to strengthen the local economy. In the case of business relocations, the range of likely additions is limited to those businesses that express an interest in the local community. On the other hand, start-ups usually reflect the full range of local needs and talents available in the community workforce. While many new businesses will not last more than a year or two, some will find their niches in the local community and become lasting members. A few will flourish widely and become regional, national, or even global businesses.

To promote start-ups, many communities have turned to business incubators. Recognizing the many challenges that confront new businesses, business incubators offer key services over a defined period to help nascent businesses survive the pains of birth. Most incubators offer clients subsidized rental space and key telecommunications, utility, and office services. In addition, many offer assistance in developing business plans, marketing their product, and acquiring capital. In this way, they relieve new businesses of some start-up costs and share business acumen with entrepreneurs who have creative ideas but little business experience. According to an industry survey, incubators in North America assisted some 27,000 businesses, supporting 100,000 jobs and generating sales of $17 billion in 2005.[10] More importantly, many become enduring members of their communities once they survive the trial period. According to National Business Incubation Association (NBIA) surveys, more than 84 per cent of the incubator graduates stay in their community and continue to earn a return for their investors.[11] Business incubators offer local officials one tool by which they can strengthen their local business community, particularly in a rapidly changing economy.

Policies that encourage redress and restoration from harm done

Despite our best efforts at prescient planning and preventative policies, we cannot fully insulate either our human or natural systems from disruptions. No reasonable manner of preparation can fully inoculate us from harm. True, the aforementioned policies can mitigate much of the potential damage, but some harm will inevitably visit our persons, homes, businesses, and communities, as well as our local and national economies. To improve system resiliency, we must consider policies that can enhance efforts to repair the damage done. To encourage restoration, we must tackle two broadly defined challenges: strengthening and broadening our social insurance programs and raising the personal wealth of the least fortunate in our communities. Improvements in these two areas can enhance the strong bonds of community trust and collaboration that are necessary in community-restoration efforts.

Extending insurance pools

We have become increasingly reliant upon different forms of insurance to protect our communities and ourselves from life's disruptions. Typically, homeowners purchase private insurance to protect themselves against a variety of natural and human-caused calamities.[12] Although the risk is small that a devastating fire will fully destroy our home, the financial and emotional costs of such an event are very high. Through annual insurance payments, we each provide the funds that assist those unfortunate homeowners who do suffer financial loss. Collectively, we spread the risk of calamity over a great number of people and create a pool of savings to draw upon to reconstruct our lives when tragedy strikes. Similarly, we insure against harm to our cars and to any persons that may result from the use of our motor vehicles. We purchase life insurance to protect loved ones and dependents from the financial consequences of our death or disability. For those of us fortunate to have jobs that provide health insurance, we gain similar protection against the vagaries of illness and the high cost of medical care. In similar ways, businesses insure their assets, both physical and human, from unpredictable harm. Lastly, our social insurance programs like Social Security, Medicare, and Unemployment Insurance offer us collective protection against such maladies as death, poor health, and job layoffs. In all of these cases, we create a pool of funds that we use to recuperate in times of crisis. The safety net is inadequate in two areas.

Already a much-discussed and visible problem, the absence of health insurance coverage for so many within our communities represents a major concern. For those without adequate health insurance or financial means, getting medical assistance can be a trying challenge. Deferring medical care today usually creates more serious and expensive problems in the future. Persistent health problems often trigger other problems, including financial insolvency, job loss, and eviction from one's residence. A recent study found that unpaid medical bills are a leading cause of bankruptcy.[13] The resultant stress only exacerbates the medical problems. Serious health problems usually accompany calamities, whether natural or human caused. Without adequate treatment, health problems will slow efforts to restore one's life. Prudence alone argues that we need to implement universal health insurance. While we can debate the form (single-payer versus private insurers) or the level of coverage, we must recognize health insurance as a necessary tool in assuring a timely recuperation of our households and communities to full health in the aftermath of disaster or disturbance.

Yet, the lack of universal health coverage is not the only hole in the social safety net. Usually, change and disturbance create opportunities as well as hardship. Even the worst natural disaster creates new business opportunities as construction and recovery services become critical needs. As changing economic circumstances abandon older industries, new businesses expand to exploit emerging needs. Growing businesses require capital and trained workers to satisfy the unmet need. While financial capital flows easily from one sector of the economy to another, workers do not relocate so effortlessly. Many displaced workers will require additional education and training to serve effectively in new jobs. Given their current income levels, they may not have the personal resources to weather such a transition. Consequently, we need to develop programs that not only assist those who are harmed by changing conditions, but also train them adequately for the emerging jobs.

One proposal calls for a comprehensive Economic Security Program that strengthens our current patchwork of policies in three important ways. First, it calls for federal and state funding to insure that communities provide truly "one stop" employment centers that offer displaced workers the full range of educational programs, employment opportunities, and available assistance, as mandated in the Workforce Investment Act of 1998. Unemployed workers should know the range of opportunities and forms of assistance available to them. Second, displaced workers should have access to adequate income and health insurance coverage during periods of unemployment. Unemployment insurance benefits should cover 50 percent of lost wages while basic health insurance coverage should be available as well. Lastly, workers whose wages decline as they return to work should receive compensation. For example, we could compensate re-employed workers half of their lost earnings up to a maximum of $10,000 payable for two years. At an annual price tag of $3.5 billion, a $25 annual insurance premium on all workers could fund this program.[14] Rather than viewing economic recessions and times of economic restructuring as anomalies that tend to surprise us, we must learn to see them as necessary, if undesired, realities of a modern economy. We must anticipate such problems and provide the kind of assistance that will help workers and business owners get back on their feet.

Redirecting the flow of personal wealth

More than anything else, what distinguishes the "wealthy" from the "poor" is the former's capacity to endure adverse circumstances with little hardship. For a person of wealth, personal savings are usually adequate to offset the loss of salary that accompanies unemployment. Under extreme conditions, the wealthy unemployed may be required to liquidate certain assets to meet expenses. In most cases, they eventually regain employment, ending the drain on their personal wealth. Natural disasters usually bring a similar response. Severe weather that wreaks havoc on property can bring devastation even to wealthy individuals. Yet, in the wake of this destruction, the availability of other undamaged sources of personal wealth offers a means to respond to adversity. Savings and other forms of wealth provide the financial means to initiate rebuilding and restoration.[15] Such financial resources can leverage additional loans to quicken and expand the reconstruction effort. Moreover, such rebuilding efforts generate jobs and other sources of income for some harmed by the disaster. The income generated can support the efforts of others in the community as they attempt to reconstruct their lives.

For those without financial means, the aftermath of economic or natural disaster is quite different. Without personal savings, income loss may jeopardize one's capacity to purchase adequate food, needed medicines, and even safe housing. Hunger, declining health, and homelessness can result. In less dire circumstances, individuals may sell their cars, tools, and other personal assets whose absence makes their re-employment even more difficult. They may find the resultant downward spiral difficult to reverse. The consequences of natural disasters are similar. Without any personal savings or wealth to draw upon, these individuals have little recourse in their response to the damage and destruction. Inadequate insurance coverage means that they have few options in responding to their destroyed homes and businesses.[16] They have no money to move to temporary housing in local hotels. The immediate drain on their limited resources leaves little to restore their damaged real estate. Nor do they have the collateral to leverage loans to supplement their efforts. With the same desire as the wealthy to restore their lives and livelihoods, they are without the financial means to do so. Without adequate personal wealth, they are unable to reinvest in their community and thereby contribute to the rebuilding effort that can lead their local economy back to health.

There is little doubt that greater dispersion of personal wealth throughout a community will enhance its capacity to respond and restore itself after any disaster of consequence. Consider for the moment two communities with equal aggregate wealth, but with different distributions among their residents. In the community in which wealth is more concentrated, those few fortunate individuals will likely recover quite rapidly, if they choose. They may also offer help to their less fortunate neighbors in their efforts to recover and rebuild. Such *noblesse oblige* may occur widely throughout the community. However, compare this community with one in which each household has some level of personal savings to draw upon. Each will have the means to initiate their rebuilding efforts. Each will contribute to expanding economic activity that will support others and supplement their wealth-based contributions. This community's rebuilding effort will likely be more extensive, more broadly based, and more rapid than the first's. Moreover, the sense of common circumstance is likely to enhance community collaboration and trust.

Targeting the home mortgage deduction

In a variety of ways, we can modify our public policies to redirect wealth creation to those households with the least personal wealth. Certainly, encouraging homeownership throughout communities is both an effective and honored tradition in our society. Currently, we expend nearly $150 billion annually through tax deductions given to homeowners; these generous tax deductions have no doubt contributed to homeownership rates that reached 69 percent 2004, an all-time high.[17] However, the vast bulk of this generous tax deduction goes to our wealthiest households since the value of the deduction increases with the size of one's mortgage, the number of homes owned and mortgaged, and the height of one's tax bracket. According to the Tax Policy Center estimates, over 80 percent of the mortgage interest deduction and local property tax deduction goes to the highest-earning households while only 0.3 percent goes to the lowest-earning households.[18] Although the mortgage deduction generously rewards homeownership, it offers only modest help to those seeking to become first-time homeowners.

With some rather simple changes to the mortgage deduction, we can redirect assistance to those who need it most. First, without raiding the taxpayer's pocket, we could replace our current mortgage interest deduction with a refundable federal tax credit equal to 1.03 percent of the value of the primary residence up to $100,000. This change would offer several benefits. Refundable tax credits effectively assist all taxpayers, even those in the lowest tax brackets.[19] Tying the credit to the home value and not to the outstanding mortgage would end the federal encouragement of mortgage debt. All homeowners would receive a tax credit, capped at $1,030. This policy change would assist all homeowners while targeting more help to those in greatest need. According to the estimates, this change would halve the share of tax benefits going to the highest-income households (from 82 percent to 42 percent), while raising the share to the lowest-earning households to nearly 8 percent.[20] This share undoubtedly would rise over time as more households attain homeownership status.

Second, a refundable tax credit could replace the current federal tax deduction for state and local property taxes, to focus assistance to those with the greatest need. Without raiding the Treasury, this federal tax credit could offer homeowners a minimum of $280 annually or 50 percent of the real estate taxes on primary residences.[21] Third, either of these proposals could be increased *without need for a tax increase* by a provision that would limit federal generosity to twenty years. After that number of years, whether consecutive or not, these benefits would end. As older households generally have increased personal wealth, they would have less need for such benefits after twenty years. The realized savings could provide more initial help to those households financially unable to make the leap to homeownership. Other tax deductions, most importantly the exclusion on capital gains when homes are sold, would remain in force and particularly benefit these older homeowners.

The recommended changes would undoubtedly increase homeownership, though they would not provide all the help that households interested in homeownership would require. Tax credits can offer needed assistance, but they require substantial patience as it takes a year before one actually receives the credit, a period beyond the capacity of many households. Further, the requirement of a downpayment precludes many lower-income households from homeownership. Although many families make rental payments that are comparable to locally prevailing mortgage payments, their limited incomes make saving for a downpayment extremely difficult. Without the help of much-improved incomes or some upfront assistance, homeownership rates will continue to lag among this group. Yet, these barriers are scalable. Local, state, and federal governments could implement modest, revolving-loan funds that would assist lower-income households in getting these needed funds. As the loans were repaid, these funds could assist new homebuyers in their quest for homeownership.

In targeting our homeownership tax incentives, we can improve access to homeownership without increasing the burden on the federal Treasury. In doing so, we have the capacity to dramatically redirect wealth-generation within our society. Given the usual rise in property values over time, extending homeownership to all who are interested offers an effective way to broaden prosperity throughout communities. Rising home equity would provide each household with a financial cushion in the face of unforeseen challenges. Further, these programs need not carry the problems associated with the sub-prime loans made in recent years, which have led to higher foreclosure rates.

Encouraging access to post-secondary education

Expanding access to post-secondary education and training offers another avenue to dispersing wealth creation across all American households. Education and training, or what economists call "human capital," represents the second most important decision facing a typical household. Substantial evidence demonstrates the value of a college education in raising future earnings. In 2001, the typical (median) college graduate earned just below $51,000 while median earnings for those with a high school diploma were only $31,500.[22] Comparable gaps exist across gender and racial differences. Even some college, short of any degree, offers substantial improvements in annual earnings. Further, this college "salary premium" has been growing in recent decades. According to the College Board, a college education can add $300,000 over the course of a typical work life, even when accounting for tuition repayment and the "lost wages" that occur during the college years.[23] In addition, college graduates are much more likely to find jobs that offer health insurance and pension benefits than are high school graduates.[24] Each of these benefits permits college-educated heads of households to increase household saving, homeownership, and broader wealth-accumulation strategies.

Still, due to the high cost of a college education, there are gaps among those able to attend college. Not only does college require tuition and related expenses, but also living expenses and, often most importantly, a substantial reduction in current earnings. Among those unmarried 18- to 24-year-olds with a high school diploma, 85 percent of those whose family incomes were among the highest quartile were enrolled in college. The college participation rate for those from families among the bottom quartile was only 57 percent.[25] Even when controlled for achievement test scores, family socio-economic status substantially influences college enrollment rates.[26] Not surprisingly, the escalating costs of attending college are beyond the financial means of many qualified students from lower-income families, even with the current array of financial aid programs. A recent study estimated that over 400,000 qualified high school graduates would not enroll in college in 2001. Over the ensuing decade, the study predicted that over four million college-ready high school graduates would not enroll in four-year colleges and two million would not enroll in any college, largely for financial reasons.[27]

In recent years, most of the changes regarding federal student aid have focused on tax policies like the Coverdell Education Savings Account and Hope Scholarships. Though important programs, they largely offer tax benefits that are of slight value to lower-income households that pay little or no federal income tax. Far more important to these households is the Pell Grant program that offers educational grants to eligible individuals and families. Unlike other college aid programs, Pell Grants are targeted to individuals and households with the greatest need. In 2000, almost half of the funds distributed to independent individuals went to those with annual incomes of less than $10,000, while a similar proportion went to dependent individuals whose parental incomes totaled less than $20,000. Along with federal work-study programs, Pell Grants provide over five million students with needed funds to enroll in college.

Yet, the value of the Pell Grants has lagged over the years compared to need. The maximum grants have grown through the years, but increases have rarely kept pace with inflation. By 2006–07, the maximum grant of $4,050 represented only 80 percent of the valued offered in the mid-1970s, when adjusted for inflation. Worse, because college tuition has increased faster than inflation in general, the problem is more acute. Whereas the average Pell Grant in 1975 paid for almost 50 percent of the tuition, room, board, and fees of the average public, four-year college, the average grant in 2006–07 covered only 30 percent. As the decision to go to college in lower-income households is very responsive to changes in cost, this reduction in aid represents a significant deterrent to higher education, and thus, broader income distribution.

Fortunately, recent increases in the maximum grant have reduced somewhat the barrier to college. After several increases, the maximum grant in 2009–10 is $5,350 and slated to rise to $5,550 the following year. Still, to ensure greater access to college for all qualified persons, Congress should authorize and fund a 50 percent increase of Pell Grants. In addition, the federal government should end the restrictions against using the funds to cover room and board expenses. These changes would mean that individuals from low-income families would meet most of their out-of-pocket expenses at the typical, four-year, public university. Given the average grant, individuals from moderate-income households could expect assistance for about 75 percent of their out-of-pocket expenses. Either modest family resources or other funding sources could fill the gap in these cases. To prevent future erosion of the Pell Grants, the maximum grant should rise according to the Higher Education Price Index (HEPI), which better measures the impact of inflation among higher education institutions.[28] Even with this increase in help, lower-income families will still need to overcome the hurdle of "lost earnings" that usually accompany the decision to enroll full-time.

An inheritance tax

For nearly a century, the federal government has taxed intergenerational transfers of wealth to limit the prevailing concentrations of wealth that mark our society. Known to its detractors as the "death tax" and to others as the "voluntary tax," it represents a nominally progressive tax that is avoidable through a variety of tax schemes and philanthropy. Under current law, most estates pass from one generation to the next without taxation. Only estates that are valued above a certain threshold ($3.5 million in 2009) are subject to any tax at all, meaning that all but 2 percent of the estates go untaxed. While estates are nominally subject to a 45 percent tax rate, most private wealth escapes unscathed. Never much of a revenue source for the federal government, the tax raised not quite $30 billion in 1999, or about 2 percent of federal revenues.

Several changes to our wealth transfer tax system could make it more effective at reducing wealth disparities. First, we should transform the estate and gift taxes to become inheritance taxes. Currently, the deceased nominally pays the estate tax; under an inheritance tax, the benefactors would pay any levy. Assuming progressive tax rates, this modest change would encourage wider dispersion of estates to more recipients as a way of limiting tax liability. Increased dispersion would limit the concentration of wealth and increase resiliency. Further, tax rates would be levied based on the recipient's circumstances. For example, tax rates on inherited wealth could be taxed at the recipients' income tax bracket plus 15 percent, causing higher-income recipients to pay higher rates than lower-income recipients. The 15 percent premium would reflect the "unearned" nature of these gifts as distinguished from income earned at work. Closure of tax loopholes could ensure that all wealth transferred from one generation to the next is subject to the tax, over some threshold limit. For example, a current threshold of $250,000 would enable any offspring the opportunity to go to the college of their choice and have enough remaining to put a downpayment on a median-priced home. Any gifts or inherited amounts below that level, over the course of one's lifetime, would be exempt from any tax; all amounts above that level would be subject to the tax.[29] In this way, each parent could ensure that their children have the means toward a generous stake in life. Certainly, wealthy parents could provide more, but the supplement would be subject to the inheritance tax.

It is likely that the changes offered here would increase the amounts raised by the tax. While decedents could avoid the tax by gifting all of their assets above the threshold to charities, tax revenues still would likely rise. The increased revenues should be used as a social covenant from one generation to the next. For example, the additional tax revenues could fund grants to young households looking to buy their first home. The program could offer matching funds ($1 for every $1 of personal savings) to be used for a downpayment. To limit potential abuse, the matching funds could be capped at 2 percent of the local median home price. In addition, the additional tax revenues could fund the proposed increase in Pell Grants. In either case, the raised funds would broaden the opportunities available to the next generation. In this way, these estates could improve the lot of the subsequent generation, without perpetuating the wealth disparities that confound our current generation.

Conclusion

No one should believe that, prior to the onset of potato blight, Ireland enjoyed a prosperous economy. Largely resulting from English conquest, much of the Irish population had been pushed to the least fertile and most marginal lands. English laws precluded Irish participation in much of the commercial life of the day, giving the Irish peasantry few options to working their meager soils. Given this state of affairs, the peasantry likely viewed the potato as a surprising blessing. The potato gave much of the rural Irish population an opportunity not only to survive their harsh conditions, but also to actually thrive. The significant rise in the island's population in the century preceding the famine gives witness to this blessing. Yet, from our vantage, we know that the potato's benefit was fleeting and insidious. In 1845, Ireland had a fragile economy, dependent on the bounty of the lowly potato. The risks of relying so much on one crop became fully apparent as the blight swept across the island.

Yet, dependence on a single crop was not the sole cause of the horrors experienced during the Famine. In the fertile eastern and southern regions, lands held mostly by English overlords, the farms grew a variety of grains and animals unaffected by the passing blight. The owners exported these crops to England and beyond to make payments on their farms. Thus, as the Great Starvation was occurring across the landscape during 1846–47, food ready for export filled the wharves of Dublin and Belfast. With little opportunity for employment and any family wealth rapidly depleted by rising food prices, the Irish peasantry had no means to pay for this food. Instead, food that could have eased the suffering went to higher-paying markets. Some imports, American corn and rice, arrived to stem the starvation but the relief efforts were too little and too late. Underlying these efforts was the belief that the Famine was providential and the Irish peasantry somehow deserving of its fate.

Given the similarities in circumstances that led to the Irish Famine and our society today, we should take warning from this nineteenth-century horror. Current socio-economic disparities are not as deep as those found then, but they are exacerbating divisions within society. Both income and, especially, wealth are becoming increasingly concentrated into fewer hands. By some accounts, the concentration of wealth in the USA is reaching levels not witnessed since the 1920s. This concentration suggests two likely consequences. First, for the wealthy, any substantial disruption to the economy, whether natural or human-caused, will have only a passing impact on their lives. Given their vast resources, they will have the means to weather and repair whatever economic damage they face. In this way, their personal wealth will insulate them from experiences felt by their less-wealthy neighbors. Second, the acute concentration of wealth among the few means that the vast majority of households will have fewer resources to endure and rebound from the same calamity. The dearth of personal wealth will deepen and lengthen the impact of any disturbance that affects these households causing their burden of pain and sacrifice to increase proportionately. While Hurricane Katrina affected every resident of New Orleans, the pace of recovery has been very different for those with significant personal resources and those without. Just as in Ireland, while the vast majority of the Irish Catholics suffered from the brutal conditions imposed by the blight, the English elites were largely unaffected.

More worrisome, the parallels between contemporary society and nineteenth-century Ireland extend beyond the rising wealth disparities. Current market forces are undermining the natural and social diversity while encouraging a homogenization of our economy and society. As already discussed, we have pursued agricultural policies that increasingly narrow the range of foods that we eat. Out of the thousands of plants that can satisfy the human appetite, we have moved to food systems in which most of the world feeds on just ten major crops and, at least in the USA, one crop – corn – is ubiquitous. Worse still, though each of these major food crops may include hundreds of different species, our food systems are increasingly relying on an ever-smaller number to meet our food needs. Recall that during the 1970s, a major blight attacked the corn crop, wreaking havoc across the Corn Belt and demonstrating our modern vulnerability. Only the discovery of a nearly extinct, blight-resistant strain of wild corn eventually stymied the blight. Despite this lesson and those of Ireland, we are increasing our reliance on hybrid species that offer substantial yields under specific conditions. We are betting our future on just a few highly selected stocks, expecting their stellar performance will continue unabated. In this way, we are emulating the Irish rural masses of the early nineteenth century, though one can argue that they did not have the same options and opportunities available to us today.

The influences of biological and cultural homogenization go beyond our critical food systems. In manufacturing, global market forces are encouraging corporate mergers and consolidations as one industry after another seeks the advantages offered by economies of scale. Basic industries like car manufacturing, steelmaking, oil refining, electricity generation, and countless others are clearly well down the evolutionary path that led from many small competitors to a few global rivals. Not only does this affect the nature of competition within each of these industries, but it also leaves each economy further vulnerable to any calamity that might befall a specific, major producer. Fueled by new technologies, similar patterns are occurring in industries that have been largely resistant to large-scale businesses. Wal-Mart is changing the face of retailing, and even production and marketing, as its sheer size conveys substantial influence to its business decisions. Over the past two decades, the banking and financial services industry has witnessed startling changes as a handful of national banks consolidate to take an increasing share of household and business deposits. In so much of our economy, key sectors are increasingly becoming the province of a few major providers, which then replicate a specific business model in the name of efficiency.

Rather than being surprised by each natural calamity or economic recession that ravages parts or the whole of our nation's economy, we must see these disruptions as inevitable and episodic. The measure of economic health should include more than the size of our economy and the level of economic well-being; we must also examine our capacity to endure and recover from irregular disruptions. To improve our system's resiliency, this chapter offers eight new specific recommendations on ways that we can better weather and recover from these disturbances. Not only will such measures, if taken, increase the capacity of human systems to meet future disruptions, but they will increase human well-being as we limit the inevitable suffering that these dislocations will bring.

Further readings

Advisory Committee on Student Financial Assistance, *Empty Promises: The Myth of College Access in America*, argues persuasively how financial barriers prevent many college-ready students from matriculating.

A. Carruso *et al.*, 'How to Better Encourage Home Ownership', offer a detailed analysis of different mortgage deductions and their likely impact on homeownership rates among different income households.

P. Gray, *The Irish Famine*, gives an extensive account of the sorrowful saga.

Seth Reice, *The Silver Lining: The Benefits of Natural Disasters*, offers a more comprehensive examination of the role of ecological succession and natural disturbances in the natural world.

11 Conclusion

Reconciling the paradox

At this point, a return visit to my local bookstore and its "Environment" section is not such a confusing experience. The array of book titles, each suggesting either an improved or degraded natural world, now is more understandable. Indeed, the wider public discourse over whether we should celebrate or mourn changes to our natural environment is clearer as well. Earlier chapters provide a framework from which we can interpret and understand this ongoing debate. Though this framework may not be fully intuitive, its key conclusion certainly makes common sense: changes to our natural world, just like those to our own lives, entail both positive and negative consequences. As simple and obvious as this conclusion is, one might wonder why the debate is framed so often as either a uniformly declining or improving environment.

The debate on the environment tends to simplify the natural world into a more manageable concept. In its extreme form, it is "the Environment," a singular entity either improving or declining as a whole. Yet, early in this book, I identify twenty-four different ecological services that we receive from nature. Even this lengthy list only hints at the complex bio-geochemical reactions, the vast variety of species, and the interrelated systems that comprise the natural world. Decline and ascendancy are ongoing features of the natural world, even in the absence of human intervention. Changing circumstances cause the waning and extinction of some species while promoting other species, even new ones to emerge. Similar changes occur at the ecosystem level. Areas long filled with water are slowly drying out as sediments slowly raise the bottom soil above the local water table; other areas fall victim to increased and persistent flooding. Ascendancy and decline is the natural state of things. Adding our heavy, human footprint exacerbates and alters these contrary changes, but is not likely to undo this natural reality. We should not be surprised to hear that some facets of our world are improving while others are declining. However, we should not draw too much solace from this insight.

Fortunately, the book's analytical framework offers more specific insights than simply that some elements of nature gain at the expense of others. It suggests which facets are likely to thrive and which are likely to founder. In categorizing the twenty-four different ecological services into four functional areas – life-support services, provisioning services, cultural services, and carrier services – we can differentiate critical features that distinguish each area. The way in which these distinguishing features interface with our market institutions, with their strengths and weaknesses, determines which ecological services are vulnerable to neglect and decline and which are not. The case study of the twin energy crises serves as an illustrative example. Markets responded effectively to the oil shortages that precipitated the 1970s energy crisis. That crisis was largely the result of inadequate provisioning services. These same market institutions have remained unresponsive to the current energy crisis, resulting from rising carbon dioxide levels in our atmosphere and their impact on global climate change. Neglect of a critical life-support service is at the core of this energy crisis. Our market institutions are not uniformly capable of encouraging prudent management of the full endowment of nature.

This dual understanding of market capabilities and the distinctive features of different ecological services allows insight into the likely future of the natural endowment. On the positive side, markets function effectively when dealing with both provisioning services and carrier services. Particularly in the case of provisioning services, property owners with clear title to natural assets generally have adequate economic incentives to maintain and even improve the natural capital. Unfortunately, several caveats to this point exist, particularly for carrier services. Until effective implementation of the "polluter pays" principle, landowners are financially encouraged to develop their property in ways that limit expenses, even as they cause harm to downstream or downwind property owners. We can expect such spillover effects to continue. Land-development decisions will continue to neglect the inevitable losses to life-support services offered by each parcel of land. Moreover, since markets reflect human values and interests, our land-use decisions will continue to undervalue refuge uses of the land, particularly when they conflict with other, more human-centric uses. While we can expect markets to function effectively in prioritizing land use among the human-centric uses, we should be worried by development patterns that continue to eradicate life-support services, whether on lands previously held for refugia or not. Those caveats aside, we can expect that most of the evidence pointing toward an "improving" natural environment will measure aspects of these two functional areas.

Market institutions function much less effectively with the remaining two functional areas: life-support and cultural services. Nature freely provides both seemingly without limit; given this generosity, we find it easy to take them for granted. Further, both sets of services operate in ways that defy the capacity of market institutions to account for their value. The vastness, complexity, and global scale of these natural assets make it very difficult to assign clear title and specific accountability for their services. Therefore, we view them as infinite and beyond our individual impact. We have difficulty avoiding the appeal of free ridership, thereby encouraging individual behaviors that only exacerbate the problem. Limitations in our market institutions make these services the most vulnerable to our misuse and therefore those that are most likely to show evidence of decline. With this understanding, we are better equipped to discern and even anticipate those environmental problems that will continue to fester.

Ways in which ecology informs economics

The value of this book stem from its co-disciplinary perspective, that of ecological economics. The inclusion of both ecology and economics offers competing, though ultimately complementary, insights. Like so many disagreements, the competing positions reflect alternative perspectives that cast different light and shadow patterns across the complex landscape, thereby highlighting some features and neglecting others. One view reveals the "young beauty" while the other sees the "aging matron." Yet, recognizing these dissimilar viewpoints and integrating their competing insights offers a richer and more nuanced understanding of the issues.

Over the past two centuries, mainstream economics has consigned nature to a seemingly prominent, though decidedly supportive role in its conception of how economies work.[1] Considered to be one of the three key "factors of production" described in every introductory textbook, nature's role frequently received scant attention as economists focused more on capital and labor. Most viewed nature's contribution as a passive provider of key resources, or simply provisioning services, as we have discussed. Recognizing nature's contribution to the economy, its full range of beneficial services, marks a significant shift in thinking. No longer can we easily dismiss the benefits of nature as simply "resources" that are either infinite or perfectly elastic as we replace one diminishing material with a more abundant one. Instead, viewing the bounty of nature as a form of capital, that we can be squander or preserve, represents a significant paradigm shift in itself.

Ecology has more to offer economics than simply the insight that we should give nature its full due. The concept of "natural capital" conjures obvious parallels to physical or financial capital. Some of the parallels hold true. Just as diversity enhances the strength of a financial portfolio, so does biodiversity strengthen natural systems. Ecosystems that are more diverse tend to offer a higher level of ecological services and greater resiliency in the face of external disturbances. Yet, some key differences exist between human and natural forms of wealth. The individual items in a given financial portfolio are largely substitutable with other assets. This is not the case with natural systems. One growth-oriented mutual fund can generally replace another without unduly affecting the investment portfolio. However, the loss of a single species, particularly a keystone species, can trigger a wave of changes within an ecosystem that can undermine its effectiveness. The complex interrelationships among the different members of a natural community along with the synergy among the different ecological services suggest that the elements of natural capital are more complementary than substitutable. This gives even more reason to maintain biodiversity in these systems.

Understanding the ecology of natural capital offers another insight as well. The general concept of capital suggests a valued asset that produces some service or benefit, often called income. For example, money deposited in a savings account, a form of financial capital, will generate interest. One can reliably count on this income source as long as the withdrawals do not exceed the interest income. Similarly, forested land, a form of natural capital, generates a number of services, including harvestable lumber. Can we simply apply this savings account analogy to harvesting the forest? Can we sustainably log this acreage as long as we do not remove more timber than grows each year? No. Removing timber at a rate equal to its annual growth will slowly starve the forest, just as our agriculture depletes the soil's fertility. Exporting timber for use elsewhere simultaneously removes the nutrients embodied in the wood. No longer are these nutrients available to decompose back into the local soil, eventually feeding young saplings waiting their turn. Without an understanding of the underlying ecology, simply applying rules that work for financial capital may lead to disastrous results when applied to natural capital.

In addition, an understanding of natural systems gives us a framework for implementing the concept of sustainable development. An important and increasingly utilized concept, nevertheless it is one that defies clear guidance for action. Yet, understanding what gives natural systems their durability offers us a useful guide in designing more sustainable human systems. To persist through time, natural systems require self-regulating cycles of key system nutrients, a plentiful and durable energy source, a capacity to adapt to changing conditions, and system resiliency. In later chapters, I explained how each of these qualities could apply to our economy and the ways that our current economy falls short.

No doubt, most observers do not find the first two criteria particularly surprising. Most policymakers recognize that our economy's current reliance on "disposable" goods and on non-renewable energy sources cannot last indefinitely. Clearly, we need to end these practices if we want to move toward a sustainable path. The significance attached to the last two criteria might be a bit more surprising. Change, both in our natural world and our constructed, human affairs, is the constant. Economies that cannot adapt to the changing conditions cannot hope to mitigate over time the harm to the natural environment. In this way, market economies may mirror natural systems in their capacity to adapt to changing circumstances in self-correcting ways. Further, disturbance plays not only a destructive role in natural systems, but also a recuperative one. In our human affairs, we use our wealth and technology to mitigate change and disturbances as much as we can. We build homes and businesses that insulate us from the vagaries of weather. Our economic policies aim to minimize the fluctuations imposed by the business cycle. We enact certain protections and offer subsidies to specific industries in order to shelter them from the ravages of changing circumstances. Though we are motivated to minimize human misery that often results from change, we may need to consider whether there are other, better ways to meet this need.

Lastly, an understanding of natural systems provides insight into the multifaceted concept of resiliency and its applicability to our human affairs. Rather than seeing episodic disturbances as random events that catch us by surprise, we should recognize their systematic nature and consider ways of minimizing and responding to their impact. Rather than building structures unable to withstand the storms that frequent a particular region, we should devise building codes that increase the structures' chances of surviving intact. Rather than encouraging business technologies that demand stability, we should encourage technologies that are adaptable and can either withstand or recover quickly from likely disturbances. Moreover, we must recognize that widening wealth disparities are undermining the capacity of our communities to undertake adequate safeguards or recuperate from disruptions that occur. We can mitigate the harm caused by natural and human disturbances, but only if we act with full awareness and anticipation.

Ways in which economics informs ecology

Just as an understanding of how natural systems function offers insights into economic affairs, so does an appreciation of economics help in developing effective environmental policy. Not all environmental problems should attract an equal measure of our effort, resources, or creative energy. We cannot attempt to meet all of these challenges at a given time. Nor should we. Rather, we should emphasize those environmental issues that are most threatening and least susceptible to easy remedy. By understanding our economy, particularly the strengths and weaknesses of our market institutions, we can discern the more vexing problems from their less pressing counterparts. As the chapter on the two energy crises illustrates, we can reliably anticipate our market institutions to function more effectively in addressing the "resource" side of our energy problems than the "emissions" side. Understanding this distinction should inform our environmental emphasis and policies. More broadly, I have explained why provisioning services and carrier services, in general, are more susceptible to self-correcting responses of market-based institutions than are life-support services and cultural services. By understanding those instances where markets are well equipped to respond to a particular environmental concern, we can devote our attention and resources to developing reasonable solutions. Further, we can anticipate where future problems might arise.

Understanding market institutions offers further insights. Most environmental problems are caused in part by some limitation of markets, whether ignorance, open access problems, or market externalities. Correctly diagnosing the problem's source leads to more effective remedies. In recognizing that the overfishing of our oceans is largely an "open access" problem, fishery officials can design appropriate policies. New Zealand fishery officials created a system of transferable fishing quotas to limit the catch and allow the fishery to recover. Strict enforcement allows only licensed fishing boats to bring fish to market and in amounts that are subject to overall limits. No longer are fishing boats allowed to catch as many fish as possible, regardless of the long-term consequences. Yet, these transferable fishing permits offer a less visible incentive. As the fishery recovers and the fish stocks replenish, possessing one of these permits provides access to easier and larger fish catches, raising their value. In fact, their value will rise and fall with the health of the fishery, giving each captain a significant financial stake in future fish stocks. In this way, these transferable fishing permits create financial incentives that promote long-term stewardship. Policymakers can design similar policies to resolve other environmental problems by creating market incentives that encourage environmentally benign behaviors.

There is a reason that the prescriptions offered in this book are market-based policies. Just as natural systems function as complex, adaptive systems, so do market economies. The critical lesson here is to understand the potential value of market-based environmental policies. Unlike the traditional environmental regulations, often referred to as "command and control" policies (CAC), market-based policies can adjust as changing conditions warrant. As discussed earlier, the price of emissions permits will adjust to a variety of changing circumstances. In some cases, these emissions permits will be highly sought after, causing their price to rise. Higher permit prices will encourage development of new emission-abatement technologies that reduce the need for these expensive permits. As businesses implement this technology, permit prices will decline thereby encouraging some businesses to purchase more permits and increase their emissions. In this case, markets appear to encourage more pollution, creating mistrust among environmentalists for market-based policies. Yet, these fluctuations in local emissions should not cause undue concern as long as the policy caps total emissions to a level that the natural environment can reasonably assimilate.[2] Market-based policies can adapt more easily to changing circumstances than can more conventional environmental regulation.

Understanding economics helps to identify current government policies that are exacerbating the very problems we want to resolve. Current energy policy offers vast subsidies to producers of non-renewable fuels, while outdated federal mineral policies encourage their depletion; this recognition should inform a reappraisal and revamping of our public policies. Less obvious is the role that our local property tax systems have on encouraging urban sprawl and low-density development. Moving toward a split-rate system could offer incentives that would soften the impact of future economic development on the environment.

Policy cascades

Both natural systems and market economies respond to changing conditions with cascading consequences. Change in one vicinity impacts other locales, that subsequently alter other areas, in a wave of successive interactions. At times, these different shocks can operate at cross-purposes and offset each other. At other times, they complement and magnify their impacts. This synergy can expand the impact of the original trigger and mitigate some of the pain and sacrifice that may be required. For example, the implementation of broadly designed emissions taxes on solid waste will do more than afflict the end consumer. Market incentives will guide manufacturers and retailers to redesign both product and packaging to alleviate the disposal costs imposed on the end user. Markets will encourage innovation and new behaviors that will reduce the burden that such changes will generate.

In certain industries, the consequences can extend beyond simple changes in product design. In the case of durable products, a solid waste disposal tax would likely transform the *relationship* between producer and customer. The manufacturer who can design a product that offers the same level of services but avoids the disposal fee will have an advantage in the marketplace. One way that this is likely to happen is if manufacturers shift from selling products to leasing them. In leasing the product, they would remove this burden of disposal from their customers. To avoid the fee themselves, they could redesign the product to maximize reuse of some components and the refashioning of other components toward new uses. As long as the manufacturers sell the product to their customers, they have less incentive to undertake the time and expense that this redesign requires.[3] By keeping title to the product, the manufacturer would be responsible for both the production costs and the disposal costs. They would now have the financial incentive to produce products that meet specific performance standards, though at a lower production *and* disposal cost.

This shift toward product leasing would alter the customer–provider relationship in a variety of ways. To the manufacturer, leasing would offer a more stable income source. Recurring lease payments would now replace uncertain repeat sales, giving manufacturers a more reliable income stream. Product leasing would encourage manufacturers to design products that were more durable. Longer-lasting products would generate a longer stream of lease payments, rather than simply delaying repeat sales. Further, leasing offers firms the opportunity to cultivate a long-term relationship with the customer, which may lead to providing additional services.

The leasing relationship offers advantages to the customer as well. Outright ownership of durable goods offers the customer few advantages as long as they capture the full services that the product offers. Instead, product leasing would preclude the upfront purchase price that many customers already borrow to avoid. Manufacturers would have further encouragement to produce quality products, since they would know that their customers would not be deterred by sticker shock. Under leasing, manufacturer responsibilities begin, not end, as the customer takes possession of the product. Customers could expect not only higher-quality products, but better customer service under leasing. Implementing these changes would truly yield the "post-consumer" society as manufacturers worked to keep their long-term customers satisfied.

Instituting emissions taxes or marketable emissions permits would trigger a cascade of changes in other ways. Businesses would revamp their operations as they adapt to the new conditions. To reduce the disposal of solid waste, liquid, and air emissions, businesses would overhaul their operations in ways that lead to increased reuse and recycling of materials. As in Kalundborg, Denmark, businesses would develop commercial relationships by which they exchange their "waste" energy and materials. To offset reduced use of materials and decreased disposal rates, employers would require more labor to maintain their production processes. Rather than disposing of or replacing a machine or household item, both businesses and households would hire individuals to service and repair the equipment. As the economy undergoes substantial "dematerialization," it would require more labor.

Increased demands for labor would generate upward pressure on wages and salaries. Though these increases would be inflationary, they would slow and even narrow the widening gap in incomes. Since most lower- and middle-income households earn a preponderant portion of their income from wages and salaries, rising real wages usually boost their earnings relative to those of higher-income households. The increased number of jobs would function to lower the unemployment rate, providing a further boost to lower-income households. While the extent of this effect is unknown, it would complement those policies recommended in the prior chapter to mitigate current disparities. Together, these effects would operate incrementally and extensively to make the economy more egalitarian and resilient.

The looming clouds

Mostly, this book suggests a hopeful future, despite the fact that so many of our contemporary behaviors, decisions, and policies generate the very problems discussed throughout this book. Much too often we are the primary source of decline in our natural world; however, this also means that we hold the solution to these problems. Many solutions to those environmental problems that often seem so daunting are largely within our grasp. Moreover, nature's vast generosity and resiliency provide us with a forgiving environment. Its recuperative powers can largely withstand our neglect and remediate our abusive behaviors. This is not to say that there is no limit to nature's patience or forgiveness. Although we are an incredibly arrogant species, we are equally creative and energetic. We can design policies that discourage our lesser selves and encourage decisions and behaviors that permit a dual pursuit of our narrow self-interest and the common good.

Nonetheless, we must recognize the remaining challenges – those that will remain even if all of the policies recommended in this book are implemented fully. Two in particular deserve discussion now. First, we should recall the neglect shown by our economic development policies and land-use decisions as they eliminate essential life-support services. Due to the complex nature of these essential services, we have great difficulty in assessing and including their value in our decisions, even as we relentlessly undermine them. While their vast reservoir stored within nature has protected us in the past, we cannot continue to count on nature's generosity without limit. This problem is particularly disturbing as it frequently results from our technological triumphs.

Over the last fifty years, the doubling of the world's population from three to six billion individuals has surprised many observers. During this period, many people familiar with Malthus have suggested that his predictions would finally unfold.[4] As this recent doubling of the human population has placed relentless pressures on the world's food production systems, many have predicted the emergence of worldwide starvation unlike any witnessed before. Yet, that calamity has not occurred.[5] Despite this incredible growth of mouths (and appetites that expand with increased income), food production has managed to keep pace, at least to this point. We have augmented our food production even as we have reduced the lands usable or suitable for farming. Through our creative genius and our innovative technologies, we have kept the specter of famine at bay.

Although the full story is more complex, much of the credit goes to the "Green Revolution" in agriculture. Over this period, agronomists developed new hybrid strains of prevailing crops that produce more "fruit" per plant, thereby boosting harvest yields. These new strains, often unable to survive on their own, thrive under conditions in which sunlight, water, and nutrients are amply provided. To insure these conditions, farmers removed rival vegetation and imported water and chemical fertilizers to supplement local supplies. Mechanized sowing and harvesting equipment produced further increases in crop yields per acre. This expensive and often highly specialized equipment required larger farms filled with identical crops to defray their expense. Farm economics directed a shift from multiple cropping toward monoculture farming. To further boost crop yields, pesticides and fungicides were used to limit pests and their share of the bountiful harvest. Though these chemicals tended to kill other plants and animals as "collateral damage," farmers found that they needed ever-increasing applications as the target pests evolved in ways to mitigate the effectiveness of these chemicals. Crop yields have continued to rise, spurred on by improved crop strains and new chemicals to combat their pests.

The same technological successes that enable us to feed our growing human appetite have taken a toll on the life-support services provided by the land. The cutting of trees and the replacement of perennials that provide buffers against wind and water during storms have reduced disturbance regulation. As a result, increased erosion has usually followed, causing valuable topsoil to be lost. Heavy machinery compacts the soils, making them less receptive to absorbing natural downpours, leading to increased flooding in local creeks and rivers. In some areas, heavy irrigation can add unwanted minerals or raise salts that reduce soil fertility. The application of commercial fertilizers can disrupt the normal nutrient cycling, often causing the downstream waters to choke with plant nutrients. The stripping of trees and other perennials eradicates natural habitats for local insect and animal species, as does the uniform cropping. In many places, natural pollinators are becoming vulnerable to eradication. Chemicals further disrupt the local biotic community, leaving it a hollow shell of itself. To boost crop yields, we prevent unwanted weeds from infesting our fields and unwanted species from eating our harvest. In our efforts to expropriate the full bounty of solar energy, we reduce biological diversity as all competitors to the selected crop are targeted for elimination. According to one estimate, we are currently taking about 40 percent of the net value of solar energy that falls on earth, and this percentage is rising.[6] As our technology enables us to increase this yield, we are leaving less energy to support the natural processes that support the broader natural community and local ecosystem services.

Our strength, our creative genius as applied through our technology, is both harvesting ample food to feed the world's human population and eroding the critical life-support services. Of course, we cannot simply walk away from these practices and these technologies. To do so would condemn tens of millions of people to death. At the same time, we cannot continue down this path blind to the perilous costs. This problem goes beyond agriculture. As we use the land more intensively, whether for homes, businesses, or industry, our technology has the same impact. As we make the land more useful for ourselves, we undermine its capacity to provide life-support services. Since our decisions consider only the benefits of increased development and ignore the lost services, we continue to make decisions that encourage one at the expense of the other. The cumulative impact of countless small and localized decisions, each using the same calculus and causing largely imperceptible damage to the local environment, raises serious concerns. Until we redress this imbalance, we will continue to see development that fosters human-created capital while undermining our declining natural capital.

The second issue that remains largely unresolved is the legacy of income and wealth disparities that lace our society. I have offered certain policy proposals to limit and even reverse the current trend toward greater wealth disparity. Limiting wealth disparities is particularly important, as this book encourages the increased use of market-based policies to achieve social aims. While markets offer numerous benefits, they can fairly assess social priorities only when the distribution of wherewithal is relatively egalitarian. Otherwise, the sacrifice of higher prices affects only those with limited means while those with ample means consume largely unhindered. Therefore, to utilize fully the potential that market-based solutions offer, we must examine and mitigate the prevailing disparities.

As the prior chapter suggests, this issue is not only one of equity, but also one that speaks to the health and durability of our communities. Wide disparities erode a community's capacity to resist and recover from the external crises that periodically occur. The differing experiences of wealthy and struggling households further reduce effective response if community bonds forged from common experience are not renewed. As increasing income and wealth disparities undercut the resiliency of a community in the face of external disturbances, they make the community less flexible and more rigid. Increased wealth disparities further privilege those who "inherit" over those born with "merit," particularly as we examine transfers of wealth between generations. If we follow such a path, fewer resources would be available to those who truly merit them, creating a less dynamic society.

Understanding our uneven record

At this book's outset, I gave evidence that suggests our uneven impact on the natural environment. Though some measures show improvement, most notably toxic releases and air quality, other measures indicate further decline. In this book, I examine the full range of ecological services that nature provides and explain their different characteristics and varied relationships with humankind. I also distinguish the specific strengths and weaknesses of market institutions, particularly as they relate to these services. In some cases, the interface between economics and our environment functions effectively. Suitable financial incentives encourage individuals and businesses to conserve our natural capital. In other cases, the complexities involving the ecological services overwhelm our market institutions, causing our economic decisions and behaviors to neglect the environmental capital and contribute to its decline. It is now time to formalize this understanding in order to discern which environmental problems are likely to persist to plague us versus those that are more amenable to effective solution.

I believe that there are three key circumstances, the first two of which are fairly obvious and straightforward. The first critical characteristic is the visibility of the problem. In our society, the old adage "if it ain't broke, don't fix it" speaks to this issue. Without a clear comprehension that a problem exists, there is little motivation or interest in solving anything. However, the issue is not simply whether the problem exists, but whether it is visibly apparent to us. Some changes or problems in our natural environment are more apparent to us than others. Some evolutionary biologists argue that we respond better to some environmental changes than to others. Among our potential ancestors, those who focused too carefully on the subtle changes in their surroundings may have been surprised by the large predator lurking behind them. Consequently, experts argue that we have evolved from those ancestors much more attuned to sudden changes in their visual fields. As such, environmental problems that lead to gradual and imperceptible changes may elude us, while those that generate sharper changes have a greater likelihood of attracting our attention and possible response.

However, I think that the issue goes deeper than this relic of our distant past. Perhaps since the advent of the printing press, Western culture has emphasized visual communication. With the prevalence of the printed word, we have become an ever increasingly "visual culture," in which other senses, most particularly hearing, have become less important. Email, text messaging, and video I-phones represent just some of the most recent developments. Visual images are more likely to grab our attention. Many have stressed the importance of that iconic picture of the earth, a sphere of blue surrounded by the black void of space, as key to the revival of the environmental movement in the 1970s. Environmental problems that are clearly visible are likely to generate more effective responses than those that are not so visible. While accumulations of smog evident in our urban skylines have encouraged air quality measures in recent decades, the invisible accumulation of carbon dioxide and other greenhouse gases has likely undermined effective responses to this problem.[7]

The second issue is cost. The costs I speak of are not simply measured in dollars and cents, though money is important. The likelihood of a feasible technological alternative becomes important as well. We can solve certain environmental problems simply by implementing a replacement technology that mitigates the offending activity or uses a substitute resource. These technological solutions require little sacrifice in the form of behavior change on the part of the larger society. Switching fuel sources or retrofitting pollution-abatement equipment often mitigates environmental harm without requiring extensive changes in the underlying production process. Much of our success to date in mitigating environmental harm has come from the introduction of new technologies that have permitted some version of having our cake and eating it too. In most cases, these technological solutions have allowed us to continue our daily lives without much change or disruption.

Not only is the likelihood of technology at issue here, but also the consequences of regulatory costs. In the wake of both Clean Water and Clean Air Acts, the regulatory authorities made the decision to emphasize limiting "tailpipe emissions," or the amount of pollution emitted from a particular source. Given the monitoring and enforcement costs, it made sense for regulators to focus initially on the larger emitters, whose fewer numbers made oversight relatively manageable. Limiting the emissions from our municipal waste water systems, industrial plants, and electrical generating plants has certainly improved the quality of our environment. Certainly, most of the improvements in our waterways and airsheds are due to reducing the emissions from these sources. Yet, our relentless pattern of economic growth has led to the proliferation of smaller, but far more numerous sources of pollution. Gas-powered lawnmowers can emit ten times the pollution of a car.[8] Chemicals flushed from our farms and household gardens, as well as from our roads and parking lots, are becoming the greater threat to our country's freshwater resources. Their widespread use and release make these sources of pollution much more costly to regulate, both economically and politically.

Third, I argue that the actual or potential role of market institutions serves as the final determinant of which environmental problems will persist to plague us. Given the focus of this book, I expect that the reader is unsurprised by this addition. Yet, we should not overlook the role that markets can and do play. Some environmental concerns have not festered, largely because market institutions have encouraged problem-solving responses. Littered throughout our economic history are fears of impending resource shortages that never occurred. Instead, markets encouraged a variety of responses that alleviated the potential shortage. Today, growers of organic produce are foreswearing the use of toxic chemicals and reintroducing techniques that work to improve the health of their soils. Rather than struggling against nature by using chemical pesticides, these farmers harness natural processes to their advantage as they adopt practices like integrated pest management. While still a small portion of the food-growing industry, organic farming is experiencing rapid growth, giving testimony that we can have both delicious produce and a healthier natural environment, albeit at a higher monetary cost to the food consumer. For the most part, our country's sub-tropical forest resources seem largely unthreatened by our vast appetite for paper and wood products. In these and other cases, market institutions currently guide economic behavior in ways that allow us to benefit from nature's services without placing undue strain on the underlying systems that provide those services.

Many other environmental problems that currently bedevil us could be solved by relatively easy public policy changes. Some have already been discussed in prior chapters. For example, the looming problem of global climate change can be mitigated by the gradual implementation of a substantial carbon tax. As discussed in Chapter Eight, such a tax would generate new economic incentives that would radically alter many short-term behaviors and longer-term decisions, each working to limit the release of carbon dioxide. Car owners would consider different habits that would limit their driving. Over the longer term, car buyers would actively seek more fuel-efficient options. Facing increased pressures, local communities would offer better public transportation and planners would examine new development patterns that limit transportation use. In a similar vein, homebuyers and appliance shoppers would select more energy-efficient purchases, encouraging builders and manufacturers to offer new designs. Industrial manufacturers and electrical generators would choose cleaner fuels, either fossil or alternative, as ways to limit the impact of the tax on their production costs. Some portion of the tax revenues could be invested in new energy sources or in improved public transportation, as rail and other options could be revitalized. By implementing market-based reforms in other areas as well, we can effectively address a variety of environmental challenges. These policies can limit the damaging behaviors and encourage decisions that conserve and foster the underlying natural capital that generates the newly valued ecological services.

Many of our current environmental challenges meet these general criteria. They are producing problems that are clearly visible, within our creative genius or economic means to solve, and subject to market-based remedies. As such, we are fully capable of preventing further harm and redressing the damage. However, not all of our current challenges meet these three conditions. In some cases, our actions are creating harm that is not easily detectable or visible. In other cases, we are unaware of the damage that our actions are wreaking. Just as past generations were unaware of the consequences of leaking chloroflourocarbons (CFCs) or ever-expanding carbon dioxide emissions, we are no doubt producing changes on our natural environment that will only become apparent to future generations. In other cases, though the problem is well known, we may currently believe that the cost of remediation is too high.[9] For example, we are unwilling to eliminate many toxic emissions or to protect all species from human-caused extinction. Lastly, not all of our current or future environmental challenges are solvable through market-based policies and institutions. In some cases, the complexities of the underlying ecological processes and their services cross spatial and temporal boundaries that befuddle market institutions. We must look to other means to resolve these difficulties.

Notes

1 Dueling Paradigms

1 When oil prices surged to the previously unthinkable price of $145 per barrel, many observers thought that this future had finally arrived. However, as subsequent events remind us, the history of oil offers many examples of cycles of oil scarcity followed by oil gluts. As I write this, the era of "cheap oil" has not yet ended.

2 During this time, agricultural jobs have declined modestly, thereby taking some luster off this employment growth figure.

3 The dollar figures in this table are in constant 2000 dollars, to make adjustments for inflation. I have used the Consumer Price Index (CPI) to make these adjustments.

4 These percentages measure the ratio of college graduates to the adult population, defined as age 25 or older.

5 Despite the lowered poverty rate, the rapid growth in the number of households translates to a higher absolute number of households in poverty.

6 Unfortunately, the Census Bureau did not report mean family income by race in 2000 at the county level. Different sources suggest that the income disparity has recently declined. The American Community Survey (ACS) does report *median household income by household race.* Though not strictly comparable to the figures given in Table 1.2, black-headed households earned a median income that was over 66 per cent of that of white-headed households in both 2004 and 2008. This income measure differs in three ways. Household income differs from the family income as the latter excludes the income of unrelated persons, while median and mean income figures offer different measures. Lastly, the ACS data are for the Greensboro–High Point, NC Metro area that includes Winston–Salem versus simply Guilford County. Nonetheless, these suggest that the income disparities may have declined relatively, if not absolutely. See ACS, Series B19013A and B19013B.

7 Some of the decline in both measures is likely the result of recent closures in local furniture and textile plants.

8 Division of Air Quality, *1972–1995 Ambient Air Quality Trends Summary* (1998). These represent statewide trends for ambient monitoring of the major metropolitan areas, in which my community is included.

9 According to the Index, measures between 50 and 100 are labeled as "Fair" air quality.

10 Modern advances in contraception could certainly be added to this list.

11 Joel Cohen, in his book *How Many People Can the Earth Support?* (1995), reviews some of the key calculations regarding potential supply, usable supply, and current demand for water.

12 Noted nineteenth-century economist William Stanley Jevons raises the alarm regarding declining coal reserves in Great Britain in his book, *The Coal Question* (1866).

13 Jared Diamond's recent book, *Collapse: How Societies Choose to Fail or Succeed*, examines how significantly ecological factors have played in the collapse of earlier societies.
14 B. Lomborg, *The Skeptical Environmentalist: Measuring the Real State of the World* (2001), p. 33.
15 J.R. Sauer, J.E. Hines, and J. Fallon, *The North American Breeding Bird Survey, Results and Analysis 1966–2006* (2007).
16 At least until we develop the capacity to migrate throughout the universe economically.
17 Energy Information Administration, *Annual Energy Review, 2006* (2007), Table 2.8.
18 Ibid., Table 5.13c.

2 Our Precious Endowment

1 G. Heal, *Nature and the Marketplace: Capturing the Value of Ecosystem Services* (2000).
2 K. Stave, 'Describing the Elephant: Multiple Perspectives in New York City's Watershed Protection Conflict' (1996), 3.
3 M. Sagoff, 'On the Value of Natural Ecosystems: The Catskills Parable' (2002), 16–21.
4 G. Daily (ed.), *Nature's Services: Societal Dependence on Natural Systems* (1997).
5 R. Costanza, *et al.* 'The Value of the World's Ecosystem Services and Natural Capital' (1997).
6 R.S. de Groot, *Functions of Nature: Evaluation of Nature in Environmental Planning, Management, and Decision Making* (1992).
7 If spread evenly around the earth, our planet's water would rise to a height of 1.7 miles. Yet 95–98 percent of this water is in our glaciers or oceans.
8 Experiments with hydroponics farming (in which no soil is used and both water and nutrients are fed directly to the plant) have achieved laboratory and commercial success in certain high-value crops. How economical this technology becomes in meeting broader food needs is unclear.
9 J. McKee, *Sparing Nature: The Conflict Between Human Population Growth and Earth's Biodiversity* (2005), p. 165.
10 G.P. Nabhan and S. Buchmann, 'Services Provided by Pollinators' (1997), p. 136.
11 Ibid., p. 138.
12 M.E. Watanbe, 'Pollination Worries Rise as Honey Bees Decline' (1994), 1170.
13 R. Ricklefs, *The Economy of Nature* (1997), p. 601.
14 E.O. Wilson, *The Diversity of Life* (1999), p. 29.
15 Ibid., p. 344.
16 C. Maser, *Ecological Diversity in Sustainable Development: The Vital and Forgotten Dimension* (1999), p. 32.
17 C. Redman, *Human Impacts on Ancient Environments* (1999), pp. 136–9.
18 H. O'Neill, 'Horseshoe Crab: Lifeblood of Today's Medical Science', *Greensboro News and Record*, 9/10/2000, p. 2.
19 N. Myers, 'Biodiversity's Genetic Library' in G. Daily (ed.), *Nature's Services: Societal Dependence on Natural Ecosystems*, Washington, DC: Island Press, 1997, p.263.
20 N. Myers, 'Biodiversity's Genetic Library' (1997), p. 258.
21 P. Kahn, Jr., *The Human Relationship with Nature: Development and Culture* (1999).
22 Myers, 'Biodiversity's Genetic Library', p. 267.
23 There are, of course, some exceptions to this rule. Rooftop gardens and solar panels on houses and office buildings are one way that we can gain multiple uses, though we do this by creating additional space.
24 At least until the timber is clear-cut and logged.
25 At one point, Secretary of the Interior Donald Hodel did call for the use of hats and sunglasses as a way of mitigating the impact of a reduced ozone layer.

3 Understanding Our Natural Endowment

1 The land was originally purchased by the Jefferson Standard Insurance that later merged with Pilot Life Insurance to create Jefferson Pilot Insurance. Since then, Jefferson Pilot has merged with the Lincoln Financial Group.
2 This is based on an interview with Camp Director and faculty colleague, Elwood Parker, Ph.D. on November 9, 2005.
3 They did eventually lead to the last-minute response of a generous benefactor, as I will relate.
4 T. Steinberg, *Down to Earth: Nature's Role in American History* (2002), pp. 66–9.
5 Market externalities are beneficial or harmful consequences of a market decision that are borne by individuals who have no role in the market decision. Their existence usually means that the market participants are not fully accountable for their actions. A fuller discussion of this concept lies in Chapter Five.
6 My local public radio station estimates that 100,000 local residents listen to their programming; only about 6,000 provide financial support to the station.
7 The "open access" problem is one where individuals can access goods or services regardless of whether they pay for them or not. As already discussed, this situation discourages markets from emerging.
8 This is an example of a self-reinforcing (sometimes called a positive) feedback loop. In our common parlance, we know these as vicious cycles. As the subsequent paragraph notes, vicious circles have the potential to become virtuous circles.
9 The exception here is waste treatment services. Our individual use of these services does "consume" some portion of the available assimilative capacity, at least until the assimilation is complete. Our overuse of this service manifests itself in different forms of pollution and environmental degradation.
10 A key exception is the provision of genetic services. Both in the past and the present, agronomists have used the diverse gene pool to develop hybrids that offer larger harvest and improved taste. As such, each of us has benefited from the provision of this broad gene stock. The provisioning of genetic resources has met many of our needs *indirectly*.
11 E.O. Wilson, *The Diversity of Life* (1999), p. 244.
12 D. Yeargin, *The Prize: The Epic Quest for Oil, Money, and Power* (1993), p. 223.
13 There is the case in which "improvements" to the land increase the yields of the provisioning good at the expense of the underlying natural system. Plantation forestry and monocultural agricultural systems are two examples. These represent cases in which the underlying life-support services are undervalued, excessively exploited, or ignored.
14 This is not to suggest that private property rights, in either conception or implementation, are flawless. Far from it. Numerous historical examples attest to the latter, human slavery only being one of many obvious examples.
15 Indeed, if Texas had remained part of Mexico, a different result would have occurred. Article 27 of the Mexican Constitution reserves all subsurface resources as part of the public domain. Such public ownership would have likely prevented the problems of wasteful drilling that occurred in Texas because of our system of private property rights.
16 There exists ample research to document that cultural learning is not a solely human attribute.
17 This quote is widely attributed to President Reagan as something he said while campaigning to become Governor of California. There is little evidence that he actually said them, though he did express this view using different words.
18 Regrettably, numerous examples abound. One is found in the alarming decline of so many of the world's coastal reefs – habitats that are unusually fecund.
19 Many of the atmospheric systems, including the water cycle, come to mind here.

20 Our nation's surface waters are generally cleaner than they were a generation or two ago. In many metropolitan areas, the local airsheds are cleaner and less harmful than in past decades, particularly with regard to industrial pollutants like lead and sulfur dioxide.
21 The exceptions such as ocean fish are notable and the problems encountered generally prove the rule.

4 A Tale of Two Energy Crises

1 D. Yeargin, *The Prize: The Epic Quest for Oil, Money, and Power* (1993), p. 698.
2 At that time, oil prices reached a price that they would not reach again for another twenty-five years. Of course, in 2008 oil prices spiraled to $145 per barrel before collapsing again.
3 When oil is used as an energy source, it is not reusable. The laws of thermodynamics prevent this. On the other hand, when oil is used to manufacture other non-energy products, such as lubricants, it is potentially reusable though rarely so.
4 This is the focus of those arguing that "Hibbert's Peak" is imminent. They argue that we are rapidly depleting the "easy to get" oil and that the world will soon witness the peaking and then decline in world oil production.
5 There is a body of evidence indicating the growing disparities in both income and wealth holdings in the USA. The US Census Bureau's *2009 Statistical Abstract of the United States*, Table 675 'Share of Aggregate Income Received by Each Fifth and Top 5 Percent of Households' and Table 699 'Family Net Worth' offer some of this evidence.
6 Energy Information Administration, *Monthly Energy Review October 2009* (2009), Table 3.5 'Petroleum Products Supplied by Type'.
7 The subsequent elimination of these regulations meant that as oil prices surged to $145 a barrel in 2008, this resulted in higher gasoline prices as opposed to gasoline shortages and long gas lines.
8 Energy Information Administration, *Monthly Energy Review October 2009* (2009), Table 1.8 'Motor Vehicle Mileage, Fuel Consumption, and Fuel Rates'.
9 The likely initial reaction would be outrage at the thought. Once people considered the alternative, I suspect that much of the outrage would subside and shift into acceptance.
10 Energy Information Administration, *Annual Energy Review 2008* (2009), Table 1.5 'Energy Consumption, Expenditures, and Emission Indicators, 1949–2008'.

5 Dysfunctional Markets

1 W. Mitsch and J. Gosselink, *Wetlands* (1986), p. 33.
2 F. Mackenzie, *Our Changing Planet: An Introduction to Earth System Science and Global Environmental Change*, 2nd edn (1998), p. 140.
3 S. Reice, *The Silver Lining: The Benefits of Natural Disasters* (2001), pp. 144–5.
4 Mackenzie, *Our Changing Planet*, pp. 146–7.
5 Reice, *The Silver Lining*, pp. 169–70.
6 S. Postel and S. Carpenter, 'Freshwater Ecosystem Services' (1997), pp. 198–9.
7 W. Lewis, Jr., *Wetlands Explained: Wetland Science, Policy, and Politics in America* (2001), p. 6.
8 Most of these protected acres, about 76 million, are located in Alaska.
9 Lewis, Jr., *Wetlands Explained*, p. 7.
10 Ibid., p. 13.
11 T. Dahl, *Status and Trends of Wetlands in the Coterminous United States 1986 to 1997* (2000), p. 82.
12 T. Dahl, *Status and Trends of Wetlands in the Coterminous United States 1998 to 2004* (2005), p. 112.
13 Ibid., p. 74.

14 Though we may prefer not to admit it, sometimes the poor performance of the system is due to "operator error." Out of either ignorance or stinginess, we may not achieve desired comfort if the temperature is set too high or too low. Markets can function poorly for the same reason. Buyers and sellers can knowingly or unknowingly ignore critical information and thereby make some dumb or even disastrous decisions. Economists give surprisingly little attention to this problem, a deficiency that this book will not counteract.
15 Lewis Jr., *Wetlands Explained*, p. 132.
16 Any substantial market price for wetlands is likely to reflect its potential developmental value rather than the innate services it provides.
17 World Resources Report, *World Resources 2000–01: People and Ecosystems: The Fraying Web of Life* (2000), p. 78.
18 These income opportunities result from the land's capacity to offer provisioning services. As discussed in the prior section, the life-support services provided by the land do not offer the property owner a revenue stream.
19 Chapter Four's brief discussion of our "cap and trade" policy to limit the use of fossil fuels is an example of a marketable emissions policy.
20 The expected market value of the land likely prevented any lengthy consideration of proposals to use the land for cultivation or for grazing animals.
21 Zoning restrictions prevent the building of energy-generation plants while market dysfunctions discourage most commercial valuation of refuge services.
22 I will examine this proposal more fully in Chapter Eight.

6 Nature as Guide

1 According to the prevailing laws in 1862, only whites could become citizens and therefore black Americans initially were excluded from this law. The 14th Amendment to the Constitution gave citizenship rights to all blacks born in the USA.
2 T. Steinberg, *Down to Earth: Nature's Role in American History* (2002), p. 134.
3 Though a different story, our attempts at commercial ranching in this region have frequently floundered. Domesticated herds selectively alter the natural grasses for the worse and the decline of cheap fodder threatens the long-term health of this industry.
4 D. Pearce, A. Markandya, and E. Barbier, *Blueprint for a Green Economy* (1989), pp. 173–85. They offer a list in 1989 that has become longer with the passage of time.
5 N. Mirovotskaya and W. Ascher, *Guide to Sustainable Development and Environmental Policy* (2001), p. 74.
6 Certain legumes are also capable of transforming atmospheric nitrogen into forms of nitrogen useful to other plants. Unlike most plants that tend to deplete the soil of available nitrogen, these plants actually add to the nitrogen levels in the soils. Thus peas and beans are used as rotation crops.
7 Commercial fertilizers are produced by transforming atmospheric nitrogen. Given its vast quantities, gaseous nitrogen represents a seemingly unlimited source of nitrogen for plant production. However, current conversion processes require substantial amounts of energy.
8 The interested reader should review W. McDonough and M. Braungart, *Cradle to Cradle: Remaking the Way We Make Things* (2002).
9 R. Putnam, *Community Ecology* (1994).
10 R. Ricklefs, *The Economy of Nature: A Textbook in Basic Ecology* (1997), p. 538.
11 Putnam, *Community Ecology*.
12 J.H. Connell, and R.O. Slatyer, 'Mechanisms of Succession in Natural Communities and Their Role in Community Stability and Organization' (1977), 1119–44.
13 E.P. Odum, *Ecology and Our Endangered Life-Support Systems* (1989), p. 188.

14 F.A. Bazzaz, *Plants in Changing Environments: Linking Physiological, Population, and Community Ecology* (1996), pp. 206–22.
15 L.R. Walker and F.S. Chapin, III, 'Interactions Among Processes Controlling Successional Change' (1987), 131–5.
16 Odum, *Ecology and Our Endangered Life-Support Systems*, p. 195.
17 Whether we humans can create systems that ignore this ecological constraint is part of the debate discussed in Chapter One. Among others, Herman Daly and his call for a steady-state economy offers a minority view that we cannot.
18 LEED refers to Leadership in Energy and Environmental Design and represents the US Green Building Council program for sustainable building practices. Energy Star is the Department of Energy's symbol of energy-efficient appliances.
19 C.S. Holling and G. Meffe, 'Command and Control and the Pathology of Natural Resource Management' (1996), 328–37.
20 C.S. Holling, 'Simplifying the Complex: The Paradigms of Ecological Function and Structure' (1987), 139–46.
21 J.K. Piper, 'Composition of Prairie Plant Communities on Productive versus Unproductive Site in Wet and Dry Years' (1995), 1635–44.
22 Holling and Meffe, 'Command and Control and the Pathology of Natural Resource Management', 328–37.
23 D. Tilman, 'Biodiversity: Population Versus Ecosystem Stability' (1996), 350–63.
24 T. Cox, J. Glover, D. Van Tassel, C. Cox, and L. DeHaan, 'Prospects for Developing Perennial Grain Crops' (2006), 649–59.
25 R. Manning, *Grassland: The History, Biology, Politics, and Promise of the American Prairie* (1995), p. 135.

7 Closing the Materials Loop

1 John Ehrenfeld and Nicholas Gertler, 'Industrial Ecology in Practice: The Evolution of Interdependence at Kalundborg' (1997), 67–79.
2 A. Moon, 'How Economic Development Leads to Environmental Protection in Kalundborg in Denmark' (2009).
3 Ehrenfeld and Gertler. 'Industrial Ecology in Practice', 67–79.
4 Ibid.
5 Ibid.
6 Based on the city of Greensboro's proposed 2007–08 Budget. Available online at: http://www.greensboro-nc.gov.
7 No doubt, some would turn to clandestincly dumping their wastes in neighbors' bins or along roadways. While the fear of being caught may limit these behaviors in urban areas, they are likely to create some problems in rural areas. Phasing in the fee over an extended period would mitigate some of this behavior.
8 Daly argues that any consumption of non-renewables is strictly speaking unsustainable, as the source is depleted.
9 This is harder than it might appear. Since the total tax reflects not only the tax rate per unit of emission, but also the total amount of emissions, one can only estimate the latter. Many factors will contribute to the actual level of emissions; most will not be easily predictable.
10 These are in addition to the formidable political challenges. Few politicians and government officials want to endorse taxes of any form. Yet, in many cases, these services are already being assessed. In those cases where they are truly new, public officials should stress the costs imposed by the waste-disposal services and the alternatives if the emissions tax is not levied.
11 In cases where the primary harm results more from the specific use or disposal of the offending material than from the magnitude of its use, this solution may not be effective.

12 Ambient measures are those that measure substances in certain environments, say the atmosphere or freshwater systems. If a substance is entering a freshwater lake at the same rate as it is being assimilated, then the ambient measure of that substance should stay roughly unchanged.
13 The cap and trade bill currently passed by the House of Representatives met much resistance on exactly this point. Bill sponsors found a compromise; initially 20 percent of the permits will be auctioned, though this figure will rise over time.
14 In some cases, the collected taxes would be fully spent in remedying any damage caused by the pollutant. However, the additional tax revenues would not always have dedicated expenditures on which they would need to be spent.
15 More municipalities are "exporting" their trash to more distant rural landfills where land costs are cheaper and local opposition to nearby landfills is less effective.
16 This is the expected consequence of Hotelling's Rule, named after the economist Harold Hotelling.
17 According to this argument, the real rate of interest will influence the rate of depletion of reserves. There exists a somewhat technical controversy whether this guide will lead to prudent or imprudent use of our current available reserves.
18 In some cases, the sustainable yield is less than the regeneration rate. Timber harvesting represents a good example of this. Since many of the nutrients of the local forest are locked up in the trees, their removal and consumption elsewhere does more than remove the annual growth. Such removal also withdraws a substantial amount of the system's nutrients needed to keep the local ecosystem healthy and durable.
19 Given the vagaries of nature, these harvesting rates may frequently be cyclical.

8 Shifting Back to Renewable Energy Sources

1 At this time, our money was largely specie based. Each discovery of gold and silver expanded the money supply, much as the Federal Reserve does today with its monetary policy. Larger gold and silver reserves permitted more currency and credit, which fostered commerce and economic growth.
2 J. Ronald, *The Roar and the Silence: A History of Virginia City and the Comstock Lode* (1998), p. 109.
3 Excerpt from the 2006 State of the Union speech, White House transcript. Available online at: www.whitehouse.gov/stateoftheunion/2006.
4 Ibid.
5 Energy Information Administration, *International Energy Annual 2006*, Washington, DC: Department of Energy, Table E.1, 'World Total Primary Energy Consumption, 1980–2006'.
6 Energy Information Administration, *International Energy Annual 2006*, Washington, DC: Department of Energy, Table E.1c, 'World Per Capita Total Primary Energy Consumption (Million of BTU) 1980–2006'.
7 Energy Information Agency, *Monthly Energy Review 2009*, Table 2, 'Energy Consumption by Sector and Source'.
8 Ibid.
9 The Energy Department considers this to be its most accurate forecast.
10 In 2030, fossils fuels will contribute a slightly smaller relative share, although their absolute contribution is predicted to increase.
11 Energy Information Administration, *International Energy Outlook 2009*, Table A.2, 'World Total Energy Consumption by Region and Fuel'.
12 Energy Information Administration, *Federal Financial Interventions and Subsidies in Energy Markets 2007* (2008), Table ES1, p. xii.
13 Energy Information Administration, *Federal Financial Interventions and Subsidies in Energy Markets 1999: Primary Energy*, 1999, p. 51.
14 Energy Information Administration, *Federal Financial Interventions and Subsidies in Energy Markets 1999: Primary Energy* (1999), p. 52.

15 Ibid., Table A2, 'Summary Comparison of Findings', p. 47.
16 Obviously, he did not anticipate the current war in Iraq.
17 Energy Information Administration, *Federal Financial Interventions and Subsidies in Energy Markets 2007*, p. 17.
18 Ibid., Table A16, p. 142.
19 Energy Information Administration, *Federal Financial Interventions and Subsidies in Energy Markets 1999: Primary Energy*, p. 108.
20 M. Goldberg, *Federal Energy Subsidies: Not all Technologies Are Created Equal* (2000), p. 14.
21 The individual plant estimates of $2.32 million and $21.75 million translate to about $4.0 million and $37 million in current dollars. Multiplying these figures by 104 plant operators equals estimates between $410 million and $3.9 billion annually.
22 N. Myers and J. Kent, *Perverse Subsidies: How Tax Dollars Can Undercut the Environment and the Economy* (2001), p. 100.
23 Ibid.
24 The US military provides many of the trained pilots who ultimately fly our commercial jets, thereby relieving the airline companies from significant training costs.
25 Quotas on carbon emissions would offer another effective mechanism for internalizing some of the unaccounted costs already discussed. Though emissions quotas offer substantial benefits, and should likely be used in tandem with the carbon tax, they suffer from several drawbacks. Though these permits can be sold to raise revenue for other projects, it is complicated to do so without creating major financial disruptions.
26 According to estimates, coal contains about 26 tons of carbon per quadrillion BTUs, the usual measure of heating potential. Petroleum contains 20 tons per quadrillion BTUs, while natural gas contains 14 tons per quadrillion BTUs. These estimates can be found in *Annex B: Methodology for Estimating the Carbon Content of Fossil Fuels*, available online at: Yosemite.epa.gov/OAR/globalwarming.nef.
27 The estimates of Table 8.1 are based on average carbon emissions of each fuel source and their prices in either 2008 (coal) or 2009 (gasoline, heating oil, and natural gas). All of the figures are from Energy Information Agency, *Annual Energy Report* (2009).
28 D. Burtraw and P. Portney, 'A Carbon Tax to Reduce the Deficit' (2004). Available online at: http://www.rff.org.
29 The additional gas tax money would be spent on road projects. Currently, most of these expenditures are financed from other tax revenue sources. These monies could then be freed for new uses and for tax relief.
30 Energy Information Administration, *Federal Financial Interventions and Subsidies in Energy Markets 2007*, p. 167.
31 It is interesting to note that initially, the town tried to capture the image shown in the TV drama. Many of the storefronts were dressed in cedar shingles, as suggested in the series. Underneath these false fronts, however, lay the brick exteriors that were the actual shells of the nineteenth-century city. Later, historical veracity was restored.

9 Economic Succession

1 C. Troxler and W. Vincent, *Shuttle and Plow: A History of Alamance County, North Carolina* (1999), p. 20.
2 Ibid., pp. 379–80.
3 For-profit wildlife areas represent some exceptions to this point.
4 Local zoning restrictions sometimes offer a haphazard, crude, and inflexible exception to this point.
5 This point assumes a growing economy. Cities suffering population and economic decline may find their tax base less stable as property values decline accordingly. At

the same time, lowered rates on new investment may encourage more of it and thereby slow or even turn around the decline.

6 Some land can be "produced" by land reclamation of local lakes, bays, and other water areas.

7 Increases in the land tax would directly reduce the market value of the land. A sufficiently high tax rate could drive the market value to zero, or even below. At a zero price, owners might "abandon" their property to avoid paying the annual property tax. As long as the market price was positive, then property owners would be better served by selling the land, than by abandoning it.

8 Obviously, poor government expenditures may lead to increases in tax rates in order to pay for the boondoggle.

9 D. Riley, *Taken for a Ride* (2001).

10 A. Hartzok, 'Pennsylvania's Success with Local Property Tax Reform: The Split Rate Tax' (1997), 205–13.

11 W. Oates and R. Schwab, 'The Impact of the Urban Land Taxation: The Pittsburgh Experience' (1997), pp. 1–21. Table 3.

12 K. Lusht, *The Site Value Tax and Residential Development* (1992).

13 Hartzok, 'Pennsylvania's Success with Local Property Tax Reform', 205–13.

14 The state of North Carolina offers an exclusion of 50 percent of one's local property tax to selected elderly and disabled property owners.

15 Alternatively, the developing business could commit corporate assets into a trust account. The funds in this account would go to the appropriate government agency in the event of damages. Obviously, the government agency would need to verify the value of these assets, especially over time.

16 J. Boyd, *Financial Responsibility for Environmental Obligations: Are Bonding and Assurance Rules Fulfilling Their Promise?* (2001), p. 30.

17 Ibid., p. 33.

18 J. Boyd, *Show Me the Money: Environmental Regulation Demands More, Not Less Financial Assurance* (2001), p. 22.

19 Another disaster has visited this parcel. The financial tsunami of 2008 stopped the proposed mixed development plan, leaving the land idle and subject to some natural healing. However, some new owners have begun construction of an outlet mall that will eventually cover much of the site in concrete.

10 Economic Resiliency

1 C. Woodham-Smith, *The Great Hunger* (1980), p. 29.

2 P. Gray, *The Irish Famine* (2004), p. 26.

3 C. Ponting, *A Green History of the World: The Environment and the Collapse of Great Civilizations* (1993), p. 108.

4 Hurricane Katrina and its impact on New Orleans offers one telling example.

5 For example, the advances that have led to the emergence and growth of the compact disc market have eroded the prior cassette tape market.

6 Schumpeter popularized this concept in his book *Capitalism, Socialism, and Democracy* (1962). Even in his explanation of the concept, he showed understanding of the biological parallels, using the phrase "industrial mutation" (p. 83).

7 Assuming that any private development would require public infrastructure and services, local governments may require local funding of similar insurance policies to protect these public assets, like roads, sewer mains, and vulnerable facilities.

8 S. Reice, *The Silver Lining: The Benefits of Natural Disasters* (2001).

9 L. Gunderson *et al.*, 'A Summary and Synthesis of Resilience in Large Scale Systems' (2002), p. 254.

10 L. Knopp, *2006 State of the Business Incubator Industry* (2007).

11 University of Michigan *et al.*, *Business Incubation Works* (1997).

12 Virtually all home mortgages require property insurance to protect the mortgager's financial interest.
13 D. Himmelstein *et al.*, *Market Watch: Illness and Injury as Contributors to Bankruptcy* (2005).
14 L. Barinard, 'New Economy Safety Net: A Proposal to Enhance the Worker Adjustment Program' (2008).
15 This includes having adequate insurance on their destroyed real properties.
16 Renters have few choices, even in the long run. The restoration of affordable rental units is the choice of the landlord and their decision on whether to use insurance funds to rebuild. Even with rebuilding, construction costs will likely require higher rents to remunerate the landlords. Affordable housing is likely to be the least resilient housing type in every community.
17 A. Carruso *et al.*, 'Making Tax Incentives for Homeownership More Equitable and Efficient' (2005), p. 3.
18 A. Carruso *et al.*, 'How to Better Encourage Home Ownership' (2005), p. 3.
19 Tax credits directly affect how much taxes you pay or what refund you receive rather than reducing taxable income. In this way, all taxpayers benefit similarly from their provision.
20 Carruso *et al.*, 'How to Better Encourage Home Ownership', p. 4.
21 Like the previous proposal, this step is estimated to be "revenue neutral."
22 US Bureau of Census, '(PINC-03) Educational Attainment – People 25 Years Old and Over, by Total Money Earnings in 2005, Work Experience in 2001, Age, Race, Hispanic Origin, and Sex' (2006). US Bureau of Census website.
23 College Board, *Education Pays, 2007* (2007).
24 Ibid.
25 E. Maag and K. Fitzpatrick, *Federal Financial Aid for Higher Education: Programs and Prospects* (2004), p. 35.
26 S. Baum, *Student Financial Aid Policies: Do They Promote Universal Education?* (2004), p. 12.
27 Advisory Committee on Student Financial Assistance, *Empty Promises: The Myth of College Access in America* (2002).
28 The US House of Representatives passed a student aid bill that links future Pell Grants to inflation, though it does not use the HEPI standard. Implementation awaits Senate action.
29 One much-discussed issue is the impact of this tax on inherited farms and businesses. While these assets may be very valuable, they often do not generate sufficient cash to pay the tax liability. Many complain that the tax would force families to liquidate these family assets. Rather than exempt these assets from taxation, the tax bill could be delayed until sometime in the future, when the asset is sold. At the time of sale, the past tax could be paid along with some reasonable interest rate.

11 Conclusion

1 The eighteenth-century Physiocrats believed that nature played a much more important role. They believed that nature rested as the foundation of economic activity and that its surplus was necessary to permit manufacturing and trade.
2 In some cases, increases in local pollution could be problematic as the emissions exceed local assimilation capacity. In these cases, the permits should include some geographic limitations. For example, water emissions permits may be limited to specific water basins to discourage inter-basin exchanges that could lead to excessive local emissions.
3 Manufacturers are unlikely to undertake the added expense of this product design unless they benefit from it. Retaining title to the product provides this assurance.
4 Most notably, Paul Ehrlich in *The Population Bomb* (1968).

5 As I edit this passage, there is increasing evidence of worldwide increases in food prices that are endangering the livelihoods of hundreds of millions of our most vulnerable neighbors around the world.
6 Peter Vitousek *et al.*, 'Human Appropriation of the Products of Photosynthesis' (1986), pp. 368–73.
7 Visible images of the consequences of climate change, like receding glaciers and struggling polar bears, may yet serve to encourage effective public response.
8 Marquita K. Hill, *Understanding Environmental Pollution* (1997).
9 Presumably, part of the standard by which "too costly" is determined is based on the known or likely benefits of remediation.

Bibliography

Advisory Committee on Student Financial Assistance, *Empty Promises: The Myth of College Access in America*, Washington, DC, 2002.

Allen, T.F.H., R.V. O'Neill, and T.W. Hoekstra, 'Interlevel Relations in Ecological Research and Management: Some Working Principles from Hierarchy Theory', USDA Forest Service General Technical Report RM-110, 1984.

American Community Survey, Series B19013A and B19013B, US Census Bureau.

Andrews, R., *Managing the Environment, Managing Ourselves: A History of American Environmental Policy*, New Haven, CT: Yale University Press, 1999.

Arrow, K., B. Bolin, R. Costanza, P. Dasgupta, C. Folke, C.S. Holling, B. Jansson, S. Levin, K. Maler, C. Perrings, and D. Pimentel, 'Economic Growth, Carrying Capacity, and the Environment', *Science* 268, 1995, 520–1.

Ashworth, W., *The Economy of Nature: Rethinking the Connection Between Ecology and Economics*, New York: Houghton Mifflin Company, 1995.

Ayres, R., 'Limits to Growth Paradigm', *Ecological Economics* 19, 1996, 117–34.

Ayres, R., and L. Ayres, *Industrial Ecology: Towards Closing the Materials Cycle*, Cheltenham, UK: Edward Elgar, 1996.

Bailey, R., *Earth Report 2000: Revisiting the True State of the Planet*, New York: McGraw-Hill, 2000.

Bak, P., *How Nature Works: The Science of Self-Organized Criticality*, New York: Copernicus, 1996.

Barbier, E. (ed.), *Economics and Ecology: New Frontiers and Sustainable Development*, London: Chapman and Hall, 1993.

Barbier, E., J. Burgess, and C. Folke, *Paradise Lost?: The Ecological Economics of Biodiversity*, London: Earthscan Publications, 1994.

Barbier, E., 'Valuing Environmental Functions: Tropical Wetlands', *Land Economics* 70, 1994, 155–73.

Barinard, L., 'New Economy Safety Net: A Proposal to Enhance the Worker Adjustment Program', *Democracy Journal* 8, Washington, DC: Brookings Institution, 2008.

Barrett, G., and A. Farina, 'Integrating Ecology and Economics', *BioScience* 50, no. 4, 2000, 311–12.

Barrett, G., and E. Odom, 'The Twenty-First Century: The World at Carrying Capacity', *BioScience* 50, no. 4, 2000, 363–8.

Baum, S., *Student Financial Aid Policies: Do They Promote Universal Education?*, Ford Policy Forum, 2004.

Baumgartner, S., H. Dyckhoff, M. Faber, J. Proops, and J. Schiller, 'The Concept of Joint Production and Ecological Economics', *Ecological Economics* 36, 2001, 365–72.

Bazzaz, F.A., *Plants in Changing Environments: Linking Physiological, Population, and Community Ecology*, Cambridge, UK: Cambridge University Press, 1996.

Bennett, J., *Human Ecology as Human Behavior: Essays in Environmental and Developmental Anthropology*, New Brunswick, NJ: Transactions Publishers, 1993.

Berkes, F., and C. Folke, 'A Systems Perspective on the Interrelations Between Natural, Human-Made, and Cultural Capital', *Ecological Economics* 5, 1992, 1–8.

Berry, W., *The Unsettling of America: Culture and Agriculture*, San Francisco, CA: Sierra Club Books, 1986.

Bingham, G., R. Bishop, M. Brody, D. Bromley, E. Clark, W. Cooper, R. Costanza, T. Hale, G. Hayden, S. Kellert, R. Norgaard, B. Norton, J. Payne, C. Russell, and G. Suter, 'Issues in Ecosystem Valuation: Improving Information for Decision Making', *Ecological Economics* 14, 1995, 73–90.

Binswanger, M., 'From Microscopic to Macroscopic Theories: Entropic Aspects of Ecological and Economic Processes', *Ecological Economics* 8, 1993, 209–34.

Bockstael, N., R. Costanza, I. Strand, W. Boynton, K. Bell, and L. Wainger, 'Ecological Economic Modeling and Valuation of Ecosystems', *Ecological Economics* 14, 1995, 143–59.

Bohi, D., and J. Darmstader, 'Twenty Years After the Energy Crisis: What Lessons Have We Learned?' in W. Oates (ed.), *The RFF Reader in Environmental and Resource Management*, Washington, DC: Resources for the Future, 1999, pp. 161–70.

Bolund, P., 'Ecosystem Services in Urban Areas', *Ecological Economics* 29, 1999, 293–301.

Boyce, J., and B. Shelley (eds.), *Natural Assets: Democratizing Environmental Ownership*, Washington, DC: Island Press, 2003.

Boyd, J., *Financial Responsibility for Environmental Obligations: Are Bonding and Assurance Rules Fulfilling Their Promise?*, Washington, DC: Resources for the Future, Discussion Paper 01–42, 2001, p. 30.

Boyd, J., *Show Me the Money: Environmental Regulation Demands More, Not Less Financial Assurance*, Washington, DC: Resources for the Future, 2001, Issue 144.

Brown, L., *Plan B 2.0: Rescuing a Planet Under Stress and a Civilization in Trouble*, New York: W.W. Norton, 2006.

Brown, L., *Plan B 3.0: Mobilizing to Save the Planet*, New York: W.W. Norton, 2008.

Brown, L., *Plan B 4.0: Mobilizing to Save Civilization*, New York: W.W. Norton, 2009.

Budiansky, S., *The Covenant of the Wild: Why Animals Choose Domestication*, New York: William Morrow and Company, 1992.

Burtraw, D., and P. Portney, 'A Carbon Tax to Reduce the Deficit' in R. Morgenstern and P. Portney (eds.), *New Approaches on Energy and the Environment: Advice for the President*, Washington, DC: Resources for the Future, 2004.

Capra, F., *The Web of Life: A New Scientific Understanding of Living Systems*, New York: Anchor Books, 1996.

Carpenter, S., J. Kitchell, and J. Hodgson, 'Cascading Trophic Interactions and Lake Productivity', *BioScience* 35, 1985, 634–9.

Carruso, A., C.E. Steuerle, and E. Bell, 'Making Tax Incentives for Homeownership More Equitable and Efficient', Tax Policy Center Discussion Paper No. 21, Washington, DC: The Urban Institute, 2005.

Carruso, A., C.E. Steuerle, and E. Bell, 'How to Better Encourage Home Ownership', Tax Policy Issues and Options No. 12, Washington, DC: Tax Policy Center, 2005.

Chertow, M., and D. Esty (eds.), *Thinking Ecologically: The Next Generation of Environmental Policy*, New Haven, CT: Yale University Press, 1997.

Chew, S., 'Ecological Relations and the Decline of Civilizations in the Bronze Age World System: Mesopotamia and Harappa 2500 bc – 1700 bc', in W. Goldfrank, D. Goodman, and A. Szasz (eds.), *Ecology and the World System*, Westport, CT: Greenwood Press, 1999.

Christensen, N., 'Landscape History and Ecological Change', *Journal of Forest History* 33, 1989, 116–24.

Clayton, A., and N. Radcliffe, *Sustainability: A Systems Approach*, Boulder, CO: Westview Press, 1996.

Cockburn, A., *An Introduction to Evolutionary Ecology*, Oxford, UK: Blackwell Scientific Publications, 1991.

Cohen, J. and C. Coughlin, 'An Introduction to Two-Rate Taxation of Land and Buildings', *Federal Reserve Bank of St Louis Review* 87, 2005, 359–74.

Cohen, J., *How Many People Can the Earth Support?*, New York: W.W. Norton and Company, 1995.

Colinvaux, P., *Why Big Fierce Animals Are Rare: An Ecologist's Perspective*, Princeton, NJ: Princeton University Press, 1978.

College Board, *Education Pays, 2007*, Washington, DC: College Board, 2007.

Connell, J.H., and R.O. Slatyer, 'Mechanisms of Succession in Natural Communities and Their Role in Community Stability and Organization', *American Naturalist* 111, 1977, 1119–44.

Costanza, R., 'Social Traps and Environmental Policy', *BioScience* 37, no. 6, 1987, 407–12.

Costanza, R., B. Norton, and B. Haskell (eds.), *Ecosystem Health: New Goals for Environmental Management*, Washington, DC: Island Press, 1992.

Costanza, R., S. Farber, and J. Maxwell, 'Valuation and Management of Wetland Ecosystems', *Ecological Economics* 1, 1989, 335–61.

Costanza, R., and B. Patten, 'Defining and Predicting Sustainability', *Ecological Economics* 15, 1995, 193–6.

Costanza, R., R. d'Arge, R. de Groot, S. Farber, M. Grasso, B. Hannon, K. Limburg, S. Naeem, R. O'Neill, J. Paruelo, R. Raskin, P. Sutton, and M. van den Belt, 'The Value of the World's Ecosystem Services and Natural Capital', *Nature*, 1997.

Costanza, R., O. Segura, and J. Martinez-Alter (eds.), *Getting Down to Earth: Practical Applications of Ecological Economics*, Washington, DC: Island Press, 1996.

Costanza, R., *Frontiers in Ecological Economics*, Cheltenham, UK: Edward Elgar, 1997.

Cox, T., J. Glover, D. Van Tassel, C. Cox, and L. DeHaan, 'Prospects for Developing Perennial Grain Crops', *BioScience* 56, 2006, 649–59.

Crocker, T., 'On the Value of the Condition of a Forest Stock', *Land Economics* 61, 1985, 244–54.

Crocker, D. and T. Linden (eds.), *Ethics of Consumption: The Good Life, Justice, and Global Stewardship*, Lanham, MD: Rowman and Littlefield, 1998.

Crosby, A., 'Ecological Imperialism: The Overseas Migration of Western Europeans as a Biological Phenomenon', *Texas Quarterly* 21, 1978, 10–22.

Culbert, P. (ed.), *The Classic Maya Collapse*, Albuquerque, NM: University of New Mexico Press, 1983.

Dahl, A., *The Eco Principle: Ecology and Economics in Symbiosis*, Oxford, UK: George Ronald Publishers, 1966.

Dahl, T., *Status and Trends of Wetlands in the Coterminous United States 1986 to 1997*, Washington, DC: Department of Interior, Fish and Wildlife Service Report, 2000.

Dahl, T., *Status and Trends of Wetlands in the Coterminous United States 1998 to 2004*, Washington, DC: Department of Interior, Fish and Wildlife Service Report, 2005.

Daily, G. (ed.), *Nature's Services: Societal Dependence on Natural Ecosystems*, Washington, DC: Island Press, 1997.

Daily, G. and K. Ellison (eds.), *The New Economy of Nature: The Quest to Make Conservation Profitable*, Washington, DC: Island Press, 2002.

Daly, H. (ed.), *Toward A Steady-State Economy*, San Francisco, CA: W.H. Freeman and Company, 1973.

Daly, H., 'Allocation, Distribution, and Scale: Towards an Economics That Is Efficient, Just, and Sustainable', *Ecological Economics* 6, 1992, 185–91.

Daly, H., 'The Steady State Economy: Towards a Political Economy of Biophysical Equilibrium and Moral Growth', in H. Daly and K. Townsend (eds.), *Valuing the Earth: Economics, Ecology, Ethics*, Cambridge, MA: MIT Press, 1993.

Daly, H., *Beyond Growth*, Boston, MA: Beacon Press, 1996.

Daly, H., *Ecological Economics and the Ecology of Economics: Essays in Criticism*, UK: Edward Elgar, 1999.

Daly, H. and J. Cobb, Jr., *For the Common Good: Redirecting the Economy Toward Community, the Environment, and a Sustainable Future*, Boston, MA: Beacon Press, 1989.

Daly, H. and K. Townsend (eds.), *Valuing the Earth: Economics, Ecology, Ethics*, Cambridge, MA: MIT Press, 1993.

Daly, H., *Ecological Economics and Sustainable Development: Selected Essays of Herman Daly*, Cheltenham, UK: Edward Elgar, 2007.

Darley, J., *High Noon for Natural Gas: The New Energy Crisis*, White River Junction, VT: Chelsea Green, 2004.

Dasgupta, P., S. Levin, and J. Lubchenco, 'Economic Pathways to Ecological Sustainability', *BioScience* 50, no. 4, 2000, 339–46.

Davidson, E., *You Can't Eat GNP: Economics As If Ecology Mattered*, Cambridge, MA: Perseus Publishing, 2000.

Davis, J., and E. O'Boyle (eds.), *The Social Economics of Human Need*, Carbondale, IL: Southern Illinois University Press, 1994.

de Groot, R., *Functions of Nature: Evaluation of Nature in Environmental Planning, Management, and Decision Making*, Amsterdam, Netherlands: Wolters-Noordhoff, 1992.

Deffeyes, K., *Beyond Oil: The View from Hubbert's Peak*, New York: Hill and Wang, 2005.

DeWaal, F., *Our Inner Ape: A Leading Primatologist Explains Why We Are Who We Are*, New York: Riverhead Books, 2005.

Diamond, J., *The Third Chimpanzee: The Evolution and Future of the Human Animal*, New York: HarperPerennial, 1992.

Diamond, J., *Guns, Germs, and Steel: The Fates of Human Societies*, New York: W.W. Norton and Company, 1997.

DiCastri, F., 'Ecology in a Context of Economic Globalization', *BioScience* 50, no. 4, 2000, 321–32.

Division of Air Quality, *1972–1995 Ambient Air Quality Trends Summary*, Raleigh, NC: Department of Environment and Natural Resources, 1998.

Dodson, S., T. Allen, S. Carpenter, K. Elliott, A. Ives, R. Jeanne, J. Kitchell, N. Langston, M. Turner (eds.), *Readings in Ecology*, New York: Oxford University Press, 1999.

Dolsak, N., and E. Ostrom (eds.), *The Commons in the New Millennium: Challenges and Adaptations*, Cambridge, MA: MIT Press, 2003.

Dresner, S., *The Principles of Sustainability*, London: Earthscan, 2002.

Dugatkin, L., 'The Evolution of Cooperation: Four Paths to the Evolution and Maintenance of Cooperative Behavior', *BioScience* 47, no. 6, 1997, 355–62.

Easterbrook, G., *The Progress Paradox: How Life Gets Better While People Feel Worse*, New York: Random House Trade Paperbacks, 2004.

Ehrenfeld, John, and Nicholas Gertler, 'Industrial Ecology in Practice: The Evolution of Interdependence at Kalundborg', *Journal of Industrial Ecology* 1, 1997.

Ehrlich, P., *The Population Bomb*, New York: Sierra Club Ballantine, 1968.

Ehrlich, P., *The Machinery of Nature: The Living World Around Us – and How It Works*, New York: Simon and Schuster, 1986.

Ehrlich, P., *Human Natures: Genes, Cultures, and the Human Prospect*, Washington, DC: Island Press, 2000.

Ehrlich, P., and A. Ehrlich, *One with Nineveh: Politics, Consumption, and the Human Factor*, Washington, DC: Island Press, 2004.

Ehrlich, P., and A. Ehrlich, *The Dominant Animal: Human Evolution and the Environment*, Washington, DC: Island Press, 2008.

Ekins, P., and M. Max-Neef (eds.), *Real-Life Economics: Understanding Wealth Creation*, London: Routledge, 1992.

Eldredge, N., *The Pattern of Evolution*, New York: W.H. Freeman and Company, 1999.

Eldridge, N., *Life in the Balance: Humanity and the Biodiversity Crisis*, Princeton, NY: Princeton University Press, 1998.

Eldredge, N., *The Pattern of Evolution*, New York: W.H. Freeman and Company, 2000.

Elser, J., D. Dobberfulh, N. MacKay, and J. Schampel, 'Organism Size, Life History, and N:P Stoichiometry', *BioScience* 46, 1996, 674–84.

Energy Information Administration, *Annual Energy Review, 2006*, Washington, DC: Department of Energy, 2007.

Energy Information Administration, *Monthly Energy Review 2009*, Washington, DC: Department of Energy, 2009.

Energy Information Agency, *Federal Financial Interventions and Subsidies in Energy Markets 1999: Primary Energy*, Washington, DC: Department of Energy, 1999.

Energy Information Agency, *International Energy Annual 2003*, Washington, DC: Department of Energy, 2003.

Energy Information Agency, *Federal Financial Interventions and Subsidies in Energy Markets 2007*, Washington, DC: Department of Energy, 2008.

Energy Information Agency, *International Energy Outlook 2009*, Washington, DC: Department of Energy, 2009.

Faber, M., and J. Proops, *Evolution, Time, Production and the Environment*, Berlin: Springer, 1998.

Fagan, B., *Floods, Famines, and Emperors: El Nino and the Fate of Civilizations*, New York: Basic Books, 1999.

Farina, A., 'The Cultural Landscape as a Model of the Integration of Ecology and Economics', *BioScience* 50, no. 4, 2000, 313–20.

Fedick, S. (ed.), *The Managed Mosaic: Ancient Maya Agriculture and Resource Use*, Salt Lake, UT: University of Utah Press, 1996.

Flannery, T., *The Eternal Frontier: An Ecological History of North America and Its Peoples*, New York: Grove Press, 2001.

Folke, C., C.S. Holling, and C. Perrings, 'Biological Diversity, Ecosystems, and the Human Scale', *Ecological Applications* 6, 1996, 1018–24.

Frank, R., *Luxury Fever: Why Money Fails to Satisfy in an Era of Excess*, New York: The Free Press, 1999.

Freedman, B., *Environmental Ecology: The Impacts of Pollution and Other Stresses on Ecosystem Structure and Function*, San Diego, CA: Academic Press, 1989.

Gabriel, Y., and T. Lang, *The Unmanageable Consumer*, London: Sage Publications, 1995.

Gadgil, M., 'Conserving Biodiversity As If People Matter: A Case Study from India', *Ambio* 21, 1992, 266–70.

Gatto, M., and G. De Leo, 'Pricing Biodiversity and Ecosystem Services: The Never-Ending Story', *BioScience* 50, no. 4, 2000, 347–56.

Georgescu-Roegen, N., *The Entropy Law and the Economic Process*, Cambridge, MA: Harvard University Press, 1971.

Georgescu-Roegen, Nicholas, 'The Entropy Law and the Economic Problem', in H. Daly (ed.), *Toward A Steady-State Economy*, San Francisco, CA: W.H. Freeman and Company, 1973, pp. 37–49.

Godoy, R., R. Lubowski, and A. Markandya, 'A Method for the Economic Valuation of Non-Timber Tropical Forest Products', *Economic Botany* 47, 1993, 220–33.

Goklany, I., *The Improving State of the World: Why We're Living Longer, Healthier, More Comfortable Lives on a Cleaner Planet*, Washington, DC: Cato Institute, 2007.

Goldberg, M., *Federal Energy Subsidies: Not All Technologies Are Created Equal*, Renewable Energy Policy Project Research Report, No. 11, 2000.

Goldstein, D., *Saving Energy, Growing Jobs: How Environmental Protection Promotes Economic Growth, Profitability, Innovation, and Competition*, Richmond, CA: Bay Tree Publishing, 2007.

Gould, S., *Full House: The Spread of Excellence from Plato to Darwin*, New York: Three Rivers Press, 1996.

Gowdy, J., and C. McDaniel, 'One World, One Experiment: Addressing the Biodiversity–Economics Conflict', *Ecological Economics* 15, 1995, 181–92.

Gowdy, J., 'The Value of Biodiversity: Markets, Society, and Ecosystems', *Land Economics* 73, 1997, 25–41.

Gray, P., *The Irish Famine*, London: Thomas and Hudson, 2004.

Gunderson, L., L. Pritchard, Jr., C.S. Holling, C. Folke, and G. Peterson, 'A Summary and Synthesis of Resilience in Large Scale Systems', in L. Gunderson and L. Pritchard, Jr. (eds.), *Resilience and the Behavior of Large-Scale Systems*, Island Press: Washington, DC, 2002.

Gunderson, L., and L. Pritchard, Jr. (eds.), *Resilience and the Behavior of Large-Scale Systems*, Washington, DC: Island Press, 2002.

Gustafsson, B., 'Scope and Limits of the Market Mechanism in Environmental Management', *Ecological Economics* 24, 1998, 259–74.

Hardin, G., 'Tragedy of the Commons', *Science* 162, 1968, 1243–8.

Harris, M., *Cultural Anthropology*, 2nd edn, New York: Harper and Row Publishers, 1987.

Hartman, T., *The Last Hours of Ancient Sunlight: The Fate of the World and What We Can Do Before It's Too Late*, New York: Three Rivers Press, 1998.

Hartzok, A., 'Pennsylvania's Success with Local Property Tax Reform: The Split Rate Tax', *American Journal of Economics and Sociology* 56, 1997, 205–13.

Hawken, P., *The Ecology of Commerce: A Declaration of Sustainability*, New York: HarperBusiness, 1993.

Hawken, P., A. Lovins, and L. Lovins, *Natural Capitalism: Creating the Next Industrial Revolution*, Boston, MA: Little, Brown, and Company, 1999.

Heal, G., *Nature and the Marketplace: Capturing the Value of Ecosystem Services*, Washington, DC: Island Press, 2000.

Heinberg, R., *The Party's Over: Oil, War and the Fate of Industrial Societies*, Gabriola Island, Canada, 2005.

Hill, M., *Understanding Environmental Pollution*, Cambridge, UK: Cambridge University Press, 1997.

Himmelstein, D., E. Warren, D. Thorne, and S. Woolhandler, *Market Watch: Illness and Injury as Contributors to Bankruptcy*, Bethesda, MD: Project Hope, 2005.

Hohl, A., and C. Tisdale, 'How Useful Are Environmental Safety Standards in Economics?: The Example of Safe Minimum Standards for Protections of Species', *Biodiversity and Conservation* 2, 1993, 168–81.

Holland, J., *Hidden Order: How Adaptation Builds Complexity*, Reading, MA: Addison-Wesley, 1996.

Holling, C.S., 'Resilience and Stability of Ecological Systems', *Annual Review of Ecology and Systematics* 4, 1973, 1–23.

Holling, C.S., 'Simplifying the Complex: The Paradigms of Ecological Function and Structure', *European Journal of Operational Research* 30, 1987, 139–46.

Holling, C.S., and G. Meffe, 'Command and Control and the Pathology of Natural Resource Management', *Conservation Biology* 10, 1996, 328–37.

Huber, P., and M. Mills, *The Bottomless Well: The Twilight of Fuel, the Virtue of Waste, and Why We Will Never Run Out of Energy*, New York: Basic Books, 2006.

Huesemann, M., 'Can Pollution Problems Be Effectively Solved by Environmental Science and Technology? An Analysis of Critical Limitations', *Ecological Economics* 37, 2001, 271–88.

Hunsaker, C., and D. Levine, 'Hierarchical Approaches to the Study of Water Quality in Rivers', *BioScience* 45, 1995, 193–203.

Hussen, A., *Principles of Environmental Economics: Economics, Ecology, and Public Policy*, New York: Routledge, 2000.

Jaccard, M., *Sustainable Fossil Fuels: The Unusual Suspect in the Quest for Clean and Enduring Energy*, Cambridge, UK: Cambridge University Press, 2005.

Jackson, T., *Material Concerns: Pollution, Profit, and Quality of Life*, London: Routledge, 1996.

Jacobsen, J., and J. Firor, *Human Impact on the Environment: Ancient Roots, Current Challenges*, Boulder, CO: Westview Press, 1992.

Jacobsen, T., and R. Adams, 'Salt and Silt in Ancient Mesopotamian Agriculture', *Science* 128, no. 3334, 1958, 1251–8.

James, R., *The Roar and the Silence: A History of Virginia City and the Comstock Lode*, Reno, NV: University of Nevada Press, 1998.

Jevons, S., *The Coal Question: An Inquiry Concerning the Progress of the Nation and the Probable Exhaustion of Our Coal-Mines*, London: MacMillan, 1866.

Johnson, A., and T. Earle, *The Evolution of Human Society: From Foraging Group to Agrarian State*, Stanford, CA: Stanford University Press, 1987.

Johnson, E., and M. Klemens, *Nature in Fragments: The Legacy of Sprawl*, New York: Columbia University Press, 2005.

Johnson, K., K. Vogt, H. Clark, O. Schmitz, and D. Vogt, 'Biodiversity and the Productivity and Stability of Ecosystems', *Trends in Ecology and Evolution* 11, 1996, 372–7.

Kahn, J., and J. McDonald, 'Third-World Debt and Tropical Deforestation', *Ecological Economics* 12, 1995, 107–23.

Kahn, M., *Green Cities: Urban Growth and the Environment*, Washington, DC: Brookings Institution, 2006.

Kahn, P., Jr., *The Human Relationship with Nature: Development and Culture*, Cambridge, MA: MIT Press, 1999.

Keddy, P., *Competition*, London: Chapman and Hall, 1989.

Keohane, N., and S. Olmstead, *Markets and the Environment*, Washington, DC: Island Press, 2007.

Knopp, L., *2006 State of the Business Incubator Industry*, Athens, OH: NBIA Publications, 2007.

Kuttner, R., *Everything for Sale: The Virtues and Limits of Markets*, Chicago, IL: University of Chicago Press, 1997.

Lawn, P., 'On Georgescu-Roegen's Contribution to Ecological Economics', *Ecological Economics* 29, 1999, 5–8.

Levin, S., *Fragile Dominion: Complexity and the Commons*, Cambridge, MA: Perseus Publishing, 1999.

Lewis, W., Jr., *Wetlands Explained: Wetland Science, Policy, and Politics in America*, Oxford, UK: Oxford University Press, 2001.

Lintott, J., 'Beyond the Economics of More: The Place of Consumption in Ecological Economics', *Ecological Economics* 25, 1998, 239–48.

Lomborg, B., *The Skeptical Environmentalist: Measuring the Real State of the World*, Cambridge, UK: Cambridge University Press, 2001.

Loomis, J., and D. Larson, 'Total Economic Values of Increasing Gray Whale Populations: Results from a Contingent Valuation Survey of Visitors and Households', *Marine Resource Economics* 9, 1994, 275–86.

Lott, D., *American Bison: A Natural History*, Berkeley, CA: University of California Press, 2002.

Lovelock, J., *The Ages of Gaia: A Biography of Our Living Earth*, New York: W.W. Norton and Company, 1988.

Lusht, K., *The Site Value Tax and Residential Development*, Cambridge, MA: Lincoln Institute of Land Policy, 1992.

Maag, E., and K. Fitzpatrick, *Federal Financial Aid for Higher Education: Programs and Prospects*, Washington, DC: Urban Institute, 2004.

McCracken, G., *Culture and Consumption: New Approaches to the Symbolic Character of Consumer Goods and Activities*, Bloomington, IN: Indiana University Press, 1988.

McDonough, W., and M. Braungart, *Cradle to Cradle: Remaking the Way We Make Things*, New York: North Point Press, 2002.

McKee, J., *Sparing Nature: The Conflict Between Human Population Growth and Earth's Biodiversity*, New Brunswick, NJ: Rutgers University Press, 2005.

Mackenzie, A., A. Ball, and S. Virdee, *Instant Notes in Ecology*, Oxford, UK: BIOS Scientific Publishers Limited, 1998.

Mackenzie, F., *Our Changing Planet: An Introduction to Earth System Science and Global Environmental Change*, 2nd edn, Upper Saddle River, NJ: Prentice-Hall, 1998.

McKibben, B., *The End of Nature*, New York: Random House, 1989.

McMahon, T., and J. Bonner, *On Size and Life*, New York: Scientific American Books, 1983.

McNeill, J., *Something New Under the Sun: An Environmental History of the Twentieth-Century World*, New York: W.W. Norton and Company, 2000.

McPhee, J., *The Control of Nature*, New York: Noonday Press, 1989.

Manning, R., *Grassland: The History, Biology, Politics, and Promise of the American Prairie*, New York: Viking Press, 1995.

Mannion, A., *Global Environmental Change: A Natural and Cultural Environmental History*, New York: Addison Wesley Longman, 1997.

Manno, J., *Privileged Goods: Commodization and Its Impact on Environment and Society*, Boca Raton, FL: CRC Press LLC, 2000.

Maser, C., *Ecological Diversity in Sustainable Development: The Vital and Forgotten Dimension*, Boca Raton, FL: CRC Press, 1999.

Max-Neef, M., *Human Scale Development: Conception, Application, and Further Reflections*, New York: Apex Press, 1991.

Meadows, D., J. Randers, and D. Meadows, *Limits to Growth: The 30-Year Update*, White River Junction, VT: Chelsea Green Publishers, 2004.

Merrifield, J., 'A Market Approach to Conserving Biodiversity', *Ecological Economics* 16, 1996, 217–26.

Millennium Ecosystem Assessment, *Ecosystems and Human Well-Being: Synthesis*, Washington, DC: Island Press, 2005.

Mirovotskaya, N., and W. Ascher, *Guide to Sustainable Development and Environmental Policy*, Durham, NC: Duke University Press, 2001.

Mitsch, W. and J. Gosselink, *Wetlands*, New York: Van Nostrand Reinhold Company, 1986.

Moon, A., 'How Economic Development Leads to Environmental Protection in Kalundborg in Denmark', WCYF Forum 2009 Conference Paper, 2009.

Moore, C., and A. Miller, *Green Gold: Japan, Germany, and the United States in the Race for Environmental Technology*, Boston, MA: Beacon Press, 1994.

Moran, E., *Human Adaptability: An Introduction to Ecological Anthropology*, Boulder, CO: Westview Press, 2000.

Moran, E., *People and Nature: An Introduction to Human Ecological Relations*, Malden, MA: Blackwell Publishing, 2006.

Myers, N., 'Biodiversity's Genetic Library', in G. Daily (ed.), *Nature's Services: Societal Dependence on Natural Ecosystems*, Washington, DC: Island Press, 1997, pp. 255–74.

Myers, N., and J. Kent, *Perverse Subsidies: How Tax Dollars Can Undercut the Environment and the Economy*, Washington, DC: Island Press, 2001.

Nabhan, G.P., and S. Buchmann, 'Services Provided by Pollinators', in G. Daily (ed.), *Nature's Services: Societal Dependence on Natural Ecosystems*, Washington, DC: Island Press, 1997, pp. 133–50.

National Research Council, *Ecological Indicators for the Nation*, Washington, DC: National Academy Press, 2000.

Naveh, Z., 'The Total Human Ecosystem: Integrating Ecology and Economics', *BioScience* 50, no. 4, 2000, 357–61.

Norberg, J., 'Linking Nature's Services to Ecosystems: Some General Ecological Concepts', *Ecological Economics* 29, 1999, 183–202.

Norgaard, R., *Development Betrayed: The End of Progress and a Coevolutionary Revisioning of the Future*, London: Routledge, 1994.

Norton, B., 'Resilience and Options', *Ecological Economics* 15, 1995, 133–6.

Norton, B., 'Evaluating Ecosystem States: Two Competing Paradigms', *Ecological Economics* 14, 1995, 113–27.

Oates, W., and R. Schwab, 'The Impact of the Urban Land Taxation: The Pittsburgh Experience', *National Tax Journal* 50(1), 1997, pp. 1–21.

Odum, E.P., *Ecology and Our Endangered Life-Support Systems*, Sunderland, Massachusetts: Sinauer Associates, 1989.

Odum, H., *Ecological and General Systems: An Introduction to Systems Ecology*, Niwot, CO: University Press of Colorado, 1994.

O'Neill, R., and J. Kahn, 'Homo Economicus as a Keystone Species', *BioScience* 50, no. 4, 2000, 333–7.

Ormerod, P., *Butterfly Economics: A New General Theory of Social and Economic Behavior*, New York: Pantheon Books, 1998.

Orr, D., *The Nature of Design: Ecology, Culture, and Human Intention*, New York: Oxford University Press, 2002.

Outwater, A., *Water: A Natural History*, New York: Basic Books, 1996.

Owen, D., *What Is Ecology?*, Oxford, UK: Oxford University Press, 1980.

Packham, J., J. Harding, G. Hilton and R. Stuttard, *Functional Ecology of Woodland and Forests*, London: Chapman and Hall, 1992.

Palumbi, S., *The Evolution Explosion: How Humans Cause Rapid Evolutionary Change*, New York: W.W. Norton, 2001.

Pastor, J., R. Naiman, B. Dewey, and P. McInnes, 'Moose, Microbes, and the Boreal Forest', *BioScience* 38, 1988, 770–7.

Pearce, D., A. Markandya, and E. Barbier, *Blueprint for a Green Economy*, London: Earthscan, 1989.

Pearce, D., and E. Barbier, *Blueprint for a Sustainable Economy*, London: Earthscan Publications, 2000.

Peet, J., *Energy and the Ecological Economics of Sustainability*, Washington, DC: Island Press, 1992.

Perrings, C., *Economy and Environment: A Theoretical Essay on the Interdependence of Economic and Environmental Systems*, Cambridge, UK: Cambridge University Press, 1987.

Perrings, C., *Economics of Ecological Resources*, Cheltenham, UK: Edward Elgar, 1997.

Perrings, C., and D. Pearce, 'Threshold Effects and Incentives for the Conservation of Biodiversity', *Environmental and Resource Economics* 4, 1994, 13–28.

Perrings, C., and B. Walker, 'Biodiversity, Resilience, and the Control of Ecological–Economic Systems: The Case of Fire-Driven Rangelands', *Ecological Economics* 22, 1997, 73–83.

Peters, R., *The Ecological Implications of Body Size*, Cambridge, UK: Cambridge University Press, 1983.

Peterson, G., C. Allen, and C.S. Holling, 'Ecological Resilience, Biodiversity, and Scale', *Ecosystems* 1, 1998, 6–18.

Pickett, S., V.T. Parker, and P. Fiedler, 'The New Paradigm in Ecology: Implications for Conservation Biology Above the Species Level', in P. Fiedler and S. Jain (eds.), *Conservation Biology: The Theory and Practice of Nature Conservation, Preservation, and Management*, New York: Chapman and Hall, 1992.

Pimm, S., G. Russell, J. Gittleman, and T. Brooks, 'The Future of Biodiversity', *Science* 269, 1995, 347–50.

Pimm, S., *The World According to Pimm: A Scientist Audits the Earth*, New York: McGraw-Hill, 2001.

Piper, J.K., 'Composition of Prairie Plant Communities on Productive versus Unproductive Site in Wet and Dry Years', *Canadian Journal of Botany* 73, 1995, 1635–44.

Plattner, S. (ed.), *Economic Anthropology*, Stanford, CA: Stanford University Press, 1989.

Pollan, M., *The Botany of Desire: A Plant's Eye View of the World*, New York: Random House, 2002.

Ponting, C., *A Green History of the World: The Environment and the Collapse of Great Civilizations*, New York: Penguin Books, 1993.

Postel, S., and S. Carpenter, 'Freshwater Ecosystem Services', in G. Daily (ed.), *Nature's Services: Societal Dependence on Natural Ecosystems*, Washington DC: Island Press, 1997, pp. 195–214.

Potts, R., *Humanity's Descent: The Consequences of Ecological Instability*, New York: Avon Books, 1996.

Princen, T., *The Logic of Sufficiency*, Cambridge, MA: MIT Press, 2005.

Putnam, R., *Community Ecology*, London: Chapman and Hall, 1994.

Quammen, D., *The Song of the Dodo: Island Biogeography in an Age of Extinction*, New York: Touchstone Books, 1996.

Randall, A., 'The Value of Biodiversity', *Ambio* 20, 1991, 64–8.

Rao, P., *Sustainable Development: Economics and Policy*, Malden, MA: Blackwell Publishers, 2000.

Rathge, R., and P. Highman, 'Population Change in the Great Plains: A History of Prolonged Decline', *Rural Development Perspectives* 13.

Raven, P., and T. Williams (eds.), *Nature and Human Society: The Quest for a Sustainable World*, Proceedings of the 1997 Forum on Biodiversity, Washington, DC: National Academy Press, 1997.

Redman, C., *Human Impacts on Ancient Environments*, Tucson, AZ: The University of Arizona Press, 1999.

Rees, W., 'Consuming the Earth: The Biophysics of Sustainability', *Ecological Economics* 29, 1999, 23–7.

Reice, S., *The Silver Lining: The Benefits of Natural Disasters*, Princeton, NJ: Princeton University Press, 2001.

Richards, J., *The Unending Frontier: An Environmental History of the Early Modern World*, Berkeley, CA: University of California Press, 2005.

Ricklefs, R., *The Economy of Nature: A Textbook in Basic Ecology*, New York: W.H. Freeman and Company, 1997.

Ridley, M., *The Origins of Virtue: Human Instincts and the Evolution of Cooperation*, New York: Penguin Books, 1996.

Riley, D., *Taken for a Ride*, London: Centre for Land Policies Studies, 2001.

Roberts, P., *The End of Oil: On the Edge of a Perilous New World*, New York: Houghton Mifflin, 2004.

Roodman, D., *The Natural Wealth of Nations: Harnessing the Market for the Environment*, New York: W.W. Norton and Company, 1998.

Ruitenbeek, H.J., 'Modeling Economy–Ecology Linkages in Mangroves: Economic Evidence for Promoting Conservation in Bintuni Bay, Indonesia', *Ecological Economics* 10, 1994, 233–47.

Ruitenbeek, H.J., 'The Rainforest Supply Price: A Tool for Evaluating Rainforest Conservation Expenditures', *Ecological Economics* 6, 1995, 57–78.

Ruttan, V., 'Constraints on the Design of Sustainable Systems of Agricultural Production', *Ecological Economics* 10, 1994, 209–19.

Sagoff, M., 'On the Value of Natural Ecosystems: The Catskills Parable', *Politics and the Life Sciences* 21, 2002, 16–21.

Sauer, J.R., J.E. Hines, and J. Fallon, *The North American Breeding Bird Survey, Results and Analysis 1966–2006*, Version 10.13.2007, Laurel, MD: USGS Patuxent Wildlife Research Center, 2007.

Schell, J., *The Fate of the Earth*, New York: Alfred Knopf, 1982.

Schneider, E.D., and J.J. Kay, 'Life as a Manifestation of the Second Law of Thermodynamics', *Mathematical and Computer Modeling* 19, 1994, 25–48.

Schor, J., *The Overspent American: Why We Want What We Don't Need*, New York: Basic Books, 1989.

Schumpeter, J., *Capitalism, Socialism, and Democracy*, New York: HarperPerennial, 1962.

Shogren, J., J. Herriges, and R. Govindasamy, 'Limits to Environmental Bonds', *Ecological Economics* 8, 1993, 109–33.

Simmons, I., *Changing the Face of the Earth: Culture, Environment, History*, 2nd edn., Cambridge, MA: Blackwell Publishers, 1996.

Smil, V., *Global Ecology: Environmental Change and Social Flexibility*, New York: Routledge, 1993.

Smil, V., *Cycles of Life: Civilization and the Biosphere*, New York: Scientific American Library, 1997.

Smil, V., *Energy: A Beginner's Guide*, Oxford, UK: Oneworld Publications, 2006.

Smith, G., *The History of the Comstock Lode*, Reno, NV: University of Nevada Press, 1998.

Socolow, R., C. Andrews, F. Berkhout, and V. Thomas, *Industrial Ecology and Global Change*, Cambridge, UK: Cambridge University Press, 1994.

Solomon, B., 'New Directions in Emission Trading: The Potential Contribution of New Institutional Economics', *Ecological Economics* 30, 1999, 371–87.

Stave, K., 'Describing the Elephant: Multiple Perspectives in New York City's Watershed Protection Conflict', Watershed 96 Conference Proceedings, 1996. Available online at: www.epa.gov/owow/watershed/Proceed.

Steinberg, T., *Down to Earth: Nature's Role in American History*, Oxford, UK: Oxford University Press, 2002.

Sterner, T., *Policy Instruments For Environmental and Natural Resource Management*, Washington, DC: Resources for the Future Press, 2003.

Stiling, P., *Ecology: Theories and Applications*, Upper Saddle River, NJ: Prentice Hall, 1999.

Swallow, B., and D. Bromley, 'Institutions, Governance, and Incentives in Common Property Regimes for African Rangelands', *Environmental and Resource Economics* 6, 1995, 99–118.

Tainter, J., *The Collapse of Complex Societies*, Cambridge: Cambridge University Press, 1988.

Tilman, D., 'Biodiversity: Population versus Ecosystem Stability', *Nature* 77, 1996, 350–63.

Tilman, D., D. Wedin, and J. Knops, 'Productivity and Sustainability Influenced by Biodiversity in Grassland Ecosystems', *Nature* 379, 1996, 718–20.

Tilman, D., J. Knops, D. Wedin, P. Reich, M. Ritchie, and E. Siemann, 'The Influence of Functional Diversity and Composition on Ecosystem Processes', *Science* 277, 1997, 1300–02.

Tilton, J., *On Borrowed Time?: Assessing the Threat of Mineral Depletion*, Washington, DC: Resources for the Future, 2003.

Tivy, J., and G. O'Hare, *Human Impact on the Ecosystem*, Edinburgh, UK: Oliver & Boyd, 1981.

Torras, M., and J. Boyce, 'Income, Inequality, and Pollution: A Reassessment of the Environmental Kuznets Curve', *Ecological Economics* 25, 1998, 14–60.

Troxler, C., and W. Vincent, *Shuttle and Plow: A History of Alamance County, North Carolina*, Burlington, NC: Alamance County Historical Association, 1999.

Tucker, M., 'Carbon Dioxide Emissions and Global GDP', *Ecological Economics* 15, 1995, 215–23.

Turner, R.K., S. Subak, and W.N. Adger, 'Pressures, Trends, and Impacts in Coastal Zones: Interactions Between Socioeconomic and Natural Systems', *Environmental Management* 20, 1996, 159–73.

Turner, R.K., K. Button, and P. Nijkamp (eds.), *Ecosystems and Nature: Economics, Science, and Policy*, Cheltenham, UK: Edward Elgar, 1999.

University of Michigan, NBIA, Ohio University, and Southern Technology Council, *Business Incubation Works*, Athens, OH: NBIA Publications, 1997.

van den Bergh, J., *Ecological Economics and Sustainable Development Theory, Methods, and Applications*, Cheltenham, UK: Edward Elgar, 1996.

van den Bergh, J., and J. van der Straaten (eds.), *Toward Sustainable Development: Concepts, Methods, and Policy*, Washington, DC: Island Press, 1994.

van den Bergh, J., and J. van der Straaten (eds.), *Economy and Ecosystems in Change: Analytical and Historical Approaches*, Cheltenham, UK: Edward Elgar, 1997.

van der Ryn, S., and S. Cowan, *Ecological Design: Tenth Anniversary Edition*, Washington: Island Press, 1996.

Vandermeer, J., *Reconstructing Biology: Genetics and Ecology in the New World Order*, New York: John Wiley & Sons, 1996.

Vermeij, G., *Nature: An Economic History*, Princeton, NJ: Princeton University Press, 2004.

Villiers, M. de, *Water: The Fate of Our Most Precious Resource*, New York: Houghton Mifflin, 2000.

Vitousek, Peter, P. Ehrlich, A. Ehrlich, and P. Matson, 'Human Appropriation of the Products of Photosynthesis', *BioScience* 36, 1986, pp. 368–73.

Vitousek, P., H. Mooney, J. Lubchenco, and J. Meillo, 'Human Domination of Earth's Ecosystems', *Science* 277, 1997, 494–9.

Wackernagel, M., and W. Rees, *Our Ecological Footprint: Reducing Human Impact on the Earth*, Gabriola Island, BC: New Society Publisher, 1996.

Wackernagel, M., L. Onisto, P. Bello, A. Linares, I. Falfan, J. Garica, A. Guerrero, and M. Guerrero, 'National Natural Capital Accounting with the Ecological Footprint Concept', *Ecological Economics* 29, 1999, 375–90.

Walker, L.R., and F.S. Chapin, III, 'Interactions Among Processes Controlling Successional Change', *Oikos* 50, 1987, 131–5.

Ward, P., *The Call of Distant Mammoths: Why the Ice Age Mammals Disappeared*, New York: Copernicus, 1997.

Watanbe, M.E., 'Pollination Worries Rise as Honey Bees Decline', *Science* 265, 1994, 1170.

Webb, S., M. Dwyer, C. Kaunzinger, and P. Wyckoff, 'The Myth of the Resilient Forest: Case Study of the Invasive Norway Maple (*Acer platanoides*)', *Rhodora* 102, 2000, 332–54.

Wenke, R., *Patterns in Prehistory: Humankind's First Three Million Years*, Oxford, UK: Oxford University Press, 1990.

Whittaker, R., *Island Biogeography: Ecology, Evolution, and Conservation*, Oxford, UK: Oxford University Press, 1998.

Wills, I., *Economics and the Environment: A Signaling and Incentives Approach*, St Leonards, Australia: Allen & Unwin, 1997.

Wilson, E.O., *The Diversity of Life*, New York: W.W. Norton, 1999.

Woodham-Smith, C., *The Great Hunger*, New York: E.P. Dutton, 1980.

World Resources Report, *World Resources 2000–01: People and Ecosystems: The Fraying Web of Life*, Washington, DC: World Resources Institute, 2000.

Worster, D., *The Wealth of Nature: Environmental History and the Ecological Imagination*, New York: Oxford University Press, 1993.

Wright, R., *Moral Animal: Evolutionary Psychology and Everyday Life*, New York: Vintage Books, 1994.

Wright, R., *Nonzero: The Logic of Human Destiny*, New York: Vintage Books, 2001.

Yeargin, D., *The Prize: The Epic Quest for Oil, Money, and Power*, New York: Free Press, 1993.

Index

Note: page numbers in **bold** refer to figures and tables.